PLOMER, William Charles Franklyn. The Diamond of Jannina; Ali Pasha, 1741–1822. Taplinger, 1970 (orig. pub. by Nelson as <u>Ali the Lion</u>, 1936). 288p il map bibl 79-107008. 7.50

CHOICE JUL./AUG. '70

History, Geography & Travel

Europe

Ali the Lion was widely acclaimed for its interesting treatment of "the Mohammedan Bonaparte" who entertained Byron and, curiously, was admired after a fashion by the likes of Napoleon, Nelson, Victor Hugo, and Dumas. Yet the romantic adulation of Ali notwithstanding, Plomer deals with his life and career as it really was, one of greed, crime, and constant intrigue. A barbarian among barbarians, he dealt with his subjects in the manner in which they were accustomed. While it cannot be looked upon as a scholarly presentation in the true sense of the word, the *Diamond of Jannina* is a factual account in essential detail, albeit lacking in documentation, of the Pasha's domestic and foreign politics, emerging as he did as the most powerful figure in Ottoman Europe with a harem of 600 to adorn the barbaric splendor of his court. Young scholars are presently laboring on the production of more scholarly and less romantic treatments of the Pasha of Jannina. Written in an eloquent and absorbing style, the work reads like a captivating novel aimed at the general reader. Seven illustrations, bibliographical note; index.

ABOUT THE AUTHOR

WILLIAM PLOMER, F.R.S.L., hon. D.Litt.,
was born of English parents in South
Africa in 1903. He was educated at
Rugby, then returned to South Africa
where he worked as a farmer in the
Stormberg Mountains and as a trader
in Zululand. In his early twenties he
went to Japan at the invitation of a
Japanese friend and lived there for more
then two years. He was offered, but
declined, the Chair of English
Literature at the Imperial University of
Tokyo, and in 1929 he returned to
England.

William Plomer has written nine
volumes of poetry, the most recent being
Collected Poems (1960) and *Taste and
Remember* (1966). In the Coronation
year, he was chosen to write the libretto
for Benjamin Britten's opera
"Gloriana," and in 1963 he was
awarded the Queen's Gold Medal for
Poetry. In addition to novels, short
stories and biographies, he is the author
of two autobiographical books, *Double
Lives* and *At Home*. He is also known as a
critic and broadcaster, and as the
editor of several books by other writers,
including the classic *Kilvert's Diary*.

WILLIAM PLOMER

THE DIAMOND OF

JANNINA

ALI PASHA 1741–1822

TAPLINGER PUBLISHING COMPANY
NEW YORK

First Published in the United States in 1970 by
TAPLINGER PUBLISHING CO., INC.
29 East Tenth Street
New York, New York 10003

SBN 8008 2190 4

Library of Congress Catalog Number 79-107008

Printed in Great Britain

CONTENTS

CONTENTS

ILLUSTRATIONS

PREFACE

WHO was Ali? A century or so ago there would have been no need to ask that question, for he played a considerable part in his time. He has been called the most romantic monster in history, the Mohammedan Bonaparte, and many other names more or less apt. Victor Hugo, writing in the eighteen-twenties, called him the only colossus and man of genius of the time worthy to be compared with Napoleon, and added that Ali was to Napoleon as the tiger to the lion, or the vulture to the eagle. Ali's story has not been lately told in English, and it seemed to me worth telling anew, mainly for the story's sake. I have not tried to tell it completely, with all its political and historical ramifications, but rather to make it as interesting as I could, and I have tried to be graphic without being inaccurate, since concise biography and not gushing fiction was my aim.

I think if Ali had lived before Shakespeare, the story of this tyrant would certainly have interested and might conceivably have been used by the poet who concerned himself so much with the destinies and characters of powerful men and with the infinitely various lives and deaths going on round them. Never was a life more full than Ali's of suggestions of plot and atmosphere for the poet, the novelist, and the dramatist. He has not been neglected. He has a significant place in history. In Greece he has figured in ballads, folk songs, and other popular writings; he caught the imagination of Byron; he furnished the motif at least of a novel, or rather a Hungarian rhapsody, by Mor Jókai; and Dumas made some use of the later part of his life in *The Count of Monte Cristo*.

PREFACE

There is nothing new in dictatorships, though with the passing of time we seem to see more power in fewer hands, and greater dangers. The story of the Dictator of Epirus offers a lesson in the working of autocracy that may well be borne in mind.

I talk not of mercy, I talk not of fear,
He neither must know who would serve the Vizier:
Since the days of our prophet the Crescent ne'er saw
A chief ever glorious like Ali Pashaw.

BYRON: Childe Harold

THE DIAMOND OF
JANNINA

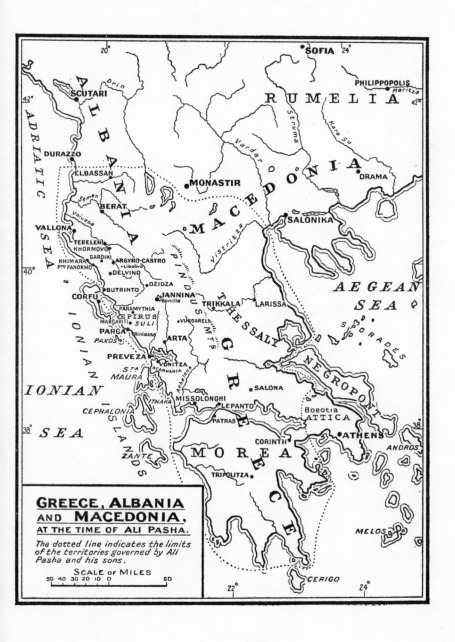

20° SOFIA 24°

SCUTARI PHILIPPOPOLIS
Maritza

ALBANIA RUMELIA
42° Drin 42°

ADRIATIC DURAZZO
ELBASSAN MONASTIR Struma
Vardar DRAMA

BERAT MACEDONIA
Semeni SALONIKA
Voiussa

VALLONA

SEA TEBELENI MACEDONIA
KHORMOVO
KHIMARA GARDIKI ARGYRO-CASTRO Vistritza
40° Pto PANORMO Liboövo 40°
DELVINO
BUTRINTO DZIDZA AEGEAN
CORFU JANNINA TRIKKALA LARISSA SEA
Bonilla
PARAMYTHIA EPIRUS THESSALY SPORADES
MARGARITI SULI VURGARELI
PARGA Riniassa
PAXOS ARTA GREECE

PREVEZA VONITZA NEGROPONT
STA CARNANIA
MAURA Achelous

IONIAN ITHAKA SALONA
MISSOLONGHI
CEPHALONIA LEPANTO Boeotia
PATRAS ATTICA
38° SEA CORINTH ATHENS 38°
ZANTE ANDROS
MOREA

ISLANDS
TRIPOLITZA

MELOS

GREECE, ALBANIA
AND MACEDONIA,
AT THE TIME OF ALI PASHA.

*The dotted line indicates the limits
of the territories governed by Ali
Pasha and his sons.*

SCALE OF MILES
50 40 30 20 10 0   50

22° CERIGO 24°

CHAPTER I

ALI'S ORIGINS

ABOUT the year 1600 an obscure religious establishment in Asia Minor contained among its inmates a dancing dervish whose name was Nazif. He did something wrong, and as a result was either turned out or thought it best to run away. He made his way out of Asia into Europe, and wandered about the Balkans, a tramp and beggar, until he came to a village in Albania called Tebeleni, where he chose to settle down. Surrounded by vineyards which produced a poor red wine, and by a few fields of wheat and barley, the village stood on a high rocky peninsula above the waters of the river Voiussa, which in that place is about as wide as the Thames at Kew, though very much more turbulent. On all sides it was over-looked by huge, wild mountain heights, bleak and desolate, and the breeding-place of violent storms. There were no trees to be seen, the wind often howled and the river came down in flood, and altogether Tebeleni was well suited to be the nursery of a race of people anything but mild, and in particular of a family which was to provide on a grand scale successive displays of all the more violent and devastating passions of which human beings are capable.

Like most villagers, the people of Tebeleni were not in-clined to be trustful of strangers, and they were not too ready to take to Nazif. They did not like the idea of a man settling amongst them who was not of their race and did not even speak their language, but they allowed him to establish himself in a wretched hut some way off. Since he spoke Turkish they soon found a use for him as an interpreter, for they only spoke

Albanian themselves, and they grew so accustomed to him that he eventually married a girl of the village.

Nazif left a son called Hussein, who managed to marry the daughter of a bey in the neighbourhood. The reason that the girl was allowed to make such an undistinguished match was that she happened to be lame and it had not been easy to find a husband for her at all. She gave birth to a son who was called Mustapha and allowed the title of bey. This Mustapha Bey, like his father and grandfather before him, acted as interpreter at Tebeleni. He did well for himself, and became a person of some consequence – nothing less, in fact, than vice-governor of the village – leaving when he died a son and two grandsons, named Mukhtar and Bekir. Mukhtar succeeded his grandfather in the post of vice-governor, and took part in the Turkish expedition against Corfu in 1716, when he was captured and put to death by its Venetian defenders, which caused him to be regarded by the Turks as a martyr. He left three sons, of whom the youngest was called Veli Bey, and his brother Bekir left a son called Islam Bey, who became vice-governor of Tebeleni.

In those days each district and sometimes each village in that part of the world was like a republic on its own, and these different republics lived in a state of anarchy, rivalry, and perpetual warfare, although in theory they were all dominions of the Turkish Empire, against the corrupt and grasping authorities of which they would sometimes combine to defend themselves. Family life was much disturbed by politics, and life in general by feuds and vendettas kept going for all sorts of private and public reasons. Now Islam Bey had not only bettered himself at Tebeleni, but had taken under his wing, in return for the payment of tribute, several Christian villages in the neighbourhood. One of these villages, called Khormovo, he entrusted to his cousin Veli

18

to be defended against enemies from outside. If the people of
Khormovo had enemies, it is not surprising, for they were
notorious as bandits, and no doubt their victims or the
relations of their victims tried to get a little of their own back.
They used to drag the victims, when they had captured them,
to a certain tree, which they said was an oracle. Actually this
tree was hollow, and one of their priests used to hide inside it
and then give out, in a suitably oracular tone of voice, instructions as to what was to be done to the prisoners: sometimes
they were stripped and hanged on the tree; sometimes,
deprived of their horses and all their belongings, they were
allowed to depart on foot. Now it happened that Veli was
jealous of his cousin Islam, and on bad terms with his own
brothers as well, and not at all in the frame of mind to do
nothing but defend Khormovo, so he put himself at the head
of a gang of brigands and began to engage in the prevailing
local industry, or sport, of highway robbery. Cousin Islam,
who was supposed to stand for law and order, was naturally
not at all pleased at this waywardness, and perhaps a little
apprehensive as to what might happen next.

Veli decided to get his brothers out of the way first. He
led his gang in a surprise attack on Tebeleni and set fire to a
building in which his brothers were taking refuge. They
were both conveniently burnt to death, and Veli came into
the family fortune of six thousand piastres a year. Money was
not enough, he wanted rank as well, and it seemed to him
absurd that Cousin Islam should continue in office as vice-
governor of Tebeleni. He soon found a way of removing the
absurdity. Islam had just been ordered by some higher
authority to punish some wrongdoers who came originally
from Khormovo, so he had them arrested and brought to his
office, where they were given the bastinado and then locked
up. Veli at once set himself to work on the feelings of the

inhabitants of Khormovo, with such success that he excited
the relations and friends of the prisoners into making an
attempt to free them by force. The relations and friends,
glowing with righteous indignation, hurried over to Tebeleni,
set fire to Islam's house, killed him, and shared out his
belongings, as a result of which Veli not only became vice-
governor, but was accorded the title of Pasha of Two Tails.
This promising career, however, seems to have gone no
further. He was so soft as to be nice to Islam's widow and
orphans, and was led such a trying life by a number of jealous
or revengeful beys and agas in the neighbourhood, that he not
only failed to enrich himself, but when he died in 1753, at the
age of forty-five, he died poor.

Veli had married, as his second wife, a woman of great
force of character, as little given to gentleness as Tamora,
Queen of the Goths,

'When Goths were Goths, and Tamora was queen.'

Her name was Khamco, she was the daughter of a notability and through her Veli had become connected with some
of the chief families of Albania, and in particular with no less a
person than Kurd Pasha, the Vizier of Berat. By Khamco Veli
had had two children, a daughter called Shainitza, and a son
called Ali, the subject of this book.

CHAPTER II

THE SKIPETARS

GIBBON said of Albania that a country 'within sight of Italy is less known than the interior of America'. The Albanians amongst whom Ali grew up (counting himself one of them) and on whom he was chiefly to rely for support in getting and keeping power, were a remarkable race, and some effort of imagination has to be made by us to understand their way of living. Perhaps of Scythian origin, they called themselves Skipetars, and spoke a mixed language with a Slavonic basis. Edward Lear, who visited Albania in Victorian times and continued to employ Albanian servants, whimsically recorded part of a conversation as sounding like 'dort beer, dort bloo, dort hitch, hitch beer, blue beer, beer chak, dort gatch', which is at least suggestive of outlandishness. And outlandish the Skipetars certainly were, a vigorous race, half shepherds and half warriors, devoted to their native mountains and inheriting heroic traits from the remote past. From those mountains came the mother of Alexander the Great, and George Castriotes, known as Scanderbeg, the national hero who in the fifteenth century waged unceasing war against the Turks for twenty-three years. It is said that entire phrases from Homer may be regarded even to-day as typical Albanian expressions, and as in their language so in their life archaic virtues were to be found.

They delighted to regard themselves as Palikars, or braves, and they were not without justification in doing so. 'In general, the Albanians are of a high stature,' observed the Baron de Vaudoncourt, 'strongly muscular, and thin waisted,

21

which is occasioned by the use of the girdles they are in the habit of binding round their bodies. Their profile is handsome . . . and tends to form the real Grecian features.' The general impression was one of alertness, and the prevailing type had a fresh colour, lively and expressive grey eyes, thin arched eyebrows, bony foreheads and high cheekbones. Their mouths were small, their necks long, their backs straight, their chests broad and elevated, and their arms and legs well made. All observers agreed that they carried themselves with a great air. They could all make their own clothes, which Byron called 'the most magnificent in the world', and usually wore a small scarlet skull-cap on the front of the head, which was shaved, while the hair at the back was worn very long; a mantle, falling loosely over the shoulders and reaching down to the knees, made of a coarse brown woollen stuff, embroidered with red; two waistcoats, the outer one open, and sometimes of green or purple velvet, the inner one laced and embroidered; a sash and a strap tightly bound round their small waists and serving to hold a pistol or two and a dagger, the handles worked with silver; a cotton shirt and drawers; a long sabre, kept as sharp as a razor; circular greaves of worked metal over knees and ankles, and sometimes coloured stockings as well; sandals; and over all a great shaggy white capote of sheepskin or goatskin with a hood and loose open sleeves. Across their backs they slung a long-barrelled musket, and round their necks they wore silver chains with amulets, silver snuff-boxes or watches in shagreen cases slung at the end of them. Besides, they often wore in their girdles, next to their pistols and daggers, silver pen-and-inkstands, of which they were very proud.

In spite of all this equipment, which of course was varied according to seasons and occasions, they were agile and athletic in their gait, being used all their lives to climbing mountains, and their energy and enthusiasm made a strong contrast with the slowness and sedateness of their overlords, the turbaned Turks, whom they thought base and cowardly. The capote served not only to protect them from the weather, but as a bed, and their only preparation for sleep was to loosen the ligatures round their middles and pull their capotes over them. They had little taste for washing either themselves or their clothes, which made them smell rather strong, and they would often go on wearing a shirt until it was worn out without ever taking it off except to hold it over a fire occasionally in order to drive out the various kinds of vermin with which they were infested. They were not in the least ashamed of this and would brush the fleas off their clothes by dozens without turning a hair: the Albanian flea, it may be remarked, has been called 'the biggest and fattest in the world'.

Owing to the hardiness of their existence they were seldom ill, their houses and furniture were primitive in the extreme, their way of living was frugal, and their diet simple and mostly vegetarian, consisting chiefly of flour, maize meal or rice, milk, cheese, butter, eggs and olives, with occasional roast mutton or goat, but never beef or pork. They sometimes caught partridges in nets, and when they could afford it they liked to keep greyhounds for coursing hares.

In temperament they were gay and lively, but apt to be hasty and violent. Unlike the Turks and other Orientals they were frank and demonstrative, and never hid their feelings, whether of admiration or contempt. They were apt to be very fond of money, partly for its own sake, but mainly because they could use it to increase their personal adornment or to buy arms. With a passion for music, they spent much of their leisure in playing, singing and dancing. In their dance, the Albanitiko, supposed by some to be a survival of the Pyrrhic dance, a line of men would hold hands, singing, moving at first slowly backwards and forwards, then hurrying round in a quick circular movement while the music got more and more exciting. The leader, or coryphaeus, would leap in the air, bend backwards till his head almost touched the ground, and leap again with the elasticity and perfect ease of a trained acrobat or ballet dancer.

> For ere night's midmost, stillest hour was past
> The native revels of the troop began;
> Each Palikar his sabre from him cast,
> And bounding hand in hand, man linked to man,
> Yelling their uncouth dirge, long danced the kirtled
> clan.

It is not surprising that Byron should have admired them. For one thing they reminded him of the Highlanders of Scotland. 'Their mountains seemed Caledonian, with a kinder climate. The kilt, though white; the spare, active form; their dialect, Celtic in its sound; and their hardy habits, all carried me back to Morven . . .' Their manner of walking he found 'truly theatrical', and their long hair reminded him of the Spartans. In all that he learnt or observed of their ways, there was much that appealed to him, and no doubt their wild and melancholy music was perfectly attuned to his romantic temper. In the mountain pastures the shepherds could be heard, as in the time of Theocritus, playing on nine-holed pipes made of the thigh-bones of eagles, which are very hard and of a convenient size: and sometimes two men would sing to the accompaniment of a pipe, a violin, and a tambourine, the song being given in alternate response by the two voices, while the pipe, very shrill and slightly harsh, regulated the pauses of the voices, and on these pauses, long and perfectly timed, the harmony was made to depend.

Circumstances helped to foster the natural feeling of the

Skipetars for poetry, which with them was, as it should be, an important part of the pattern of the people's life and thoughts. No hard and fast line could be drawn between Albania and Epirus, or between Epirus and the rest of Greece, and since many of the songs of those times and places have been preserved, we can consider the imagery that was familiar to the people. These songs and the people who sang them did not conform to Christian ideals, or as a rule to those of Western Europe, but the fact that the Skipetars were pagan does not mean that they deserve to be either condemned or idealized out of hand: the horrors and splendours of modern civilization in the West have been on a larger and more complex but not necessarily on a higher or lower moral scale than those of European Turkey a century or two ago, for the behaviour of human beings in all times and places is distinguished by varying blends of ferocity and idealism. Sometimes, if one asked a Skipetar what his occupation was, he would reply, 'I am a Klepht', which means simply, 'I am a robber', and although this may sound shameless, are those who rob us to-day on the Stock Exchange and elsewhere anything like as honest? Or as picturesque? There was an Albanian proverb to the effect that 'the Devil is not as wicked as people believe, neither is the Skipetar'.

The influence of Greek Christianity on the old paganism of the people of Epirus and Albania had been slight, and most of the inspiration of their poetry is quite obviously non-Christian. They had, for instance, a profound feeling of oneness with nature and a habit of attributing human feelings to all kinds of natural phenomena; they did not associate sexual love with any idea of 'sin'; they did not believe in any future system of rewards and punishments; and they believed so firmly in the propriety of revenge that the vendetta was often a sacred tradition handed down to successive generations in family, village and tribe. To read their songs is to realize how their animistic view of nature lent to their everyday lives that element of magic which people need. The sun, in one poem, speaks in pity to a deer whose fawn has been killed by a hunter; in another a widow's daughter desires only the dawn for a husband; the moon is prayed to by a child; a man speaks of himself as the son of the lightning and of his wife as the daughter of the thunder; mountains are asked questions, to which they reply; one mountain courts and embraces another, which gives birth to a hero; the moon tells the ocean that she has seen two lovers kissing, the ocean tells an oar, and the oar tells a sailor; ink, of its own volition, traces questions on paper, addressed to the man who carries it; a forsaken wife asks her bed and pillow where her husband has gone, and they reply; a bridge breaks in two and a stream stops flowing because of a young widow's sorrow; and a ship stops sailing because it is horrified by the groans of a prisoner. Trees, especially the cypress, apple, and rose, are endowed with feelings and the power of speech, and by the condition of a rose tree and a carnation a mother knows of the health and finally of the death of her son. Birds give warning of death or betrayal, a partridge reproaches a girl for killing her baby, an owl heralds the approach of vampires in the form of corpses that have come to life, ghastly embodiments of necrophilous instincts. The whole landscape is haunted by elementals, malevolent nymphs, snake-women or lamias, sirens, witches, dragons and gorgons. As for the sense of sin, rape and murder occur as a matter of course, and there is a song about a girl who bribed St. George to hide her from a pursuing Turkish lover, whereupon the saint, bribed more lavishly by the amorous Turk, gave away her hiding place – a significant illustration of the usefulness of money, which was to be highly appreciated by Ali himself.

If the Skipetars were not good Christians, nobody could have called them good Mohammedans, and indeed they were known as Men without a Creed: a man would marry a Christian, take his sons to the mosque and let his daughters go to church, or go to both alternately himself, or to neither, would eat forbidden foods, drink wine, and remain uncircumcized. Most of the men married, as it was useful to possess a domestic slave, and gave them status. They were usually too poor to keep more than one wife, and a bride brought no dowry to her husband but was purchased at a stipulated price, on which a deposit was made at the time of the engagement, usually arranged when the contracting parties were still children. Women were regarded as cattle, and when lazy were punished with blows – although amongst them Byron saw the most beautiful he 'ever beheld'. While their husbands were out hunting or tending the flocks they cultivated the ground and looked after household affairs. They led no soft harem existence like the Greek and Turkish women, but shared the hard life of the men, and would go with them to the battlefield in order to attend the wounded and carry away the dead. Hobhouse, the travelling companion of Byron, observed that the men had 'rather a contempt and even aversion for their females, and there is nothing in any of their occasional inclinations which can be said to partake of what we call the tender passion. In short, their habit of life . . . appears to render them quite independent of the other sex, whom they never mention nor seem to miss in their usual concerns or amusements. The same habit is productive of a system which is carried by them to an extent of which no nation, perhaps, either modern or ancient, unless we reluctantly except the Thebans, can furnish a similar instance . . . After this information it may be considered very singular that the Albanians are exceedingly decent in their outward manners and behaviour,

27

never admitting an immodest word or gesture in their conversation, nor indulging in that kind of talk which is the
delight of some, even above the lower orders, in more civilized
parts of the world'.

In other words, they were much given to homosexual
practices, and were quite uninhibited about them. Parallels
to this can easily be found amongst other races in various ages,
living a formalized or stylized military life, keeping women in
subjection or at least in the background, and having always
before them as an image of perfection the young warrior:
one thinks of the ancient Greeks, the Germans, the Zulus at
the height of their power, the Japanese as described by Saikaku.
No question of degeneracy is involved, the Skipetars being a
race noted for health and physical perfection and living a
strenuous life in a rugged country with a pretty severe climate.
Nor can a hopeless moral turpitude be ascribed to them,
whatever Christianity may say, for they were celebrated not
merely for their bravery, their love of liberty and their devotion to their native mountains and villages, but for their
faithfulness and gratitude to friends and benefactors, and their
general liveliness of feeling. Byron describes how an Albanian
servant said good-bye to him. After receiving his pay the
Skipetar suddenly 'dashed it to the ground: and clasping his
hands, which he raised to his forehead, rushed out of the room,
weeping bitterly. From that moment to the hour of my
embarkation, he continued his lamentations, and all our
efforts to console him only produced this answer, "He is
leaving me!" '

A Skipetar meeting an acquaintance, even after a short
absence, would exchange with him a handshake and a kiss,
which would be repeated at parting, and after each of them
had gone a little distance on their respective ways, each would
fire into the air a pistol shot as a signal of farewell. It was

customary for young men who were closely attached to each other to swear eternal vows, and that this was not simply a matter of mere sentimentality or sensuality, or both, is shown by the fact that the contract was regarded as sacred and proved more durable than marriage often is with us, or friendship either, for it is said that no instance was ever known of its violation.

CHAPTER III

ALI GROWS UP

'WHEN my father died,' Ali used to say long afterwards, 'he left me nothing but a wretched hole of a place and some fields.' It seems, however, that he also inherited the sum of sixty paras and a musket. At ten years old he was ungovernable. From early childhood he had not only shown great restlessness and energy, but a kind of nervous irritability unusual amongst members of his race though characteristic of his mother. His one idea had always been to get out of doors and wander in the mountains and forests, and although his father had once engaged a tutor for him he had always run away and had never learnt to read until forced to by his mother.

When Veli was alive, Khamco's forcefulness had not found enough scope: she had lived in the seclusion of his harem, looking after domestic matters and jealously guarding the rights of her children Ali and Shainitza against the children of her husband's first marriage. She must have been a formidable stepmother, and now she was a widow she determined to let herself go. There was a good deal of unpleasantness with Cousin Islam's widow (to whom Veli had been so kind, and who was still living in Tebeleni), so Khamco decided to move away from the village and do her best to defend her children against her late husband's enemies. She therefore took up arms, gathered Veli's partisans around her, and putting herself at their head, took to the open country, where she shared their dangers and hardships, and fought and robbed with the best of them. Her new headquarters were at Carniani, near Argyro Castro.

Islam's widow concentrated on plotting to avenge the murder of her husband, and in Tebeleni she made as much propaganda against Khamco as she could. She suggested to her supporters that it would be a good idea to attack the people of Khormovo, who had not only helped in the murder but were still devoted to Khamco. As it happened, Khamco got wind of this project, and told the people of Khormovo that if they did not want to be blotted out they had better strike first. This they did. Led by an unfrocked monk, they marched suddenly on Tebeleni and in one of the usual surprise attacks massacred Islam's widow and her children. The people of Tebeleni naturally blamed Khamco, but she denied all responsibility in the matter. All the same she was afraid of reprisals, and decided to stay at Carniani in the midst of her faithful bodyguard, several members of which shared not only her anxieties but her bed.

Her affairs now went badly. First of all she put up the backs of the people of Khormovo by demanding an increase in the amount of the annual tribute which they paid her. Then she took a fancy to a little Christian village and thought she would like to obtain it for herself. This village was subject to the Mohammedans of Gardiki, who were as much afraid of her growing influence as they were of losing their revenues from the village in question, so they decided to enter into an alliance with the disgruntled Khormovo. As a result of this they were able to lay an ambush and take Khamco prisoner. They thought the time had come to teach her a lesson she would not forget, and indeed she did not forget it. They treated her very badly, shut her up in a dungeon by day, and took her out each night and forced her to submit to the embraces as well as the insults of the men of each house in turn. A Greek merchant of Argyro Castro heard of her misfortunes and felt so sorry for her that he paid her ransom of 23,000 piastres.

As soon as she was free she retired to Kiata, an estate of Veli's, but the local inhabitants, who were Christians, took a dislike to her, and she decided to return to Tebeleni – which was just as well, for she had no sooner left Kiata than her house there was burnt down.

Her two stepchildren now died suddenly within a short time of each other, and it was said, no doubt on excellent authority, that she had poisoned them. She applied herself next to putting her affairs in order and bringing up her own children. She had the most powerful influence over them, and with her very milk they drank in ambition, greed and hatred. When people behave in a way that other people dislike or do not expect, they are sometimes said to be not quite right in the head, but this is usually a charitable excuse for bad behaviour. There is no reason to suppose that Khamco was mad, but she was certainly anything but normal, and the violence of her passions may perhaps be ascribed partly to some physical peculiarity. She was especially careful to inspire her children with the idea that it was their sacred duty to avenge the wrongs that had been done to her by her enemies during her widowhood, and above all by those who had imprisoned and outraged her at Gardiki. She told Ali that a man who does not defend his inheritance deserves to lose it, and that in this world might is right and everybody obeys the strong. Her teaching was like that of the apparition conjured up by the witches in *Macbeth*: 'Be bloody, bold and resolute'.

'I owe everything to her,' said Ali in later days. 'Twice she gave me life, as a man and as a ruler. She kindled my imagination and showed me my destiny. From then I only thought of Tebeleni as a place from which to swoop out on my prey. I only dreamt of power and treasure and palaces, which time gave me and will give me still, for I have not yet gained all I hope for.'

The country was ripe for the incursion of an ambitious man. It was badly governed, roughly on the principle of 'Divide and rule'. Pashas, appointed by the Ottoman Porte with the Sultan's authority, acted as governors in various important centres like Jannina and Delvino, but under their sway various districts and towns, like Khimara, Gardiki, Argyro Castro and Suli, were allowed to keep their independence on the condition of paying tribute. Some of the people were Mohammedan, some Christian, some just Men without a Creed; some spoke Greek, some Albanian, and some Turkish. Rebellions were frequent, feuds incessant, and brigandage universal in a country perfectly adapted for guerilla warfare, and remote from the capital. In short, the general state of affairs was almost anarchy, but this did not greatly trouble the Porte, so long as tribute streamed into Constantinople and the supreme authority of the Sultan was acknowledged.

At fourteen, Ali was already stealing sheep and goats and organizing raids on neighbouring villages, a brigand like his father and mother, a member of a profession recognized, lawful, and almost respectable in that part of the world in those days, so long as it did no damage to the local authorities. If Ali's enterprises often prospered, that was largely due to his energy, perseverance, courage, memory, unscrupulousness, dashing leadership, heroic luck, and cunning, and to the fact that he was one of the finest horsemen, swiftest runners and most expert shots in a country where every man could ride, run and shoot. But he was by no means invariably lucky and successful. When at the head of his gang he attacked Khormovo to punish the people for having sided with the Gardikiots against his mother, he met with an unexpectedly firm resistance, and returned home, disheartened and alone. Khamco was furious and told him that he would be better employed with a distaff

than a gun, and that the proper place for such a cissy was in
the harem.

The taunts of his mother and his neighbours were too much
for him, so he left Tebeleni with thirty of his comrades and
took service with the Pasha of Negropont. As leader of a
company of irregular police, he was set to guard the frontiers
of the district, but the job did not interest him and he went
off with his men on looting expeditions in Thessaly and elsewhere. His exploits were already becoming legendary, and a
purely fictitious story was made up according to which he had
taken shelter, once when his fortunes were very low, in the
ruins of a deserted monastery, and was grumbling about his
bad luck and discontentedly prodding the ground with a stick
when he heard a hollow sound as if it had struck something;
scraping away the earth, he found a casket full of Venetian
gold coins, and with this treasure was enabled (so the story
ran) to make a new start.

His activities came to the notice of Kurd Pasha of Berat,
who was head of all the police in Southern Albania, Thessaly
and the Morea. His name Kurd, which means Wolf, had been
won by his bravery and skill in war, and he was a man of
immense authority and prestige. He ordered the beys under
his administration to round up Ali and his gang, which they
did, and Ali himself was brought as a prisoner to Berat. Most
of his comrades were hanged, and Ali was afraid the same
might happen to him, but the Wolf took a liking to him, and
perhaps decided that this was a life too remarkable to be
wasted. Ali at twenty was irresistible, handsome, with long
fair hair and blue eyes, full of fire and charm, intelligent,
graceful and talkative. He was not very tall, but finely made,
in perfect condition, and obviously a personality. The Wolf
(who was related to Khamco, a circumstance which may have
helped him to decide to be lenient to her son) scolded him but

treated him kindly, and he stayed at Berat for several years. It was a pleasant place as well as an important one, with its famous citadel on the top of a cliff, its gardens, its wealth, its thirteen mosques, its river which swam under the eight arches of a graceful bridge in the Turkish style, and its women dressed mostly in blue, with blue bonnets two feet high shaped like mitres, stuffed, and tied with ribbons under the chin.

Ali at last felt himself so much in favour that he made bold enough to ask for the hand of the Wolf's daughter in marriage. When this request was made, the Wolf's treasurer, a man of deep policy and great experience, advised his master either to make sure of Ali's fidelity by letting him marry the girl, or to remove him as a likely source of danger by killing him at once. The Wolf did neither. He had in any case already chosen as his son-in-law a man of better birth and position than Ali, namely Ibrahim Pasha of Vallona, and in 1764 the marriage duly took place. Ali, like his mother, was never half-hearted. He was now furious, and conceived towards Ibrahim a violent hatred, which lasted till the end of his life. He was so embittered that he fled from Berat dressed as a beggar, rejoined his old companions, and took to banditry in the mountains again.

The Wolf, after warning him not to expect any mercy if he persisted in this sort of behaviour, now put a price on his head of 5000 piastres. Ali went into hiding with his gang. It included two of his best friends, two Christians, his adopted brothers, called Skanto Boya and Lak Doro. He suggested to these two that they should drape some of his clothes over a ram, take a few shots at the beast, and then carry the clothes to the Wolf, showing him the bullet holes and bloodstains as evidence of their having killed Ali. This they did, and succeeded in getting the 5000 piastres, which they at once handed over to Ali. He used the money to start a new gang, whose

exploits soon became a matter of serious concern to the Wolf.
He was now sick of being worried by Ali, and sent out a strong
force to suppress him. Ali was sheltered for a while in a
Christian village and then took refuge with Caplan Pasha of
Delvino, whom he knew to be the Wolf's bitterest enemy.
Caplan received him with open arms.

Weary of his agitating life and of the many dangers he had
narrowly escaped, Ali was glad to settle down quietly for a
time with his new protector. Khamco thought this a suitable
moment to provide him with a wife, so she asked and obtained
for him Caplan's daughter Eminé, who was also known by the
luscious-sounding name of Umm-Gulsum. The marriage was
celebrated in grand style at Argyro Castro in 1768, and added
greatly to Ali's prestige. That the ceremony was not wanting
in picturesqueness may be gathered from some hint of the
surroundings. Argyro Castro (a mixture, remarked an English
traveller, of 'the pleasing with the grand') was a town of
mosques and minarets, with fine trees, whitewashed houses,
and a black castle, all built at different levels on three high
ridges with deep ravines between, against a panorama of
magnificent mountains. The men took care to appear splendid, and the women wore, as their ordinary dress, tight white
linen masks over the face with two small slots for the eyes,
voluminous white robes with broad buff stripes, short full
trousers of purplé calico, and canary yellow top-boots with
rose-coloured tassels.

At the time of his marriage Ali was twenty-four. Khamco
congratulated herself on having allied her son with a rich and
powerful family, and in due course two sons were born,
Mukhtar in 1769 and Veli two years later.

CHAPTER IV

HIS PROGRESS

CAPLAN PASHA thought that by getting for a son-in-law a man already well known for his enterprising and ambitious nature he would be gaining a very useful ally who would strengthen his own position and alarm his enemies. Ali, however, was much more interested in promoting his own fortunes than those of his father-in-law, whom he considered simply as an obstacle to be got out of the way as quickly as possible. He very soon found a suitable opportunity. The people of Khimara, who lived in the wilds of the Acroceraunian mountains, had been causing some annoyance to the authorities at Constantinople: presently the Porte sent orders to Caplan Pasha to go and punish them. Caplan did not like the idea, partly because the job would be a difficult one and partly because he wanted Khimara as an ally in his schemes for extending his own power. Ali knew this, and encouraged his father-in-law to postpone making any expedition: at the same time he wrote to the governor of Rumelia, denouncing Caplan's delay and hinting broadly at the reasons for it. Caplan was accordingly sent for to Monastir to come and explain himself. This alarmed him so much that he hesitated to obey, but Ali knowing very well what the consequences were likely to be, urged him to go to Monastir, which he did. Everything, from Ali's point of view, worked perfectly, for as soon as Caplan got to Monastir his head was cut off.

Ali was of course hoping that he would be rewarded with the vacant pashalik and part of Caplan's fortune, but he was doubly disappointed, for Caplan's eldest son Ali Bey of Argyro

Castro was appointed Pasha of Delvino and the fortune was sequestrated. Not only was Ali upset by the failure of his plans but his mother Khamco saw that a bitter enmity was likely to arise between Ali and the new Pasha unless something was done quickly to put them on good terms with one another. She therefore arranged a marriage between Ali Bey and her daughter Shainitza.

Shainitza bore her husband a son, Elmas, and a daughter, Hasbié, but the marriage, needless to say, did not bring about any reconciliation between the two Alis. Ali of Tebeleni made so little secret of his hatred for Ali of Delvino that he proposed to his sister that she should poison him. Although she was just as violent a character as her mother, Shainitza was too loyal to her husband to do what was asked of her, and at the same time too loyal to her brother to give away his wicked intentions. Finding her unaccommodating, Ali pretended to be sorry and said he had given up the plan, but gradually gained a great influence over one of the Pasha's brothers named Suleiman, who was only sixteen. He promised Suleiman that if he would help to get the Pasha out of the way he should have Shainitza and her fortune, while Ali should have the pashalik. Ali and Suleiman accordingly swore vows to aid each other. It was a pretty arrangement: a brother was to kill a brother, while another brother was to reward this deed by encouraging his sister's marriage with her deceased husband's brother, who was at the same time her deceased husband's murderer.

And the deed was accomplished. Suleiman, alone with his brother the Pasha at Argyro Castro, shot him dead. Ali immediately appeared on the scene, and Shainitza, who had heard the shot, rushed in to find out the cause and effect of it. Ali forbade her to cry out or he would kill her too. He then ordered Suleiman to wrap her in his pelisse, by which simple

ceremony he declared her his wife. Just as a finishing touch
the marriage was consummated on the spot, beside the still
warm corpse. It was given out that the Pasha had died of
apoplexy, but everybody said that he had been murdered.

It was expected that Ali, as the brother-in-law of the
victim, would attack Argyro Castro to avenge the crime, but
when he did nothing of the sort people naturally said that he
had instigated it. He lost no time in trying to get himself
nominated as the new Pasha of Delvino, but again had no
luck. The title went to a local dignitary named Mustapha Aga
Koka. But Ali was nothing if not persevering, and Mustapha
died shortly afterwards, mysteriously assassinated by an
unknown hand.

Mustapha again was not succeeded by Ali, but by another
local worthy named Selim Bey, who was given preference
owing to the size and regularity of the contributions he had
been sending to Constantinople. Ali was the first to call and
congratulate the new Pasha: he made friends with him, and
for some time lived as his guest, watching intently for the
very first opportunity of putting him, like his predecessors,
out of the way. It was his usual plan:

> I under fair pretence of friendly ends . . .
> Wind me into the easy-hearted man
> And hug him into snares.

Now it happened that Selim had sold to the Venetians,
who were still in occupation of parts of the coast, the right to
cut some standing timber, and had also done what he could to
promote friendly relations with them. This was Ali's chance.
He reported that Selim had at the same time actually sold the
land on which the timber stood. Making this accusation, he
well knew that the sale of Turkish territory to a Christian
power would be regarded as a crime of high treason against the

Ottoman Empire and of sacrilege against the Mohammedan
faith. Ali did not make the report entirely on the strength of
his own word, but got some local enemies of Selim's to back
him up, and in order to lend additional weight to his charges
he pointed out how painful it was for him to have to make
these accusations against a man who was his friend and said
that he only did it from an overmastering sense of duty to
Faith and Empire – religion, like patriotism, often being useful
not only as 'the last refuge of a scoundrel' but as his first excuse
for immoderate behaviour. His stories were believed at Constantinople, where it was so often best to believe the worst, and
an imperial decree was sent to Ali by a secret messenger, con-
demning Selim to death for high treason and ordering Ali to
carry out the sentence himself.

The messenger found Ali at Tebeleni. Armed with the
decree, and not only with the decree, Ali went straight to
Delvino, where Selim welcomed him in his usual friendly way
and put him up as his guest. According to custom, Ali had
with him an armed escort of Skipetars. Every morning he
went to pay his respects to Selim in the audience-chamber,
and one day, when the weather was very hot, complained of
not feeling well, and asked Selim if he might go and rest in
another room.

'By all means,' said Selim, 'and I'll soon come and join
you and see how you are, and I hope you'll soon be feeling
better.'

Ali thanked him and withdrew, with several of his men,
to Selim's private room. In this room there were some cupboards without shelves, of the kind that are used in Oriental
countries for storing the bedclothes which at night are spread
out on the floor, or divans, and in these cupboards he hid his
men, telling them that when he dropped his coffee cup on the
floor that would be a signal for them to pounce out on Selim.

40

Everything worked perfectly. Selim came in. After a few minutes' conversation Ali dropped his coffee cup. The men sprang out. Selim in falling had time to utter an *Et tu, Brute* – 'So it's *you*, my boy!' – when his own guards, hearing the sounds of a scuffle, rushed in and began fighting with the assassins. Several on both sides were killed before Ali could separate them which he did by dramatically waving the unrolled decree and announcing that he had come by the Imperial order to execute a traitor. The guards withdrew, and Ali, nothing if not thorough, at once had an official document drawn up to say that the terms of the decree had been carried out, and sent Selim's two sons away under escort to Tebeleni.

He was rewarded for this murder with the rank and title he had so long coveted, and was nominated Pasha of Delvino. Unfortunately, however, the people of the district, who had been much attached to Selim, refused to put up with their new ruler, for it was common knowledge that he had engineered the murder, and Ali had to send a deputy to Delvino to govern in his name. Soon afterwards, one of Selim's sons, Mustapha by name, managed to escape from Tebeleni, returned to Delvino, and raised a rebellion against the deputy, who was lynched: he then proclaimed himself Pasha of Delvino, and was soon recognized as such by the authorities at Constantinople, who had no doubt learnt in the meantime how unjust they had been to believe all they had heard about his father.

Ali had to wait and watch for another opening. He soon found one. By means of lavish bribes he got himself appointed an assistant to the chief inspector of roads in Rumelia and then, instead of suppressing the bandits, which was his chief duty, he started what Chicago has taught us to call a racket, and sold them licences to pursue their calling unmolested, in return for which they paid him regular tribute and gave him a share of their loot. They did so well that Ali grew rich, the roads became quite impassable to travellers, and the chief inspector was recalled to Constantinople where his head, evidently considered a poor one, was cut off.

A year or two later, the old Wolf died, being then Pasha of Vallona and also a chief inspector of roads, responsible for public safety and for guarding strategic points like mountain passes. The pashalik of Vallona went to the Wolf's son, Mehmet, but Ali put in a claim for the chief inspectorship. He persuaded some Epirot merchants in Constantinople to press his claims and make him out to be the only man with enough energy and knowledge of the country to free Thessaly and the district round Jannina from bandits, and he promised in return to protect them if he were successful. He was successful, and not only obtained the chief inspectorship but was appointed Pasha of Trikkala in Thessaly.

'The mountains of Greece,' says Mr. John Mavrocordato, 'had always been the haunt of a semi-nomadic class of pastoral warriors, who took the name of Klephts from their occasional occupation of brigandage, and had never submitted to the Turkish authorities except in so far as they had themselves from time to time been invested with a sort of constabulary authority as Armatoles – poachers turned gamekeepers.' The Armatoles, supposed to be a survival of a militia that had existed under the Byzantine Empire, were pledged by treaty to help the authorities to maintain law and order, but they were often no better than brigands themselves, and sometimes went so far as to join their more independent countrymen, the Klephts, whom they were supposed to put down. The Klephts, amongst whom all sorts of odd men were to be found, adventurers, fugitives from justice, and wild creatures with no taste for steady work, lived in a state of romantic outlawry and perpetual hostility against the Turks. They were hostile to the Turks as the oppressors of their country and enemies of their religion, and they were romantic because they took a pride in heroism, because they were picturesque freebooters, because they were fond of dancing and singing, because they had a chivalrous code of behaviour, because as enemies of an oppressor they were themselves friends to the oppressed, and because theirs was a Robin Hood-like existence of dashing and daring. They were often hospitable to travellers who sought their protection, they were kind to women prisoners, they seldom or never turned Mohammedan; their lives were hard but by no means without compensations, and much of their spare time was taken up with singing and dancing, running, wrestling and shooting. Making sudden descents from the heights of Pindus into villages in the plains of Thessaly or in Epirus they would rob the houses of rich Turks and take hostages for ransom. Many were caught and killed or tortured, and some found the strain of their existence too much and deserted, but others gained a legendary fame, like Buffalo Bill in the West, and their names and deeds are remembered and written and sung about until the present day, not least because they fostered the ideal of liberty, the right of self-determination, and the early beginnings of Greek independence.

As chief inspector Ali no longer behaved like a racketeer, but set about his duties in earnest. With a force of 4000 Skipetars he scoured the whole countryside, chasing Armatoles and Klephts, beheading their leaders, breaking up their gangs, and forcing them to take to the least accessible mountains and stay there.

'I found nothing but an exhausted country,' he said, describing his activities when Pasha of Trikkala. 'The agas of Larissa had pretended that the poor peasants were rebellious, in order to have an excuse for seizing their sheep, which they ate, and their wives and children, whom they sold. I saw at once that there were scarcely any other rebels and thieves but the Turks, so I was soon at loggerheads with the agas of Larissa. However, my first step was to pounce on the Armatoles, who were infesting the plains, and drive them back to the mountains, where I kept them penned up till I should need their services. At the same time, I sent some heads to Constantinople to amuse the Sultan and the people, and some money to his ministers, for water sleeps, but envy never sleeps.'

He knew he would be envied for being in a position to lay hands on the wealth of those agas of Larissa, and he did in fact greatly enrich himself at this time. On the other hand he managed, by ruthless methods, to impose order where it had been lacking, so that people who had left that part of the world for safety's sake now came back and settled down again.

The year was 1787, Turkey was at war with Russia and Austria, and Ali, having done so well in Thessaly, was given an important command under the Grand Vizier, whom he joined with his army of Skipetars. As troops they were not, in the European sense, disciplined, but they were mobile, brave, and enterprising, and were found very useful: they were also remarkable for the energy they showed in looting the Danubian districts through which they passed. They certainly enabled Ali, who was already regarded as a successful administrator, to make some name as a general. In the course of the campaign a young relation of Ali's was taken prisoner by the Russians and during the negotiations for his release Ali and Potemkin met and exchanged presents, and took the opportunity of discussing the future: Potemkin of course had a peculiarly Russian *folie de grandeur*, and was indulging in visions of himself seated on the Imperial throne of Constantinople. If those visions should come true, Ali hoped to be recognized as the ruler of Epirus.

Before the war was over, he was ordered to take part in an expedition against a rebellious Pasha, Kara Mahmud of Scutari. This individual had taken advantage of the war, and of the fact that the Porte was fully occupied with the conduct of it, to do a little land-grabbing on his own, and had occupied several strongholds belonging to his Bosnian neighbours and to the Venetians. Nor had he stopped there, for he had tried to set up an independent principality on a grand scale, to include part of Albania, part of Bosnia, Montenegro, and Northern Macedonia. Ali felt secretly sympathetic towards Mahmud, rather unwillingly helped to besiege him in Scutari, and returned to the war as soon as he could. This sympathy with an important rebel, which implied a certain contempt towards the Sublime Porte, may be regarded as highly significant in view of Ali's later career.

When at last he got back to Trikkala he began to take an interest in the affairs of his neighbour Ali Izzet, the Pasha of Jannina, who was still away at the war. The beys of Jannina wanted to get rid of their Pasha and were plotting against him but could not agree as to who should take his place. Serious fighting had broken out between rival factions and vas upsetting the whole neighbourhood; the town itself was in a state of anarchy; the houses were heavily fortified, and the occupants busy sniping at their opponents; and murders were done in the streets in broad daylight. In all this Ali saw the greatest chance that had yet presented itself to him. As master of Trikkala he commanded the trade route between Constantinople and Jannina: as master of Jannina, if he could make himself that, he would be in a perfect position to centralize, consolidate and increase his power. But before he took any action he heard that his mother, who for some time had been suffering from cancer of the womb, was dying at Tebeleni, so he hurried off in order to be with her at the end. Khamco

spent her last moments in having her will read to her by her
daughter Shainitza. She had expressed in it the wish that Ali
and Shainitza should at the earliest possible moment do their
best to exterminate the people of Gardiki and Khormovo, who
had formerly captured and outraged her, and added a curse
on her children if they should fail her in this. She had also
ordered that a pilgrim should be sent in her name to Mecca
to make an offering there for the repose of her soul. (This was
never done, because the source of her fortune and of her late
husband's was theft, and according to religious law the money
could not be used for such a sacred purpose.) Finally she had
prepared a list of individuals she wanted assassinated and of
villages she wanted burnt. Towards the end of her time she
lost control of herself and went into paroxysms of rage against
her sufferings and her bad luck in dying before she could
revenge herself on the Gardikiots. In the midst of her ravings
she fell back dead in Shainitza's arms. Ali arrived too late to
see her alive, but he clasped hands with his sister over the
corpse and together they swore a solemn oath to carry out
their mother's wishes.

And now for Jannina. Ali had been paying agents to
keep the troubles going, and at the same time, by means of
bribery and promises, had raised a strong party there in his
own interest: his supporters were mostly Greeks who thought
he would prove as useful a protector to them as he had been
to the Greeks in Thessaly. He felt that with their help and the
use of force, he might well be able to obtain possession of the
citadel and get himself acknowledged master of the town, and
he knew he had the greater chance of success since the town
had for long been weakly governed or a centre of sedition, so
that the coming of a strong man, already distinguished for his
public services, would at least be approved of in high places.

At the head of his forces he suddenly appeared outside

the town. He did not feel strong enough to make an immediate attack but contented himself with taking up a good position and looting some of the surrounding villages. The beys of Jannina were thoroughly alarmed, for they knew of his intentions and his power: their common fear drew them together, they called the people to their support, and sent a message to Ali inviting him to return at once to Trikkala. He refused, so they came out and attacked him. The battle ended in a draw, and both sides retired, Ali to bide his time and the beys to go on with their quarrelling. Ali had managed to link himself with the most important family in the place by fetching away one of its daughters in a boat across the lake at night and marrying her. He then persuaded his supporters in the town to send a deputation to Constantinople to petition that he might be made Pasha of Jannina, but he got word that his enemies were working actively against him in the capital, and were making some headway. He felt that the time for delays and half measures was gone, so he took the simple step of forging a decree announcing his appointment to the pashalik, for he was statesman enough to know that a *fait accompli* cannot easily be explained away. He had the announcement made in the town; the beys came out to meet him, and with much ceremony the decree was produced and drawn out of its crimson case; each bey touched it with his forehead in token of obedience; and Ali entered the town and occupied the citadel. On the following morning a second faked document was drawn up, confirming his appointment. His boldness was rewarded, for he presently found himself recognized by the Porte as Pasha of Jannina.

CHAPTER V

THE CITY OF JANNINA

ALI could not have chosen a more suitable place to establish himself in than Jannina, its appearance being half splendid and half squalid, its climate subject to sudden changes and violent extremes, its situation of great strategic value, and its history consisting largely of acts of tyranny and cruelty. Focal point of many a feud and rebellion, the town had been fortified since the eleventh century, and some of its governors had set such an example of ferocity and extortion as to make Ali in his turn seem at least nicely traditional. In the Middle Ages, for instance, there was at Jannina a tyrant of Serbian origin named Thomas with his wife Angelina. The lady is said to have been amiable, but Thomas simply set himself to plunder the churches and torture and squeeze the rich on a grand scale. The plague broke out twice, twice the town was invaded, and Thomas came entirely under the domination of a certain Michael Apsaras, who led him away from Angelina and into 'the most enormous and unnatural vices'. There were two more invasions and Thomas either murdered or mutilated his prisoners. Encouraged by Apsaras, he killed a bishop, had a prominent citizen chopped into small pieces and another dragged to death at a horse's tail, while others again he deprived both of their eyes and their incomes. Although he fortified the town and made some successful attacks on his enemies, he made life so unendurable with his cruelties, his imposition of forced labour, and his profiteering monopoly of all the necessities of life, that one winter's night he was stabbed

48

to death in bed by four members of his bodyguard. The neglected Angelina married again and found her second husband a considerable improvement on the first: in order to get her own back on Apsaras she had his eyes gouged out. A few years later the Sultan put in a Turkish garrison, but as they suffered from loneliness they waited outside the cathedral one night during an important service until the congregation came out, and then helped themselves to the girls they fancied, a caprice which led to a marked rise in the Mohammedan population.

At the beginning of the seventeenth century, about the time when Ali's ancestor the dancing dervish settled at Tebeleni, there occurred in Epirus the curious episode of Dionysius the Skelosoph, or Dog-Philosopher. This individual having been turned out of the bishopric of Trikkala for practising astrology and necromancy, announced that he had had a dream. In this dream he saw no less a person that the Sultan, the King of Kings, rise from his divan to receive him, from which Dionysius deduced that he must be fated to deliver his people from the Turks. On the strength of this he went hiking, with a knapsack containing a flask of wine, frequently refilled, and by relating his dream and preaching with some fervour managed to collect more and more adherents to what had rapidly become his cause. Eventually he led them to Jannina, which they entered singing hymns. They then attacked the Turks, killed about a hundred of them, burnt down several houses, and began to loot and to drink. When they were rather more than merry, the Turks rallied and began to kill them, and Dionysius Dogsbody thought it best to make himself scarce. He hid in a deep cave in the rock under the citadel, where he would probably have starved but for a sympathetic baker who delivered bread at the cave every day. The Turks eventually found him, flayed him alive, stuffed his skin with straw, and sent this trophy to Constantinople, where it was received with loud applause. The Sultan, hearing a noise of shouting, rose from his divan and went to the window to find out the cause of it, thus nearly fulfilling Dionysius's dream. There were further reprisals at Jannina against his followers, many of whom were impaled, sawn in half, or burned alive.

Yet another insurrection broke out in the seventeenth century, instigated, this time by the Venetians, one more in that long series of revolts so cruelly suppressed by the Turks. It was firmly believed in Constantinople that the people of Albania and Epirus were not fit to govern their own country, and as far as Jannina itself was concerned, that place had been governed, ever since the Turkish occupation in the fifteenth century, by a continuous succession of pashas chosen from the same local Turkish family, old and loyal. With the arrival of Ali this tradition was broken: here was an outsider, a vigorous and ambitious man from the mountains, more an Albanian than a Turk, with an insatiable appetite for power and wealth, ready to do anything to get what he wanted, backed by a large following, and showing some signs, at the end of the eighteenth century, of behaving very much in the medieval way of Thomas the Despot.

Jannina at this time was the most important town in Albania, if not in the whole of Greece, with a population of about thirty thousand, mostly Greek and mostly engaged in trade. It was built beside a lake at the foot of Mitzikeli, a mountain of grey limestone, whose gigantic precipices were furrowed by the courses of torrents. The lake was about six miles long and from one to three miles wide, and into it there jutted a rocky peninsula a hundred feet high, on which stood the citadel of Jannina, known as the Castro, a sort of Kremlin, strongly fortified and containing a variety of buildings. The

Castro may have been the site of the great Oracle and Sanctuary of Dodona in ancient times. 'In place of the dirty streets and bazaars of the modern town,' says Leake, 'we may imagine a forest, through which an avenue of primeval oak and ilex conducted to the sacred peninsula' with its temple and the sacred oak tree hung with garlands and ornamented with a golden dove. The Castro contained a mosque, one of the nineteen in Jannina, which contained as well six churches, five Turkish monasteries, and two synagogues.

As one approached the town it seemed peaceful and beautiful. For one thing it was full of trees, especially planes and cypresses, unlike the surrounding hills, from which the forests had been cut to build the town. Then the minarets and domes of the mosques seen against the snowy peaks of Pindus lent it a remote and enchanted air, half Oriental, half Alpine. But when one entered the place, and had passed the gardens and orchards and cemeteries, there was a feeling of heaviness and tension. The streets were narrow and medieval and though many of the houses were large and handsome their high and almost windowless outer walls and massive double gates made them look like prisons. Of real prisons, the most important and Bastille-like was known as the Buldrun: it was beneath the Castro and could hold two or three hundred people. There was a large bazaar with very good shops, especially for jewellery and clothes; at the entrance to the Castro an indescribably squalid and poverty-stricken ghetto; and on the outskirts of the town a settlement of gipsies. The Turks, of whom there were about five thousand, were remarkable for haughtiness, prejudice, indolence and apathy, except when they were roused to violence; the Greeks, who so greatly outnumbered them, were more enlightened. They spoke good Greek, and a school was supported by a family of rich merchants named Zosima, who had branches of their business in Leghorn, in Moscow, and other distant places. Another school, also endowed, was in charge of a man with some reputation for culture, Athanasius Psalida. There were also a number of smaller schools, both Greek and Turkish, and in summer one would often see thirty or forty boys sitting out of doors, having their lessons under a tree.

Women seldom appeared in the streets, and when they did were wrapped from head to foot in dark cloaks and kept their faces veiled. In walking, all but peasant women (who were too busy for such affectation) cultivated a waddle as a proof of refinement, and it was a compliment to tell a woman that she walked like a goose: there was even a love-song in Greece in those days which ran:

> May the mountains fall down
> So that I may see Athens,
> So that I may see my love
> Who walks about like a goose.

Mostly uneducated, the Greek women lived in a state of subservience, as in ancient times. Young women seldom or never went out of their houses before marriage, except to church, and that generally at night. They stayed at home doing endless embroidery. Owing perhaps to a want of exercise, amusement, work and power, their beauty faded early and they spent much time in cultivating it. At ten years old a girl would have her hair dyed a deep mahogany colour, and on the top of it she would wear a headdress covered with pearls and gold wire and gold and silver coins. Then she would learn to colour and thicken her eyebrows, often joining the two together with a heavy black line, to blacken her eyelashes, stain her finger nails and paint her face. The eyelashes were done with a mixture of oil and antimony, and the face rather crudely daubed with a white paint made of powdered cowrie shells mixed with lemon juice and a red paint from the roots of a wild lily washed, dried and preserved in pots. Sometimes on festival occasions girls wore a spot of gold leaf under each eye. For dress they wore an open silk gown with full sleeves, heavily embroidered; various undergarments, including muslin drawers, coloured stockings and shoes, a furred pelisse, and a girdle with silver buckles. As they had little else to think of, their one object in life was to get married. Marriages were generally arranged by parents without consulting the daughter, and no girl could marry without a dowry: if the parents were unable to give her this, it was often provided by a brother, who would not marry until his sister or sisters were safely settled.

In spite of its wealth, the town was dirty. Bugs and fleas abounded, to say nothing of rats. Fortunately there were no mosquitoes, but there were plenty of other insects, and on fine summer evenings after a shower moths and gnats would rise in clouds from the reeds round the lake and flock to the lamps in the houses in such numbers that they sometimes put them out. The reeds round the lake were used for thatch, and passage-ways were cut through them for the benefit of sportsmen who would go out in light boats called *monoxyla* to shoot the wild duck of several kinds that were to be found there in great numbers, or to fish for carp, eels, pike, perch and tench. Apart from eels, water snakes were often to be seen swimming on the surface with 'the most elegant undulatory motion'.

Out in the lake, opposite the Castro, was a very agreeable island with a village of clean white houses among plane trees, a pleasure resort in summer, when the women used to sit spinning at their doors while the men, wearing broad straw hats against the sun, caught fish for the visitors. Although snow sometimes fell as late as May, and much rain besides, the heat soon became intense. In June the hay was brought in, and by the middle of July the barley and wheat were already reaped. Violent thunderstorms and even earthquakes were not uncommon, and in any case one had to expect extreme cold in winter and heat in summer, and frequent and sudden changes of temperature at any time. Under the rule of Ali, whose temperament was subject to sudden disturbances, who was hot at one moment and cold at the next, the citizens soon learnt to expect sudden changes in the political temperature or in the favour shown to them by their dictator.

CHAPTER VI

THE SAGA OF SULI: I

WHEN Ali took possession of Jannina, his first act was to put a strong garrison in the Castro. He made some show of graciousness, promised protection to the people and rewarded those who had supported him. At first he was civil even to those who had been against him, but as soon as he felt himself firmly established he took care to make them pay heavily for their past misdeeds. Unlike his predecessors, he surrounded himself with Albanians and Greeks. He liked the Greeks because many of them were rich, and he appreciated their adaptability and suppleness of character. As for the Skipetars they were proud of him and looked on him as their fellow countryman. He had grown up with them, in his early years had played and fought and raided with them, sharing their hardships and good or bad fortune, and of late years had been continually their leader. He would talk to them in a gay and familiar way and ask for news of their families and villages, and for their services he would reward them freely. By descent a Turk, he was by experience a Skipetar, and the Skipetars were to be the mainstay of his power.

Although he had many important things to do, one of his first cares was to begin to put into effect the terms of his mother's will. He sent some friendly messages to the people of Khormovo and as they were afraid of him they sent back equally friendly messages in reply. He then proposed that he should visit the place as their guest just to prove to them how amiable he was, and said he would only bring a couple of hundred men with him as escort so that he need not put them to

too much expense and inconvenience. They replied that he
would be most welcome. He then went to Khormovo with
no fewer than 1200 men, who were quartered on the inhabitants. Ali was handsomely entertained and seemed very
affable, even going so far as to punish some of his men for not
showing sufficient consideration for their hosts. After some
days he said he was afraid that his stay in Khormovo must
really be putting the people to too much expense, announced
that he would retire to a monastery in the mountains a few
miles away, and invited them to come out there and draw up
a treaty of alliance and friendship. He went to the monastery
and then summoned a hundred of the leading citizens to a
conference. It was arranged that the treaty should be drawn
up and signed in the church attached to the monastery, and
according to custom the citizens deposited their arms at the
door before going in. As soon as they were safely inside, their
arms were seized by Ali's order. The treaty was about to be
signed at the altar, when one of the Khormovites who had
occasion to go outside discovered that the arms were missing
and at once gave the alarm. A detachment of Ali's Skipetars
then rushed in, seized and bound the vistors, and carried them
off to Tebeleni. With the rest of his men Ali then marched
on Khormovo, massacred most of the men, had the women
and children taken away to be sold into slavery, and set fire
to the houses. For one of his particular enemies, a certain
Chaoush Prifti, who had been responsible for the murder of
Islam's widow and children, a special fate was reserved. He
was handed over to Ali's mulatto foster-brother, Yusuf Arab,
the son of a black slave in his father's harem, a man whose
character may be guessed from his nickname, for he was known
as the Blood-Drinker. Yusuf ran a spit through the body of
Chaoush and roasted him alive. So, as a heroic ballad in
honour of Ali tersely expressed it:

The dark Khormovo became a ruin,
And Chaoush Prifti roast meat in the frying-pan.

With Khormovo in ruins and Khamco avenged, at least
in that direction, Ali felt free to concentrate on matters of
policy. His main object was to increase his own power, and his
method was to unify and extend his jurisdiction. He had
retained his inspectorship of roads, and continued to control
Trikkala, though he had managed to get the pashalik of that
place transferred to his son Veli, then barely seventeen. He
took care to ensure good communications between Jannina
and Tebeleni, and then began to seek means of increasing his
territory. He conquered the Pasha of Arta and annexed his
land, which gave him control of the gulf of Arta, where he
intended to maintain a small fleet. While enriching himself
and extending his influence, he felt that he could justify his
rapacity towards his neighbours by telling his agents at Constantinople to pretend that his enemies were secretly in league
with foreign powers: at the same time he himself did not mean
to hesitate to enter into secret understandings with foreign
powers if he thought such a policy likely to prove useful to him.

He had never forgotten his grudge against Ibrahim, who
had married the old Wolf's daughter and succeeded his
father-in-law as Pasha of Berat, and he now annexed several
villages which were under Ibrahim's protection. Ibrahim
asked for explanations, but Ali took no notice of him, so he
sent some troops against Ali under the command of a relation,
Sefer Bey. Some raids and skirmishes took place, some villages
were burnt, corn was stolen and snipers on both sides picked
off unwary enemies, until Ibrahim got tired of this desultory
warfare and suggested to Ali that they should sign a treaty of
peace. To this Ali agreed, on condition that he should be
allowed to keep the places he had already taken. In order that

Ibrahim might not lose face, it was arranged that his daughter Pasho should marry Ali's son Mukhtar and have the conquered villages bestowed on her as a dowry.

Ali very much disliked Sefer Bey and knew him to be hostile to his interests, so he thought of an ingenious plan to get him out of the way. He sent for a quack doctor and ordered him to go and ingratiate himself with Sefer and then poison him. The doctor was to represent himself as a fugitive from Ali's displeasure: to lend colour to this, Ali put the doctor's wife and children under lock and key and made him leave Jannina alone. The doctor told his tale and asked to be taken under Sefer's protection, was soon taken into his confidence, and when Sefer was ill he gave him poison instead of medicine. He then returned to Jannina to claim from Ali the large reward he had been promised. Ali said he was delighted with the success of his plan, and gave the doctor the reward, but directly the man had left his presence he ordered that he should be arrested and hanged. This enabled Ali to save the money and to get rid of the instrument and only witness of the crime, after which he spread a story that Ibrahim and his wife had been responsible for the murder.

Now all through the eighteenth century the Pashas of Jannina had been trying to subdue the little republic of Suli in the wild mountains of Thesprotia, some fifty miles to the south-west. They had never succeeded, and the Suliots had stolen from them about sixty villages, from which they exacted tribute and produce. At the time when Ali was made Pasha of Jannina the Suliots were particularly active and annoying, for they were in the pay of Ibrahim and of Catherine of Russia as well. Ali knew perfectly well that the Suliots would not be easy to conquer, but decided all the same to attack them.

Suli itself was a natural fortress in some of the most

spectacular scenery in the Balkans. The settlement consisted
of a few villages on a plateau about two thousand feet above
the river Acheron, the Black River, which flowed through a
deep chasm full of forbidding rocks and woods, 'one of the
darkest and deepest of the glens of Greece'. A cultivated
English traveller of the period let himself go in his descriptions of 'a spot which Mythology had selected as the scenes of
her wildest fantasies', and exulted in the 'perpendicular rocks,
broken with every form of wild magnificence', and 'the huge
precipices like the ruins of a disjointed world'. His romantic
but not inaccurate phrases, foaming with adjectives, tumbled
forth like a cataract – if the woods were gloomy and the
mountains wild, the chasms were terrific and the magnificence
awful. A topographer, writing more calmly, conveys in his
different way an impression of equal value: 'The river in the
pass is deep and rapid, and is seen at the bottom falling in
many places in cascades over the rocks, though at too great a
distance to be heard, and in most places inaccessible to any
but the foot of a goat or a Suliot.' If in its wilder aspects Suli
might be called Dantesque, it had also some resemblances to
the craggy, wooded landscapes we see in Chinese paintings:
there were thickets of ilex and holly-oaks, great numbers of
birds, especially storks and eagles, and in marshy places a pro-
fusion of yellow irises. The villages on the plateau itself,
which could only be reached by one steep and narrow passage
three miles long, had even something gentle and domesticated
in their appearance, for there were cultivated terraces planted
with corn and vegetables and fruit trees, and amongst them
stood the houses, small square buildings with pitched roofs
and two storys, the lower used as a store or stable, and the
upper containing two or three rooms.

As for the people, perhaps 12,000 in number, they had
a character and traditions of their own. They had probably

been in Suli since the time of Scanderbeg, were Christians, and had at one time been concerned in a plot to free Greece from the Turks. In general, they had many points in common with the other mountaineers of Greece. They were principally concerned to maintain the freedom of their little confederation, and to aid in its defence they thought their first duty. Males were conscripted and trained in arms from the age of ten, and they were of course experts in guerrilla warfare, skirmishes and sorties and stratagems, sudden attacks and quick retreats. They were renowned for their courage, as Byron noted:

> Oh! Who is more brave than a dark Suliote,
> In his snowy camese and his shaggy capote?
> To the wolf and the vulture he leaves his wild flock,
> And descends to the plain like a stream from the rock.

It was said of them that to show how brave they were they would send only a small force against a large one, while against a small force they would go in great numbers, because by that means they would be able to take more prisoners and loot. So much did they value personal courage that the women had precedence, when they went to draw water at the well, according to the acknowledged bravery of their husbands. The women themselves were brave, and in time of war would carry food and ammunition, attend to the wounded and sometimes take part in the actual fighting. There were no written laws in Suli or courts of law, and differences were settled by the heads of clans. There was an excellent rule that men, owing to their tendency to start fighting, must never interfere in any quarrel, but the women were encouraged to act as peacemakers. On feminine frailty the Suliots were just as hard as the Turks and the Albanians, and on the slightest suspicion of adultery women were sewn up in sacks and thrown over the cliffs into the Acheron. When the men had nothing better to do they used to look after their flocks of goats and sheep. They never engaged in trade, but would live, like the Klephts, by brigandage, or upon the tribute paid to them in money or kind, rice or maize, by their sixty subject villages in the plains below. Like Klephts and Skipetars, they were known for their love of dancing and singing, their activity, their quickness in difficult country, their straight shooting, and in particular for their extraordinarily keen eyesight – it was even said that they could see in the dark, like cats.

It was in the spring of 1790 that Ali decided to launch his first attack on Suli. He sent an army of 3000 men but they were able to achieve nothing, for the Suliots simply retired to their almost impregnable heights; the attackers had to content themselves with looting the villages in the plain that were known collectively as Parasuli; and then, as a result of Suliot sorties from above, they had to retire to Jannina. Ali's attention after this being engaged by other matters, he decided to wait a little before making a second attack.

To avoid being troubled at all by Ibrahim Pasha of Berat he had made further friendly overtures to him, and these had led to a marriage between Ibrahim's second daughter Zobeidé and Ali's son Veli, while a third daughter was paired off with Ali's nephew. It happened that Shainitza had married her daughter to one Murad Bey, who was a devoted member of Ibrahim's household, a circumstance which had brought upon him the hatred of Ali. Ibrahim, now that his family and Ali's were becoming so closely allied, wished to end this ill-feeling and in order to try and bring about a reconciliation he entrusted to Murad the duty of conveying Zobeidé to Jannina to be married: actually he was only sending him into a lion's den. While the wedding festivities were going on, Ali had a rumour put about that an attempt had been made on his life, that his assailant had escaped without having been identified, and that a conspiracy had been formed against him. A faked inquiry was set going, and false witnesses were easily procured to give evidence. Ali then announced that he would stop giving audiences in the Castro, and appointed for the purpose a small building by the lake: this house had an upper room reached by a ladder and a trap-door, and anyone wishing to be received by him was to come there unarmed.

After a day or two he sent for Murad Bey, his nephew by marriage, to come and see him, and the young man at once obeyed, thinking that he was to be given the presents which were due to him according to custom for having escorted the bride and having helped to give her away. He was shown up the ladder and found himself in the upper room, where the light was dim. There seemed to be nobody there, so he turned as if to go down again, when a shot was fired from a dark corner. He was hit in the shoulder, and fell to the floor. As he fell, his uncle Ali Pasha pounced out on him like a wild beast. He made some effort to defend himself, but Ali suddenly seized a red-hot log from the fire, jabbed it in Murad's face again and again, and finished him off with a knife. When he was dead, Ali dabbled himself with Murad's blood, and then began to groan and shout and call for help. When his guards came rushing up, he showed himself covered with blood and said he just managed to kill the would-be assassin. After this he arranged for a service of thanksgiving for his 'escape' to be held in the principal mosque, granted an amnesty to some of his prisoners to mark the occasion, and thoughtfully sent some troops to take over the possessions of his murdered nephew.

He now began to make great preparations for another attack on Suli, and included in his army, which numbered not less than 8000 men and probably more, some troops belonging to Ibrahim. Naturally the Suliots were informed of the mobilization, but Ali pretended, in order to put them off and catch them unawares, that he was going to attack Argyro Castro, which had not yet submitted to his authority. He therefore sent the following letter to the Suliot leaders, Captains Botzaris and Tzavellas:

'My friends, Captain Botzaris and Captain Tzavellas, I, Ali Pasha, salute you and kiss your eyes, for I well know your courage and heroic cast of mind. It seems to me that I am much in need of your services: I beg therefore that when you receive this letter you will at once assemble all your braves and come and join me so that I may go and fight my enemies. This is the hour and the time when I need you. I look forward to your showing your friendship and the love you have for me. Your pay shall be double what I give to the Skipetars, because I know that your courage is greater than theirs. I shall not go and fight before you arrive, and I hope you will come soon. This only, and I salute you.'

The Suliots had no intention of abandoning their country in order to follow Ali, but at the same time they thought it prudent not to risk offending such a powerful neighbour, so they decided to send Tzavellas to Jannina with seventy men. Ali gave them a hearty welcome, attached them to his own army, and then marched at the head of the whole force in a north-easterly direction, as if making for Argyro Castro. After four hours he ordered a halt, and while the Suliots were resting his Skipetars made a rush at them, disarmed them and then tied them up. Two were killed in resisting, and one escaped. He leapt into a river that ran near by, and swimming strongly under a hail of bullets, managed to get safely away. Travelling as fast as he could, he brought the news to Suli the next day. The Suliots at once expected the worst, and decided to evacuate Parasuli and withdraw to their mountain fastnesses.

Botzaris had pigs and lime and filth thrown into the wells and cisterns to prevent Ali's troops from using the water, and ordered a six months' supply of corn to be carried up to Suli.

It would have saved Ali a great deal of trouble if he could have persuaded the Suliots to surrender, and he decided to see what he could do by negotiation before using force. He therefore sent for Tzavellas, his leading prisoner, and asked him to act as a go-between, promising him a large reward if he could persuade his fellow-countrymen to surrender and death if he failed. Tzavellas said he would go back to Suli and see what he could do, but he had to leave with Ali as a hostage his son Photo, who although only twelve years old, had accompanied him and been taken prisoner at the same time. Directly he got to Suli, Tzavellas urged resistance to the tyrant at any cost, and composed a defiant letter which was at once sent off to Ali:

'Ali Pasha, I am glad to have deceived a traitor, and I am here to defend my country against a thief. My son will be put to death, but I shall desperately revenge him before I die. Some men, like you Turks, will say that I am a cruel father to sacrifice my son for my own safety, but I answer that if you had been able to take the mountain my son would have been killed, together with all the rest of my family and my countrymen, and then I could not have avenged his death. If we are victorious, I may beget other children: my wife is still young. And if my son, young as he is, is not willing to be sacrificed for his country, then he is neither worthy to live nor to be acknowledged as my son. Advance, traitor, I am impatient for my revenge. I am your sworn enemy, Tzavellas.'

Ali can scarcely have received this letter with equanimity. He hesitated, however, to kill the boy Photo, and kept him a prisoner at Jannina. One day Veli sent for Photo, and there exists an eye-witness's account of the interview. Photo

A JANNINOT GREEK

ALI PASHA

ON THE LAKE AT JANNINA

A SULIOT AT CORFU

returned brave answers to the questions that were put to him.

'I'm only waiting for my father's orders,' said Veli, 'to have you roasted alive.'

'I'm not afraid of any of you,' said Photo. 'My father will do the same to your father or your brother if he captures them.'

It was in July 1792 that Ali launched his second attack on Suli. He made his men such a forceful speech that some of them broke their scabbards in token of their determination to conquer, and the whole army set out, part of it under the command of Ali's eldest son Mukhtar and part under a general called Pronio Aga of Paramythia, eighty-five years old, of gigantic stature and with a long snow-white beard, who had with him his eleven sons, all between the ages of thirty and sixty and as tall and strong as their father.

At first the attack went well, for Ali's army managed to overcome the Suliot outposts. But the Suliots, who probably had no more than 1500 men in arms, put up a desperate resistance. None of them was more heroic than Moscho, the wife of Tzavellas and mother of Photo: she distributed ammunition, organized and armed the women, rushed out with them to stop some of the men retreating, and then led an attack on some of the enemy who were climbing up. In a fortified tower near the entrance to the pass sixteen of the defenders had all been killed, and amongst them she came upon the body of her favourite nephew.

'I may have arrived too late to save your life,' she cried, 'but I'll get my own back for your death!'

And off she went to lead another attack. Part of Ali's army had managed to enter one of the ravines, and when Moscho and the Suliot women discovered this they rolled rocks down on the middle of the invading column, which cut it in half, caused a panic, and enabled their menfolk to attack the front half. After the fighting had lasted for ten hours the

invaders retreated in disorder, some of them throwing away
their arms and equipment in order to escape more easily over
the rocks, some hiding in the woods, and some making for the
plain as fast as they could.

The Suliots had lost less than a hundred men and their
enemies nearly a thousand. Greatly upset by the rout of his
army, Ali joined in its hasty retreat to Jannina. He sent on
ahead to order the inhabitants to remain indoors, and the
greater part of his men came straggling back downhearted at
night. The Suliots, reinforced by their allies from Khimara,
took the offensive and forced Ali to make peace. They gained
some territory and had their prisoners returned to them unconditionally, but Ali's prisoners were only returned to him
after he had paid a ransom of 100,000 piastres. He was so
overcome by this blow to his prestige and his ambition that he
shut himself up and refused to see anybody or do any business
for a fortnight.

CHAPTER VII

MONEY MATTERS

ALI's retirement for a fortnight gave him time enough to convert his humiliation at the hands of the Suliots into a bitter and unalterable resolve to revenge himself upon them in the end at all costs, but it must also have resulted in a considerable accumulation of business, for in his government he held every portfolio (as other dictators have done) and was in the habit of attending as far as possible even to details himself. His energy, his knowledge of places and people, and his memory were all prodigious, and ambition and cupidity drove him on at full speed. He usually got up before six in the morning and attended to his affairs all day long, with only a break at twelve for dinner and another at eight for supper. Like most Turks of high rank, he usually ate alone, and sometimes after supper would go on receiving reports, making plans and giving orders.

His position was quite clear. He had to recognize the authority of the Sultan and to maintain a steady flow of tribute – and of bribes – to Constantinople, but otherwise was as good as independent, free to levy or disband armies, make wars or alliances, regulate taxes and duties, and govern without appeal. In short, his word was law, and like most men who have had absolute power, he can scarcely be said to have made the best conceivable use of it. His education was distinctly limited: he once proposed to have a warship fitted out in Paris, and another time expressed a wish that the French army would have a fair wind to carry them to Vienna. But of course mistakes of this kind are not confined to barbarians.

Sir John Warren was urged in 1813 to send a frigate to the Canadian lakes, for the Government of the day were apparently unaware that the Niagara Falls 'are not suited for sailing up or down!' It is also alleged that the Admiralty suggested during the Boer War that the commander of a certain warship should 'anchor off Pretoria'. At any rate, if Ali's geography was shaky, he had a great knowledge of the human heart, and managed to keep himself so well informed on political matters that Constantinople often got its news of European affairs from Jannina, while nothing of importance could occur at Constantinople without Ali getting to hear of it within a week. A master of cunning intrigue, he kept both Greek and Turkish agents in the capital to support his influence and keep him informed, and he had spies and *agents provocateurs* everywhere. It was because everybody knew that he managed everything himself that nothing escaped him, and it was because he was known to be entirely unscrupulous that there seemed to be an atmosphere of undefined terror always brooding over Jannina. As Metaxa, one of his doctors once remarked, 'There is a cord tied round every individual in his dominions, longer or shorter, more or less fine, and every one of the cords goes to him and is held in his hand'. One or two examples may be given of the 'royal memory' which was so helpful to him in the control of his subjects. On one occasion, when he was reviewing some troops near Jannina, he recognized and singled out, at a distance of more than three hundred yards, a Skipetar in the ranks who had offended him twenty years before. The man had been arrested and imprisoned at the time, but had escaped, wandered all over Greece, and at last enlisted among the troops of a bey in Ali's service: Ali now condemned him to death. Another time, at Preveza, a man was arrested and brought before Ali, who at once described in correct detail, with dates and names, all the acts of brigandage of which the man had been guilty during a period of fifteen years.

Ali's revenue was made up from various sources. Every village had to pay a tax equal to one-tenth of its produce: this was due to the Sultan, but Ali generally increased it to one-fifth and kept the additional tithe for himself. The collection was enforced by a detachment of Skipetars quartered in each village. The soldiers were given a free hand, and their injuries to the civilians were encouraged in order to keep the people down by fear. He imposed taxes quite arbitrarily on towns and villages, and from Jannina alone obtained about £12,000 a year, reckoning the pound at its value in those days. There were duties on all exports and imports. He made a law to establish his right to all the property of those who died without leaving any male heirs. He imposed a duty on all decisions in cases of law, amounting to 10 per cent. of the value of any property of which the ownership might be in dispute. He saved himself expense by means of forced labour and various kinds of exploitation, exactly in the manner of Thomas the Despot centuries before. He held a partial monopoly of the corn trade. He kept his troops in board and lodging as far as possible by billeting them on his subjects, who also had to provide free accommodation for all civil and military officials and for travellers, native or foreign, with a passport. He practised extortion in all kinds of ingenious and capricious ways, and was never above plain and simple theft. Besides all this, he had a rent roll of £200,000 a year.

With a real gift for rigging the market, he would have been an ornament to the capitalist system of our time that has produced a Kreuger and a Stavisky. For instance, when he had to pay his troops or make any other large disbursements he would buy up gold coin on a large scale at the ordinary Constantinople rate until his dealings had considerably raised the price, and would then pay it out at the new price. As soon as he had put a lot of gold into circulation again, and so reduced its value, he would order that all the revenues due to him should be paid in gold. With all this ingenuity in high finance, he had also from the first a very strongly developed miserly side to his nature, a 'tyranny for trifles'. He kept all the keys of his stores and would only allow things to be given out under his own minute supervision, and he would never allow any worn-out piece of furniture or old pots and pans to be thrown away, but would hide them, and would know at once if the smallest things were lost. In the passages and antechambers of his palace in the Castro could be seen all sorts of junk, old rusty sabres or the worn-out stock of a pistol, or even rags, which nobody would dare to move, for fear of his noticing. Once when some Greeks escaped from him and took refuge in the Ionian Islands he asked that they should be extradited: this being refused, he formally applied for the restitution of some property which he said belonged to him – a few articles of clothing that had been carried off by the refugees. He sent a list minutely describing each item, specifying not only the number of shirts and stockings in the possession of each individual, but even those which had been patched or mended.

To increase his wealth he would stop at nothing, and there was ever a kind of grim humour in his rather too practical jokes. He would buy a bunch of cheap, mendacious watches from a pedlar, and then re-sell them at a large profit to people who did not want them, or give them away as presents, in return for which he expected valuable presents to be given to him; or he would send people 'presents' which had to be paid for at two or three times their real value; or he would sometimes honour people by being shaved in their houses, which meant that they must give him a complete set of silver jugs and bowls. In bad times he would send for some merchants and say, 'Well, boys, there's a bit of a slump just now, isn't there? I expect you're having a job to make ends meet. Well, now, I'll tell you what I'll do. I'm going to help you with a loan. You turn it to account and pay me back whenever it suits you. The interest, by the way, will be only 20 per cent'. Then once after buying very cheap a cargo of coffee that had been damaged by sea-water he sent for some Jewish coffee-dealers in Jannina.

'And how much is coffee now?' he asked them.

'We're selling it at four and a half piastres the pound,' they replied, 'and that hardly allows us any profit.'

'Well,' he said, 'I've got some excellent coffee which you can have for five piastres and that will save you all the bother of importing the stuff and paying duties and freight and so on.'

'But we've got a lot on hand,' they protested, looking at each other in consternation, 'and just at present coffee's a drug on the market.'

'Get out, you cuckolds!' shouted Ali. 'Now I'll make you pay *six* piastres a pound!' And he did.

Another time he sent for the Greek archbishop.

'Your Holiness, I hear, has forbidden the women of Jannina to wear false hair?'

'Sir, the laws of our Church forbid our Christian women to wear it.'

'Ah, so I suppose you'll threaten them with excommunication?'

'Pasha, it is my duty.'

'Very well,' said Ali. 'Now let me tell you that the duty on this hair, which is, as you know, imported from Naples, brings me in a very tidy sum every year. If you like to pay me an equivalent amount, you can run your affairs any way you like.'

The women of Jannina continued to wear false hair.

When any rich citizen died, Ali's hands itched to take hold of the dead man's estate. He once married for a day the widow of a rich Turk in order to obtain the property she had been left. Then there was the Argyri case. Anastasi Argyri was a Greek of Jannina who had made a lot of money in trade and had used it well in various charitable and public services: he had founded a hospital, established a fund for poor prisoners, to whom he sent a hot dinner every Sunday, and built roads and bridges. He had been on excellent terms with Ali, who had treated him as a friend. When he died, Ali sent for Argyri's son Nicolo in order to offer him his condolences. In the course of conversation he spoke of old Argyri's will.

'I'm so pleased to hear,' he said, 'that I've been remembered in it, and to know that Anastasi, whom I thought so highly of, has left me, as he promised me when he was alive, all those fine lands and orange groves of his near Arta.'

Poor Nicolo was quite overcome at the thought of losing the lands near Arta, for they made up the best part of his inheritance, so he said he had not noticed this provision in his father's will, but Anastasi had certainly left Ali a very valuable diamond ring. Ali was furious at this, and cried out that a son who could not respect the last wishes of his father was not fit to live. Nicolo began to fear for his life, and begged that Ali would accept the lands as well as the ring, since his father's intentions had been clear, though *unaccountably* no document had been found. After this blow Nicolo was so disheartened that he took to an extravagant and debauched way of living. Ali continued to prey on him, and he was soon living in much reduced circumstances.

Ali's fondness for money enabled him to estimate the same quality in other people, as is shown by a story of the way he settled a dispute between two litigants, with a judgment worthy of Solomon. A Greek priest of Jannina had lent a large sum of money to a merchant and had foolishly omitted to get any receipt or IOU in return. When he wanted his money back the merchant denied ever having borrowed it, so the priest decided to lay the case before the Pasha. Ali heard the statement of both parties, announced that he could come to no conclusion, and dismissed the case – but ordered that both the plaintiff and the defendant should be weighed before they left the palace. After a week or two he sent for them again and had them re-weighed, when it was found that the merchant had gained several pounds, while the priest, distracted with worry, had lost weight proportionately. Ali then turned to the merchant and asked him if he would rather restore the money or have his head cut off. The merchant at once prostrated himself, confessed the loan, and promptly repaid it with interest.

CHAPTER VIII

ALI PASHA

IT might be supposed that Ali's tyrannies would have exposed him to attempts at assassination and that he accordingly lived in some fear and seclusion and only went about strongly guarded, but human beings are on the whole so masochistic and so fascinated by the sight of great power concentrated in the hands of one of them that they will let him go free and even cheerfully immolate themselves to increase his freedom. Thus a man once threw himself with an ecstatic cry under Ali's carriage wheels, and was crippled for life, receiving a minute pension from the Pasha in acknowledgment of the motive that had prompted the act. The man was a Greek, and it appeared that he had lain in a hole in the road, and that his motive was to prevent Ali being jolted. . . .

Ali was not in the least afraid of his people, or, if he was, he never showed it. He would sometimes ride about Jannina with only a single attendant, and was in the habit of admitting all sorts of people, armed and unarmed, into his presence even when he was alone. His confidence in himself was his best protection. He was once asked if the story about his having found a buried treasure by chance at a critical moment were true.

'Oh no, of course not,' he replied. 'It was made up by that liar of a schoolmaster Psalida. And now they come and repeat it to me. I can't help it, can I? But of course, it's quite a good thing that this fairy story should be believed. It makes my rise to power seem miraculous. Oh dear, why didn't I

come into the world sooner? With the aid of a few madmen,
I might perhaps have been hailed as a prophet . . . but
Mohammed got in first and shut the door, and the trick's been
done once and for all.'

He was never backward in blowing his own trumpet: he
liked to describe himself as the Modern Pyrrhus (which he
pronounced Bourrhous) and as 'a burning torch that shines as
brightly as the sun'. People thought he had a charmed life,
and he probably thought so too. Once in later life when he was
inspecting some repairs to the palace in the Castro a large
block of stone fell from a scaffold, caught him on the shoulder,
and laid him flat on the ground. Everybody thought for a
moment that it had killed him, and there was at once what
newspapers call a sensation. Ali was in fact seriously hurt, but
he called for a horse and mounted and rode through the city
with only one man in attendance, and showed no sign of
injury or pain, though he actually had received a wound which
kept him to his room for some weeks. When he got well he
said he had done this to assure the people of his safety, and to
deprive his enemies of the pleasure of thinking that he was
going to die.

'Every man has his enemies,' tactfully remarked a
foreigner who was in Jannina at the time, 'but I shouldn't like
to think that those of your highness would go so far as to wish
for your death.'

'What!' said Ali. 'Why, there isn't a minute of the day
when they aren't offering up prayers to heaven for my
destruction. How can you expect anything else? For forty
years I've been doing everybody as much damage as I can, and
I must have been the cause of at least thirty thousand people
being hanged or killed, and of course everybody knows that if
I go on living I shall account for a great many more. So you
think they don't hate me? Of course they hate me! but it

doesn't affect my health, you know.' And he laughed in his
usual sardonic way.

Although without religious feeling of any kind – for he
could be a Moslem with Moslems, a pantheist with the
Bektadgi dervishes, a Christian with the·Christians, ever ready
to drink to the health of 'the good Virgin', or a Man without
a Creed like his Skipetars – he was very superstitious and
probably ascribed his luck in part to an amulet which had been
given him by a dervish when he was a boy, and which he
always wore. Though almost everybody else was afraid of
him, the dervishes never were. There were many in and
around Tebeleni, where they were said to have corrupted
both the doctrines of Mohammed and the public morals, and
ever since he was a boy he had regarded them as holy, a fact
of which they took the fullest advantage. They would stroll
into his audience room and seat themselves beside him on the
divan, speak to him in the most insolent way, dun him for
money to pay for their debaucheries, and when he gave it to
them would abuse him for his meanness. Once a ragged, half-
naked dervish forced his way into the palace and into the very
room where Ali was sitting, sat down uninvited beside him,
and called for a pipe, although none of Ali's subjects except his
chief minister were allowed to smoke before him. No one
brought the dervish a pipe, so he turned round and said, 'Ali,
I want a smoke'. Ali ordered a pipe to be brought, but the
dervish waved it away, and said he wanted a hookah with rose-
water and the best Persian tobacco. Everybody was scan-
dalized, but Ali ordered the hookah. The dervish then insisted
on using Ali's own hookah and said he would not accept it
unless Ali himself handed it to him. This Ali did, and the
dervish took it without a word of thanks, had his smoke, and
then strolled out without taking any notice of anybody. Super-
stition apart, autocrats are apt to derive an exquisite pleasure

from deliberately allowing themselves at times to be
humiliated by certain privileged individuals.

Naturally Ali lived in great splendour. When he first
went to Jannina he always lived in the palace in the Castro,
where he made numerous alterations and improvements, and
where some of his furniture was sumptuous, including
Sèvres porcelain and later a Gobelin carpet with the cypher of
the King of France which he bought in Corfu. As his power
and wealth increased he built himself another palace called
Litharitza a little way out of the town, one at Tebeleni, one
at Preveza, and others less splendid in various parts of his
dominions. The palace at Tebeleni, described by an Englishman as one of the most romantic and delightful country houses
imaginable, was built on a grand scale. It had a vast hall with
columns and fountains of white marble and silk-covered divans,
and there, while taking one's ease, it was possible to hear the
rattling of the chains on the prisoners in the underground
dungeons. In an immense tower three storys high were
strong-rooms containing Ali's treasures: of these places he
wisely kept the keys himself. The gardens were laid out by
two Italians, who had been provided with wives from Ali's
harem and given houses and salaries. A traveller tells how he
saw Ali at Tebeleni buying two dozen large pearls from a
Greek jeweller and having them made up into a chaplet for
his own personal adornment. Another time, in midwinter,
when the Voiussa was in flood, Ali sat all the afternoon in a
kiosk at the corner of the harem anxiously watching to see how
the bridge over the river would stand the strain. A dervish
who caught sight of him went out and danced on the bridge,
addressed excited remarks to the trunks of trees that were
being swept under it, and then, after sacrificing one black
lamb and two white ones and pouring the blood on one of the
piers, came and assured everybody that the bridge would be

safe. It was only a temporary wooden bridge put up to replace an earlier one of stone that had fallen into ruin. An attempt was later made to replace it by an individual known as Selim Aga, who was really an Englishman named Bailey. His father had sent him on his travels to prevent him making an unsatisfactory marriage. The results were surprising. Bailey was a welcome guest at the British Embassy in Constantinople, but one day he came to a party and announced that he had turned Mohammedan, and added cheerfully that he had just been circumcized. He was at once shown out. Later he married a beautiful Turkish wife and tried to set himself up as a civil engineer, but while at Tebeleni to put up a bridge he died.

Ali's palace at Litharitza was only about half a mile from the Castro and commanded every approach to the town: it stood on a solid stone base, and the upper stories were of wood, brightly painted and somewhat Chinese in appearance. Both here and at the Castro splendour was sharply contrasted with squalor, for at the entrance to the Castro was a most miserable ghetto where some of the dwellings consisted of nothing but tattered blankets supported on props, and near Litharitza was a huge encampment of very poor gipsies. They were idle and given to crime. Some lived by robbery and some by fortune-telling, others were employed by Ali as executioners. Near their camp was a large plane tree in which ten or even twenty corpses could sometimes be seen dangling.

On the outskirts of the town Ali built a summer retreat in a garden full of fruit trees – oranges, lemons, figs and pomegranates – with planes and cypresses besides. Through a long alley of vines one approached a pavilion or kiosk built in the best Turkish style. It consisted of a large octagonal saloon surrounded by small latticed rooms. The saloon had a marble floor, in the middle of which was a marble fountain in the form of a fortress, decorated with models of lions, parrots,

and other birds and beasts, and mounted with small brass
cannon which, at a signal, spouted out jets of water, while a
mechanical organ in a recess played Italian tunes. The small
rooms round the saloon were furnished with divans covered
with silk, and the lattices and cornices were gilded and polished.
Here Ali used to retire in hot weather with his favourites, and
here women from his harem used to dance for him to the
music of the mandolines, or he would otherwise indulge, as
one of his visitors delicately phrased it, 'in the enjoyment of
whatever accomplishments the fair ones could display for his
gratification'.

'Notwithstanding he is almost exclusively given up to
Socratic pleasures,' wrote Vaudoncourt, 'and for this purpose
keeps up a seraglio of youths, from among whom he selects his
confidants, and even his principal officers, he had five or six
hundred women in his harem.' A large harem befitted his
rank and dignity. The women were kept in strict seclusion,
guarded by eunuchs, and spent their time in bathing, dressing
and beautifying themselves, embroidering, gossiping, dancing,
playing on musical instruments, and sometimes amusing
themselves with 'the exhibition of idiocy or the frantic acts of
women drugged with wine'. The Pasha was always pleased to
give a woman to any retainer to whom he wished to do a good
turn, or to any foreigner who entered his service and seemed
likely to prove useful, as an encouragement to remain.

His harem, like his treasury, was stocked by the most
ruthless methods. One of his greatest beauties was dragged
from the altar on her wedding day, and the bridegroom shot
himself in consequence. Whenever the Skipetars heard of a
specially beautiful child of either sex they would kidnap it for
their master's pleasure, and if the parents or relations resisted
they massacred them and set their houses on fire. Both as
sadist and sensualist, Ali was a man of gigantic appetite. An

English doctor who once attended him later hinted darkly at the existence of a carefully guarded Antinous, and remarked, with all the obvious relish of a moralist, that 'in the gratification of his depraved appetites, Ali Pasha, of all modern sensualists the most sensual, exceeded whatever the most *impure imagination can conceive*, whether it may have drawn its sullied stores from scenes of high-varnished debauchery, or from the obscurely tinted perspective of the low haunts of infamy and vice'.

Ali's chief minister, or secretary of state, was Mehmet Effendi, a man of very bigoted character, with a taste for astrology, and one of his closest and most faithful intimates was his favourite general, Athanasi Vaya, a native of Tebeleni, who spoke to him with complete familiarity and always slept outside his bedroom, when he did not sleep inside it, a pair of loaded pistols by his side. Vaya had a brother named Lucas whom Ali sent to Vienna to study medicine. The Pasha was always interested in doctors, and had as a rule at least four attached to him, including Metaxa, a Cephalonian who had studied in Paris, and Sakellario, who had studied in Vienna, was of a mildly literary turn, and kept in a leather bag a collection of antique coins, which he used sometimes to play with in rather a childish way. Of an older generation was an aged gentleman from Savoy, Jérôme de la Lance, who had long ago had to leave home on account of 'an unfortunate affair', had taken refuge with Ali's father, and still practised medicine in Jannina.

Ali's health was robust, but he suffered at certain times of the year, especially at the approach of the rainy season, from a violent fever, perhaps of malarial origin and popularly known as 'the Lion's fever'. Sometimes it attacked him during the last quarter of the moon, or when a particularly hot wind was blowing, a wind which was thought likely to have a bad effect

ONE OF VELI'S PAGES

A SULIOT WARRIOR

VELI'S SONS, ISMAIL AND MEHMET

ALI ON THE LAKE AT BUTRINTO

on people strongly susceptible to electrical changes in the air. At the best of times he showed a nervous restlessness, and when his fever was on him he looked for relief in exaggerated acts of terrorism: suffering from a great fear of death at such times, it pleased him to cause death to others, and everywhere his subjects could be heard making anxious inquiries about his health. He sometimes resorted to quacks and charlatans, and as he was in some ways credulous as well as superstitious, such men were never lacking to take advantage of his trust in them.

Besides doctors and various counsellors, secretaries, and minions, he was attended by two Greek under-secretaries of bad character, several Greek interpreters (he only knew Greek and Albanian, did not speak Turkish well, and knew no foreign language), and a swarm of ceremonial officers, including a sword-bearer, a standard-bearer, and silver sticks in waiting, to say nothing of other personal attendants, door-keepers, flatterers, and dervishes. His two palaces in Jannina, where meals were cooked daily for about 1500 people, naturally swarmed with hangers-on, and the gates and courtyards were thronged with petitioners, many carrying their petitions fixed on long sticks as if to attract his attention, some spending whole days kneeling and salaaming under his windows, whatever the weather, and some spending years waiting for a hearing, nursing some well-founded persecution complex, and in many cases growing old and dying without ever seeing him to speak to. In any case it was always necessary to pay to get audience with him. In his early days a lamb or a basket of figs was enough, but as his power grew, gold and precious stuffs were needed.

As might be expected, a number of foreign adventurers, renegades, deserters and rascals had been attracted to his service, and conspicuous among them were two ex-officers of the Neapolitan army who had turned Mohammedan; a French

F

deserter named Michel, originally from Paris, employed by
Ali as his chief carpenter and married off by him to a local
Greek girl; a Corsican ex-pirate named Passano, at one time
in command of Ali's ships; besides a French engineer, a
Dalmatian watchmaker, and a Milanese who built a foundry.
Ali was always ready to welcome foreigners if he thought he
could make use of them. He would receive them with great
charm and kindness and a show of generosity, with a twinkle
in his eye and a jovial laugh, but once he had them in his power
would neglect them or treat them with meanness and severity.

In appearance Ali was extremely handsome. He had an
air of frankness and honesty, and a smiling, humorous
expression. He had a good forehead, broad and open; a clear
eye, described as keen and seductive; a well-formed nose, and
a fresh complexion. His mouth and chin were now hidden
by a beard. Nothing was more characteristic than the vivacity
of his manner, his quick change of expression, and his deep,
guttural laugh, a trifle ogreish in its cheerfulness. He was an
absolute master of the art of cajolery and persuasiveness,
plausible, logical and eloquent. The Greeks had a very good
phrase to describe his blandishing talk: they used to say, 'He's
throwing honey'. 'It is difficult,' said Vaudoncourt, 'not to
be convinced or borne away by him when he enters into a
conversation for the purpose of furthering some object or
view. To resist him, it is necessary to be possessed of a perfect
knowledge of his character, and always to hold the picture
before one's eyes; and still his dissimulation is so disguised and
so profound, that one almost feels self-reproachful for being on
one's guard and acting with a salutary distrust.' If he were
thwarted or grew suddenly angry he was apt to lose control of
himself and his features would become distorted and convulsed.
He was selfish and cruel on a gigantic scale, a thief and a liar,
jealous, vindictive, miserly, and mad with ambition. His

faults cannot be overlooked or explained away, but they can be to some extent accounted for, and are to some extent set off by his good qualities. He was something more than what Gordon, the historian of the Greek revolution, calls him, 'a satrap who, by his talents and crimes, acquired unbounded sway over the western part of the Turkish Empire, and crushing the wild independence and innumerable factions of his native Albania, converted her sons into engines of his ambition and rapacity'. It must be remembered that he had been brought up to be ambitious and rapacious, and that to such a man any display of good faith would seem a weakness. According to the ideas which his mother had put into his head, he was a paragon among men. By any standards whatsoever one cannot but admire his extraordinary courage, and even in his wicked adroitness there is a curious fascination, for the sardonic smile that lurked in his beard was not the smile of a fool. Let us admit that he admired talent, that he was not intolerant of religious differences, and that he understood the value of education. As a ruler, his achievement may be compared to that of other dictators. By pretending to be secure and all-powerful he made himself so, he substituted unity for diversity, and if unity is strength he certainly made his government strong. 'His avarice,' says Gordon, 'pressed heavily on trade and agriculture, but he maintained a strict police, and cleared the roads of robbers. It was better for the merchant and cultivator, in so melancholy and inevitable a choice of evils, to sacrifice a part of their gains in buying protection, rather than to lose all by lawless outrage.' In other words, better one official robber than a mob of unofficial ones. And there is no denying the fact that Jannina, in Ali's time, became the most civilized town in Greece, superior even to Athens, as Byron noted, 'in the wealth, refinement, learning and dialect of its inhabitants'.

CHAPTER IX

'WHEN PREVEZA FELL'

THE treaty of Campo Formio, signed in 1797, gave Ali something to think about, for it put the French in possession of the seven Ionian Islands – Corfu, Paxos, Santa Maura, Ithaca, Cephalonia, Zante and Cerigo – as well as the four Venetian towns on the mainland – Preveza, Vonitza, Parga and Butrinto. The change-over from the Venetians to the French meant that a lax and decayed power was being replaced by a thrusting and ambitious one, inspired with revolutionary and Napoleonic energy, already successful, and eager for conquest and *la gloire*. Ali's first fear was that the French might turn the four coast towns into strong bases, and he arranged to meet and confer with the newly-appointed French governor, General Gentili, at Butrinto. He had been diplomatic enough to write and congratulate Napoleon on his successes in Italy, and Napoleon had now told Gentili to keep on the right side of Ali so that in case of need he could be relied on to help the French. Napoleon's occupation of the Ionian Islands and this conference with Ali alarmed Russia, which feared the growth of French influence in the Balkans, and an alliance was soon signed on behalf of the Czar Paul and the Sultan, and shortly afterwards acceded to by the English.

Gentili's successor, General Chabot, sent his chief of staff, Adjutant-General Roze, to Jannina to sound Ali and win him over to the French side as far as possible. Roze was welcomed with all that warmth and flattery which Ali knew so well how to display towards unsuspecting people whom he intended to use and victimize. He gave the Frenchman presents, called

84

him his friend, assured him that he would be a faithful ally to the French, and quickly discovering Roze's Gallic susceptibility to the opposite sex produced a seventeen-year-old Greek beauty known as Black-Eyed Zoitza and married the two off without any delay. The wedding was celebrated with great fuss; Ali's eldest son Mukhtar acted as best man. There were banquets, a balloon was sent up, a great deal of indiscriminate enthusiasm was expressed for the French Réboublika, as the Turks called it, and the archbishop of Jannina was persuaded to join in dancing the carmagnole. Roze's head was completely turned. He began to have visions of himself playing a great part in international affairs, and returned in triumph to Corfu to report the success of his mission, as a result of which Chabot sent Ali arms and munitions and granted him a privilege which the Venetians had always refused him – permission to maintain armed ships in the Ionian Sea.

Of this favour he hurried to take advantage. He fitted out some ships in the Gulf of Arta, and sent an expedition under his mulatto foster-brother, Yusuf Arab the Blood Drinker, to attack the people of Khimara, who had supported the Suliots against him. Two thousand men were disembarked secretly at night and marched on Khimara. The moment was well chosen, for it was Easter, and the people were all at church, holding a midnight service to celebrate the resurrection of Christ, while at the same time a number of young couples were being married. 'Christ is risen!' cried the priest, and the Blood Drinker's troops burst into the church and began to slaughter the congregation. It is said that six thousand people were killed, and in the morning fourteen were seen hanging in one tree, which was afterwards known as the Martyrs' Olive. The survivors were obliged to turn Mohammedan to save their skins. Ali had mosques and monasteries for dervishes built for them in each village, and sent missionaries to complete his conquest. For the whole exploit the Porte awarded him the title of Arslan, or the Lion.

Soon afterwards he was called to take part in an attack on a formidable rebel, Pasvan Oglu of Vidin. The proceedings were under the command of the Grand Vizier, who regarded Ali with dislike and suspicion, and thought him to be in secret league not only with the French at Corfu but with the rebel he was supposed to be attacking. He decided that Ali would be better out of the way altogether and invited him to a council in his tent, meaning to have him assassinated. Ali replied that he would be delighted to attend the council and mentioned quite casually that he would be bringing with him an escort of 6000 Skipetars. He kept his word and the council went off bloodlessly.

By this time the French were in Egypt, but Ali assured them that he did not mean to let that affect his friendly feelings towards them. He even offered to go into rebellion like Pasvan Oglu, if the French would send him an army of 10,000 men and a heavy subsidy, but the offer was not accepted. When he learnt that the Sultan was going to declare war on the French and that the Russians and Turks were going to combine in an attack on the Ionian Islands, he made a further offer, saying that he would side with the French, if they would give him, in the event of victory, the island of Santa Maura and the four coast towns. Again he found them unsympathetic, so he changed his tactics and informed the Porte that he proposed to help the Empire (by which he meant, to help himself) by attacking the coast towns on his own. The French had naturally foreseen this possibility, and Chabot had been busy fortifying Preveza. Ali invited him to a conference near Butrinto, but Roze came instead. Ali received him with great consideration, gave him an excellent dinner, and was altogether friendly, though he did not omit to ask some leading questions about the military condition of Corfu. After dinner he had the over-confident Frenchman seized, tied to a horse, and taken off to Jannina *en route* for Constantinople, where he was to be conveyed as a prisoner, in earnest of Ali's good faith towards his sovereign: Roze was duly taken there, and died not long afterwards. There could no longer be any pretence of amity between Ali and the French, so he attacked Butrinto without further ado. Chabot hurried over to direct the defence, but had to abandon the town, and, after setting fire to it, retired to Corfu.

It was known that Ali meant to attack Preveza, for he had already given out that any inhabitant of that place who might be captured in arms would be killed, and many of the people had already left to take refuge in the Ionian Islands, carrying their valuables with them. Chabot decided, however, that Preveza must be defended. General Lasalcette, who was in command of the town, had only 400 of his own men and 300 Prevezan Greeks, and was hoping that some Suliots would come and join him. He did what he could to strengthen the defences, while Ali approached with an army of six or seven thousand men, of whom about a third were cavalry. Lasalcette's position was alarming and pretty hopeless. The Suliots failed to arrive, and agents of Ali's were doing their best to destroy the morale of the remaining Prevezans.

On the night of October 12th, 1798, Mukhtar led an attack, which was repulsed, but a morning or two later, at daybreak, the whole of Ali's army suddenly showed themselves on the heights round the town. It was the custom of the Skipetars to work themselves up into a frenzy before going into battle and to call out threats, insults and war-cries to the enemy. While they set up their usual din, they could now be seen waving their heads, it is said, 'like a vast field of corn'. Brandishing their arms and shouting, they suddenly rushed down into the town like a wave. Lasalcette was cornered in a redoubt, and surrendered, but a French sub-lieutenant and some grenadiers went on fighting till they were all killed. The exultant Skipetars looted and set fire to the houses and carried off the women and children. By the next morning they had built a pyramid of heads cut from the French and from 160 armed Prevezans who had been taken alive. The beheading was done by a giant negro executioner in Ali's employ, but his wrists began to swell from the exertion, and overcome by fatigue and the smell of blood, he had to leave off.

There still survived 155 French prisoners, of whom 8 were officers. By Ali's orders, they were led to the pyramid of bloody heads and were forced with blows from bludgeons and the butt-ends of muskets, to flay the heads, salt the skins, and put them in sacks. Carrying these sacks, they were sent off under escort to Jannina, where they were received with jeers and showers of stones. The winter had already set in, but they were made to march over the mountains of Pindus in the direction of Constantinople. Many died on the way of cold, hunger and fatigue, and sometimes when a man showed signs of weakening his head was cut off and given to his comrades to carry. The survivors were imprisoned.

The fall of Preveza made a great impression in Europe and lent extraordinary prestige to the name of Ali. Nelson, who was cruising in the Ionian Sea, sent an officer to compliment him and to tell him how much he regretted not being able to go in person to congratulate 'the hero of Epirus'. At the same time Ali was publicly thanked by the Sultan for his services and made a Pasha of Three Tails.

Directly after taking Preveza Ali wrote some ingratiating letters to the people of Parga, a desirable town which had often sided with his enemies, suggesting that they should submit to his authority. He was met with a point blank refusal, to which he replied in a threatening tone: 'The letter you sent me is very unwise and haughty . . . God will punish you, and the sin will be upon your heads, for that which will inevitably happen.'

Towards the end of the year he was at the coast, taking a great interest in the fate of Corfu, now being besieged by the Russians and Turks in alliance, when a Tunisian privateer cast anchor off Butrinto. He heard a rumour that there were some important prisoners on board, and thinking that they might be useful to him he got into a quick, light sailing boat of the kind called a *kirlanguitch*, that being the Turkish word for a swallow, and went skimming over the water to pay a call on the corsair. Rumour had not lied. The corsair had managed to intercept an Italian tartan, the *Madonna di Montenegro*, on its way from Alexandria to Toulon, and had taken as prisoners a number of Frenchmen who had been serving with Napoleon's army in Egypt – a General Beauvais de Préau; a scholar named Bessières; Poitevin, a colonel of engineers; Charbonnel, a colonel of artillery; a certain Pouqueville; and an unfrocked monk named Guerini, who had been at one time a missionary in Syria and Palestine, where he had studied oriental languages and had in consequence been able to obtain employment with Napoleon in Egypt as an interpreter. The privateer had already dropped some of his prisoners, including Pouqueville, at Navarino, in order that they might be sent captive to Constantinople. The rest he had kept in chains at the bottom of the hold, where they had been fed on wormy biscuits and a little dirty water, besides being subjected to various other indignities and discomforts.

As soon as Ali came on board and discovered what sort of people the prisoners were he decided to carry them off with him. However doubtful they may have felt about their prospects, they were no doubt glad to go ashore. On landing they were met by one of Ali's doctors who acted as a secretary and also, it was said, as a paid poisoner at times. His name was Tozzoni, he spoke French well and was able to be of use to the new arrivals as an interpreter, though they found it difficult to be enthusiastic about his knowledge of medicine, for they soon learnt that for any and every complaint it was his custom to prescribe laudanum, more laudanum, and nothing but laudanum. Ali was kind to his prisoners and 'threw honey', for he meant to make use of them. To please them he pretended to be friendly towards France and the French, and when he left for Jannina he took them with him. He put Colonel Charbonnel in charge of a military school he had founded at a place called Bonila not far from the town, and allowed Bessières to live in the palace and travel about with him.

His fellow-passengers, or fellow-captives, had tried their best to be civil to Guerini, although they neither liked nor approved of him: at Jannina he went off every day into the country with a new friend he had picked up, and when they presently learned that he had turned Mohammedan their manners grew even more constrained.

'Of course all religions are all right in their way,' Guerini remarked to Bessières, 'and far be it from me to condemn anybody for his creed. Speaking for myself, I may say that up till now I have strayed, but at last Mohammed has appeared to me and opened my eyes.'

Like so many converts he wanted others to follow his example. He told Bessières and Charbonnel that it would pay them to do so, and boasted of his own good standing with Ali, but when he made a public profession of his new faith, had himself circumcized, and took the name Mehmet, they showed not the slightest eagerness to copy him. Ali appointed him to be one of his secretaries, he was later made an imam, and

became quite a familiar figure in Jannina as Mehmet Imam
Effendi – the Reverend Mr. Mehmet, as it were. Later in his
somewhat chequered career he turned Christian again, and
died in Paris in 1825.

After a time Ali sent word to Charbonnel that he intended
to come and inspect his new military school at Bonila, and on
the appointed day set out in state, taking his sons Mukhtar and
Veli with him. Charbonnel had pitched a little tent to serve
as a target for the artillery. He fired the first two shots himself:
the direction was perfect, but the range not quite exact, for the
first shot fell a trifle short and the second just beyond the
mark. He was getting ready to fire a third time, when Ali
ordered that some of his men should try their hands instead.
Six in turn tried, but every shot fell wide. Ali shouted to them
to stop, called them a pack of blockheads, and asked Charbonnel
to continue. After a nice calculation, the colonel fired his third
shot, which blew the tent to smithereens. Loud cheering
broke out on all sides, and Veli went and took Charbonnel by
the hand and led him to Ali, who congratulated him, presented
him with a pelisse, and made him master of the ordnance.

Ali was already thinking of a more interesting target for
the guns, for he had heard that Mustapha Pasha of Delvino,
the son of Selim, whom Ali had murdered, was plotting
vengeance against him. He accordingly sent Charbonnel to
bombard Delvino, which gave his artillerymen some useful
practice, and also brought about Mustapha's submission.

Shortly afterwards he heard that Corfu had surrendered
to the Russians and Turks, and immediately asked to be
allowed to put in a garrison, but this was refused as the
Corfiots strongly objected to him. The Ionian Islands were
turned into the Septinsular Republic, which was to be under
Russian protection and Turkish suzerainty. A republic
controlled by the two most despotic autocrats in Europe! Was

there ever such a mockery? The four coast towns were to be governed by Turkish commissioners appointed by the Porte, but the Christian inhabitants were to be allowed to keep their laws and customs. Ali did all that he could by means of bribery and argument, but was only allowed to keep Butrinto. By way of compensation he was made governor of Rumelia, with the title of Vizier, and the Sultan sent him the traditional presents for victorious proconsuls, a sable pelisse and a handsome ceremonial sabre. Ali went off to Monastir for a time to see to his new administration, which took the form of imposing heavy taxes and robbing the richer inhabitants right and left, so that he was able to send back to Jannina and Tebeleni whole consignments of valuables, including twelve bronze busts, eleven of which were melted down for military purposes, while the twelfth is supposed to have been eventually brought to England.

When he returned to Jannina he found that the Russians had been intriguing with Parga and Suli against him, and had been gun-running as well. This had encouraged the Suliots to make raids into Ali's territory in the neighbourhood of Jannina, looting and stealing sheep. He remembered his previous humiliation at their hands, he recalled that they had offered to help at Preveza, he counted up his grievances against them. They stood for all that he was out to crush, and he decided that the time had come to reduce them once and for all. Parga could be dealt with later.

CHAPTER X

THE SAGA OF SULI: II

IT was in the spring of 1800 that Ali began his preparations for a grand final assault on Suli. In June he called a conference of his Mohammedan neighbours and vassals. He assembled them in a monastery in the Castro, and produced a venerable old sheik who was willing to cite scripture in support of his purpose and proceeded to interpret some obscure passages of the Koran in such a way as to make them refer to the state of Albania. After some bitter references to the way in which the French and the Russians were menacing the Turks, Ali suggested that the least he and his hearers, as orthodox Mohammedans, could do in the meantime was to wipe out the Suliots, that nest of unbelievers in their very midst, and he invited them to join with him in swearing on the Koran, in the name of the Prophet and the Empire, to conquer Suli or perish. His oratory, thus given a colour half patriotic and half religious, had all the persuasive effect of a recruiting speech, and he soon found himself at the head of an army of 15,000 men.

The Suliots were of course well aware of his mobilization, but he was careful to spread rumours that he was going to lead an expedition against the French in Egypt. Some said that he was really going to attack Corfu. He was much aided in putting the Suliots off the scent by one of his agents, a man named Palaskas, whom he had sent to Suli some time previously. This Palaskas, pretending to be a deserter from Ali's army, had so well managed to worm his way into the confidence of the Suliots that he had married the daughter of

Captain Botzaris. Once he was sure of his position he managed by flattery to win Botzaris gradually over to a friendly attitude towards Ali. Botzaris enjoyed immense fame for his heroism in the Suliot cause years before, but unfortunately this had given him a swollen head, and now, when Palaskas conveyed fulsome compliments to him from Ali, and an offer of large sums of money and an exalted position if he would desert his country, he was too weak to refuse, and went over to Ali with seventy families of his clan. Directly he had taken this unworthy step he regretted it, and when Ali ordered him to march against Suli he refused, went away into retirement, and died very soon afterwards: he is supposed to have been overcome with shame and to have poisoned himself.

The Suliots suddenly learned that Ali was advancing against them at the head of a large army. They did not lose heart. Captain Tzavellas was no longer living, but his son Photo, nicknamed Kalilyros owing to his musical abilities, had grown up into the perfect Palikar. Photo had proved his courage when a boy: he was now physically strong, quick-witted, and of a generous and honourable nature. His mother Moscho was at hand to encourage him, and the Suliots turned to him as their natural leader. A careful ambush was quickly planned, and then they awaited the attack. Ali was too confident and headstrong and marched straight into the trap that had been laid for him. His troops were exposed to some straight and rapid shooting, and as in former days the women began rolling rocks down on them from the heights. The fighting lasted for seven hours, and at the end of that time the Skipetars retired, leaving 170 dead and many more wounded, while the Suliots had hardly suffered any losses at all.

Ali's next step was to send half his army to a place called Sistruni under one of his favourite generals, Mustapha Zyguri by name. Photo, at the head of 200 men, advanced some way to meet them, and then lay in hiding. After a time he sent out a few of his men to insult and taunt the enemy, a detachment of whom then advanced rapidly only to be shot down without even having seen the Suliots. Zyguri himself rushed forward at the head of his men and was shot down by Photo, who drew his sabre and led a counter-attack. Suddenly leaderless, the enemy got into a panic, and hastily retired. For two hours they beat a much harassed retreat, leaving many dead behind them, and Photo was able to return home in triumph, carrying with him the head of Zyguri.

Ali promptly ordered that another attack should be made on the following day by his combined forces under that now aged giant, Pronio Aga of Paramythia. As it happened, Pronio was secretly in sympathy with the Suliots, so he sent to warn them of the attack and advised them to attack first, and boldly. Photo and his friend Dimo Draku therefore took 250 men and started an offensive three hours before daylight, forcing the enemy to retreat with a loss of twenty-two men, while they only had one man killed and one wounded. When the enemy were trying to rally, a tremendous hailstorm suddenly came on and the hail was driven by the wind into their faces. This was taken by both sides as an omen and hastened the retreat. Ali found his men extremely discouraged but spoke to them mildly, for he had realized that there was little chance of taking Suli by storm and had already decided to change his tactics and see what could be done by a blockade. But first of all a short truce was declared in order that he might ransom his prisoners and wounded. The Suliots thought this a splendid chance to insult him, and took the ransom in kind, accepting one goat, sheep or donkey as the equivalent of each Mohammedan they surrendered.

Ali now gave orders for little forts and blockhouses to be built on the heights all round Suli, so that the passes could be overlooked and the Suliots prevented from obtaining supplies from outside. At the same time he wished them to be injured and demoralized by constant bombardments. For this he was counting on Charbonnel. The colonel duly organized the disposal of the artillery round Suli, but was not greatly interested in the outcome. The truth was that on first taking into his service the captured passengers of the *Madonna di Montenegro* Ali had promised to let them go after two years. That time was now up, and since Ali had not shown the slightest sign of keeping his promise Charbonnel, Poitevin and Bessières decided to take matters into their own hands and escape. They were bound by no oath or duty, and no doubt longing for home. Charbonnel now got leave from Ali to go to Jannina, no doubt on some military pretext, and as soon as he arrived set off secretly for the coast, while Poitevin and Bessières hurried away by separate routes to the same destination. Ali was enraged when he heard of their escape just when he needed them most. He put a price on their heads and hanged a muleteer who had helped them. They managed to reach Corfu, but the Russians handed them over to their allies the Turks and they were sent as prisoners to Constantinople.

Ali collected three hundred masons to put up his forts, but many of them were killed while at work. However he managed to put up no fewer than sixty-four small forts on high strategic points round Suli, the Suliots meanwhile making sudden attacks and laying ambushes, which enabled them to capture both prisoners and stores.

At this juncture Ibrahim Pasha of Berat, the father of Ali's daughters-in-law and a somewhat reluctant ally, arrived on the scene with 2,000 men and took up a position some way off from Suli, to the north. Photo marched against him with 1000 men, and the fighting had lasted for three hours when

Photo was wounded by a sniper. Lying on the ground, he called out to his companions to cut off his head to prevent his being taken alive to Ali, but after some hard hand-to-hand fighting all round him they managed to carry him back with them to safety.

While he was waiting for his wound to heal, his men were not idle. One day a Suliot deliberately put himself in the way of some of Ali's troops and allowed himself to be taken prisoner. Soon afterwards a sound of firing was heard up in the mountains, and when the Suliot was asked what it was, he said some fighting was going on up there and advised his captors to go and help their own people. Off they went, straight into another ambush, from which they only got away with heavy losses. Then on the day that Photo was well enough to take up arms again, the Suliots showed their joy by firing off their muskets. The enemy heard the firing, concluded that a quarrel must have broken out among the Suliots, and attacked with 2000 men, of whom seventy were killed.

By this time Ali's troops were in a bad way. They were tired of the war and of living on black bread and garlic, a good many were dying of an infectious disease, some no doubt thought it hopeless to go on attacking Suli, and some deserted. Among the last were many Greeks who had been conscripted into the Vizier's service and feeling naturally reluctant to side with Turks against Christians helped the Suliots secretly. Even Ali's generals were inclined to be disaffected. Men like Pronio Aga and Ibrahim Pasha saw quite clearly that if Suli were to fall Ali would enjoy absolute power in Epirus and would be able, if he chose, to put an end to what was left of their own independence. They were so busy hesitating and feeling downhearted that there was a lull in the fighting, which made it possible for the Suliots to lay in fresh supplies from Parga.

By the end of the year the Suliots were secretly negotiating with the malcontents. Besides Ibrahim and Pronio they won over Mustapha Pasha of Delvino. A pact was made and hostages were exchanged, and Ali found that a powerful league had been formed against him. He made up his mind to smash it at all costs, and is said to have spent 4,000,000 piastres for that purpose. He always believed that money could do anything, and by using his favourite device of bribery he promoted rebellions in the pashaliks of Berat and Delvino which for a time took up all the attention of their rulers.

Like women and elephants, Ali never forgot an injury, and his hatred of the Suliots was beginning to be something more than an obsession. He now offered them a truce and said he would require twenty-four hostages as a proof of good faith and a security against any invasion of his territory. The Suliots might have reminded themselves of his former treacheries, but they were badly in need of an armistice, accepted his offer, and delivered up the hostages. No sooner had Ali received them than he threatened them with death by torture unless Suli surrendered unconditionally.

'By treachery of this sort,' they replied, 'you only damage your own reputation and make us all the more determined to resist you. Kill us if you like, but that won't make Suli surrender. And from now on we shall make no pretence of feeling any friendship towards you, for you have shown that in everything you undertake you are incapable of straight dealing'.

He sent them off to Jannina and ordered them to be interned in a monastery on the island in the lake. At first they were allowed a certain amount of freedom but Ali did not mean to let them enjoy it long. One morning they all went to church, and according to custom left their arms outside, though one man, Photomara by name, took his in with him.

When the service was over they found that they had been disarmed, and were instantly surrounded by a troop of Skipetars who were waiting to seize them. The leader of the troop ordered Photomara to give up his arms.

'I'll show you how a Suliot gives up his arms,' he replied, and shot himself through the heart.

Meanwhile Pronio, who knew that Ali suspected him of double dealing, sent word pretending that he must return to Paramythia in order to prevent supplies being sent to the Suliots, but when he got there he found that Ali had put in a garrison of his own men, and Pronio was obliged to send one of his sons to Jannina as a hostage. The Suliots were badly in need of food, and an offer of help came from Ibrahim Pasha of Berat, but when Ali heard of this he was alarmed at the thought of the campaign being prolonged, and hurriedly made the Suliots an offer of peace. He suggested that they should evacuate Suli and said he would give them in compensation a large sum of money, a fertile part of the country to live in, and exemption from taxes. They sent him an answer in their traditionally defiant style:

'Our country is infinitely sweeter to us than either your money or the pleasant lands you offer us. You are wasting your time. Freedom cannot be bought with all the treasure on earth, and we shall go on fighting until not a single Suliot is left alive.'

Ali now thought his best plan would be to try and divide them, so he sent an agent to Dimo Zerva, one of the Suliot leaders, with an offer of 800 purses and honours besides if he would desert with his followers.

'Thank you, Vizier,' Dimo replied, 'for your kind regards, but please don't send the 800 purses, for I shouldn't know how to count them, and even if I did, believe me that one single pebble of my country would be too great a return for them. You can keep your honours. The honours of a Suliot are in bearing arms. With these I hope to make my name and my country endure.'

Desultory fighting was still going on. As a result of sickness and casualties and wholesale desertions, Ali's army had been reduced to about 8000 men, and these found themselves having a worse time than the people they were supposed to be besieging, for the Suliots often attacked their fortifications. Ali knew that the Suliots had sometimes managed to obtain supplies from Parga, so he brought pressure to bear on the archbishop of Jannina and tried to get him to obtain secret information from the bishop of Parga. A monk, whose turpitude earned for him the name of Kako-Joseph, acted as go-between, but the bishop of Parga proved unhelpful.

In spite of help from their Parghiot allies, the Suliots had suffered greatly from want of food, and had sent away many of their women and old men to take refuge in Corfu. By the end of the year they were reduced to eating grass, bark and acorns mixed with flour, but Moscho, the mother of Photo, led an immense procession of 413 men and 174 women to Parga to fetch provisions, and after five days they returned all laden. On their way back they laid themselves open to attack by about 1000 of Ali's troops, and the fact that no attack was made shows what a mixture of fear and sympathy was felt by the besiegers.

The war had now been dragging on for eighteen months, and still Ali had been unable to smash the confederation against him consisting of Pronio Aga of Paramythia, Mustapha Pasha of Delvino and Ibrahim Pasha of Berat (the last two of whom had especial reasons, as has been shown, for regarding Ali as a great enemy) and of some lesser chieftains besides. These associates now sent money to the Suliots so that they could buy food and munitions. When Ali heard of this he was so furious that he first hanged two of the Suliot hostages at Jannina, one a boy of twelve who was a cousin of Photo Tzavellas, and the other a nephew of Dimo Draku. Redoubling his efforts against the allies, he managed by lavish bribes to turn some of Ibrahim's and Pronio's vassals against them. With a faked letter and the help of a traitor he made Mustapha set out on a journey from Delvino and then sent 1000 of his own men to occupy the town. Ibrahim was so harassed that he made a separate peace, but Pronio, although his son was still in Ali's power, remained faithful and continued to resist. Ali sent an army against Paramythia, but Photo and Dimo, the Suliot heroes, rushed to Pronio's assistance with 300 men, and the attackers were driven off.

CHAPTER XI

THE TERROR BY NIGHT

WHILE the Suliot War was going on there were some remarkable domestic complications at Jannina. Ali's eldest son Mukhtar was engaged in a passionate love affair. Mukhtar, who had lately been given the pashalik of Lepanto and made a Pasha of Two Tails, in some ways took after his father, but had not anything like his father's ability. Large, strong, and aggressively masculine, he had a gross face without the slightest hint of good humour in its expression. His manners and pleasures were rough, he liked hunting and blood sports, and was good at *djerid*, a kind of jousting on horseback with lances of willow wood. It has been said that the leading features of his character were 'brutal ferocity, degrading sensuality, and monstrous perfidy'. He was used in any case to having his own way. Like his father, his aunt, and his grandmother, Dark Mukhtar, as Byron calls him, was a person of violent passions, and he was so little given to delay in gratifying them that he had been known to rape women publicly in the streets in broad daylight.

His attention was now engaged by a young and extremely beautiful Janninot woman named Phrosýne. She was twenty-eight, married, and the mother of two children. Her husband was a Greek merchant who was obliged for the sake of his business to be often absent in Venice for long periods. Not only beautiful but witty and accomplished, she might in an earlier age have shone as a hetaira or in a more liberal civilization have presided over a salon, but in Jannina women were not valued for their intellectual attainments. Mukhtar

took advantage of her husband's absence to make very determined advances to her and she became his mistress. He does
not seem to have met with any resistance, and even if he had,
would no doubt have rapidly overborne it. Phrosýne was not
unnaturally flattered to have been singled out for the favours
of such a powerful and important person as the eldest son of
the dictator, and she had no difficulty in realizing that he was
madly in love with her.

Mukhtar made no secret of his obsession and it became
common knowledge that he was altogether neglecting his wife
Pasho, and that she was getting exceedingly jealous. Phrosýne's head was turned. Confident of her hold over Mukhtar,
she grew bold, and made up her mind, for she was of a practical turn, and a Greek, to squeeze every possible material
advantage out of him that she could. He was in the habit of
wearing a ring set with a large gem that was very handsome
and valuable, and she begged him to give it to her, which he
did. Directly she had got it she sent for a jeweller and tried
to get him to buy it or at least to sell it for her. He could not
think of anybody in Jannina who would be likely to be in a
position to buy it except one of the ladies at the palace, and
in all innocence he showed it to Pasho. She of course at once
recognized her husband's ring and made the jeweller tell her
how it had come into his hands. When she heard who had
given it to him her jealousy completely overmastered her, and
she became obsessed with the one idea of revenge against
Phrosýne.

Circumstances aided her. Just at this time Ali was ordered
to proceed against the Pasha of Adrianople, Gurdji Osman, who
was in rebellion. But he was unwilling to go while his affairs
were still in such an unsettled state and Suli still unsubdued,
so he pretended to be ill, and ordered Mukhtar to go instead,
putting Veli in temporary command of the blockade of Suli.

It cannot have been easy for Mukhtar to leave his mistress when his passion for her was at its height. His farewell to Phrosýne was later made the subject of a romantic poem, in which he compares himself to a yellow leaf carried away by the wind, the summer being over and winter threatening, while Phrosýne is compared to a departing swallow overtaken by darkness. The poem ends, after conveying something of that sense of yearning sorrow and impending disaster which often accompanies a too intense sexual passion, on a note of warning and farewell, which may be a true suggestion of what the parting lovers actually felt. At all events, directly Mukhtar had gone, Pasho, raving with jealousy, decided to go straight to Ali and complain of the wrongs done to her by Phrosýne. She was careful not to go alone, but took her sister Zobeidé, the wife of Veli, with her to back her up, partly because Ali was fond of Zobeidé, and partly because the two sisters had managed to be helpful to Ali in maintaining his influence in Upper Albania and had even helped him to cheat their father, Ibrahim Pasha of Berat, out of some important territory. After hearing what they had to say about Phrosýne, Ali raised them up from the floor, where they were kneeling at his feet, and swore by the beard of the Prophet that Pasho should get her revenge.

Ali felt that he could not trust any of his officers to carry out his orders, for there was a danger that they might warn Mukhtar. So he took matters into his own hands. At dead of night he went secretly with his bodyguard to Phrosýne's house. Having got in, and being provided with a lantern, he went straight to her room and woke her up. She started up in alarm, and naturally when she saw who her visitor was the alarm turned to terror. With the light of the lantern shining upwards on his face and bringing his features into dreadful relief, he held out the ring and asked her if she recognized it. Seeing the ring, she lost all hope and expected the worst. She threw herself at his feet, confessed her fault, and begged and prayed for mercy. She offered Ali, as a bribe, all her jewels and other treasures. His avarice, unlike his clemency, was never appealed to in vain, and with a gleam in his eye he took possession of them all. But if she imagined that she had bought immunity from his anger she was at once disillusioned, for he sternly ordered her to get up and dress and go with him. He allowed her to bring her maid with her, and at the door of the house handed them both over to the guard.

The next day he told Pasho what he had done and asked her if she thought there were any other loose women to whom her husband had been paying attention. She must have replied with the Albanian equivalent of 'And how!' for without a moment's hesitation she wrote down the names of fifteen of the most beautiful women in the city. A detachment of Skipetars were accordingly sent to arrest them (one was pregnant, and only one month from her time) and together with Phrosýne and her maid they were thrust into the horrible Buldrun, the dungeon under the Castro, where they were made to serve the pleasures of the men in charge of them. While Ali was hesitating to condemn them all to death a poor Greek came to beg for the life of his wife who was among them. This appealed to Ali's sense of humour.

'What!' he cried. 'Do you like being the husband of a prostitute?'

The man said he did, so Ali, with a hearty laugh, gave an order for her release. The rest, including Phrosýne, he sentenced to death.

Three nights later the guards came and unlocked the Buldrun and fetched out the prisoners, and took them along a dark underground passage to an opening where some steps led down to the lake, and there some boats were waiting. A thunderstorm was going on, and when the women saw by the light of the torches the water cruelly lapping against the shore, and the expanse of the lake livid under the lightning, they struggled to turn back and uttered shrieks of terror which were lost in the angry roar of the thunder. They were forced into the boats, tied up in sacks, and thrown into the water: it was the conventional punishment for adultery on the part of a woman. It is said that Phrosýne and her maid, taking advantage of a moment's inattention on the part of the guards, clasped each other in their arms and threw themselves into the lake. Her body was later recovered by some Christians and given proper burial, and in later days her tomb was pointed out, romantically isolated under a wild olive tree and covered with white irises.

Time was kind to the reputation of this woman who had been unfaithful to her husband, vain, and grasping. She came to be regarded as a Christian martyr and even as an early heroine in the struggle for Greek independence. She has been celebrated in legend, in poetry, in popular songs and historical fiction, and surrounded with the glamour which so often attaches to women whose love affairs have been of an intense nature and have involved men of political or historical importance. Her children were turned out into the streets, from which they were rescued by the archbishop, who happened to be their mother's uncle.

CHAPTER XII

THE SAGA OF SULI: III

ALI's attacks on Suli had never been much approved of in Constantinople, and he had even been given some hints to discontinue them, for the Suliots had always been regular in paying their tribute to the Sultan and he had no reason to feel ill-disposed towards them. Besides, the Porte had not abandoned its old policy of 'Divide and rule' and had no wish to see Ali too powerful. Ali, for his part, spoke openly of the Sultan's advisers as a pack of fatheads, and it was one of his jokes to call the Sublime Porte the Low Porte. Being now able to establish that the Suliots were getting some support from the French – the supplies they had fetched from Parga, for example, had been landed there in a French vessel – he made the most of this information in a dispatch to Constantinople, with the result that the Porte authorized him to go on with his campaign and make it a fight to the finish.

When Mukhtar came back from Adrianople Ali put him in charge again of the operations against Suli, where he tried no sensational feats, but contented himself with strengthening his position. The Suliots had done what they could for themselves in the way of revictualling and fortification, but their hardships and the incessant nervous strain had begun to tell on them, they were suffering from disease as well, and tended to quarrel amongst themselves. Mukhtar managed to occupy the banks of the Acheron and cut off their water supply, so they had to depend on rain-water, and when that ran short they let down over the cliffs big sponges on ropes weighted with lead and got what they could that way. At this time, when they so badly needed heartening, they were pulled together by the influence of an extraordinary man, a monk called Samuel, nicknamed 'Last Judgment' Samuel, who had appeared as if from nowhere to lead them. He has been neatly, if insufficiently, described as 'a man of wild enthusiastic character, who ran about animating the citizens, with a bible in one hand and a sword in the other, cutting off heads and explaining prophecies'. Simple people said that he had been sent from God, and suspicious ones asserted that he was a distinguished foreign officer in disguise, but everybody agreed that he was extremely energetic and had become the life and soul of the resistance. He seemed to be everywhere at once, now firing a gun, now making a speech, then darting through the enemy lines on missions to Parga, Paramythia, and Preveza. On Kunghi, one of the highest points of Suli, he built a fort.

Ali repeated his overtures of peace. This time he suggested that the Suliots should retain their country, but that he should be allowed to build and garrison a fort there, and that Photo Tzavellas should be banished. Photo consented to go to Jannina for a conference, and Ali then sent him back to discuss with his people the terms to be agreed on. They decided to reject all the Vizier's offers and tried to persuade Photo to stay at home, but he thought it best to return with their answer to Jannina. Before he left he put a torch to the roof of his house and burnt it down, saying that no enemy should ever cross his threshold. Then he buried his sabre and went back to Ali, who imprisoned him.

In May 1803 the Suliots received some munitions from the French and this heartened them to further efforts. One of the enemy's strongest posts was a square fort favourably placed on the top of a peak for bombarding Suli. This fort had a tower at each corner and one in the middle like a keep, which was used as a magazine. One dark and windy night a party of 200 Suliots set out to destroy it. Two men with picks and shovels went on ahead, dug a hole under one of the corner towers, filled it with explosives, and then lighted a slow fuse. They rejoined the rest of the party behind some rocks not very far off, and all began to shout, which drew the greater part of the garrison to the fatal corner tower, up which they came crowding to see what was the matter. They soon found out, for the tower blew up. The Suliots then rushed in and surrounded the lower part of the central tower, or keep, from which they removed all the stores and ammunition, which were carried off to safety by their women and children. Meanwhile the remnant of the garrison, numbering 160, had taken refuge in the upper story. At daybreak they said they would surrender, but suddenly began to shoot at the Suliots below, who accordingly made a large fire on the ground floor and burnt them all alive.

All through the summer the deadlock lasted, and Ali grew more and more exasperated. His wife Eminé, the mother of Mukhtar and Veli, and a woman of benevolent character, was much alarmed at the atrocities which were being committed against the Suliots: she knew how desperate they were, and how ingenious, and was afraid they might carry out some awful act of revenge on her sons. She was rash enough to mention her fears to Ali, and even to plead with him. She begged him to stop exposing his sons to such great danger, to stop his army from murdering Suliot prisoners as soon as they were taken, and to spare the survivors of a people who had shown such heroic courage.

'I've been warned in a dream,' she said, 'that you ought to spare the Suliots . . .'

'Ach, the Suliots!' cried Ali. 'How dare you even name them to me!'

'Yes, I dare. Remember that I am the daughter of a pasha. I name them, and may their blood, and the blood of Caplan, my unlucky father, that you caused to be shed when I was little more than a child, be upon your head!'

Ali was very fond of his wife, but she had touched him on a raw spot. He was furious at the idea of a woman advising him and trying to interfere with his plans, and the mere mention of Suli was now unbearable to him. He flew into one of his ungovernable rages, and all who saw him agree that when angry he was more than terrifying – his eyes flashed and his features were twisted with passion. He shouted and stormed at Eminé, uttering threats and curses until he had worked himself up into a perfect paroxysm, when he seized hold of a pistol and fired it off at random, meaning no doubt to relieve his feelings and terrorize his wife. Eminé's women came running in when they heard the shot, found her lying unconscious on the floor, and carried her off to her own apartments. A few minutes later Tozzoni came to Ali and told him that Eminé had not been hit and had only fainted. The news calmed the Vizier, and he began to weep.

In the night, feeling himself again and uneasy about Eminé, he decided to go to her. He went and knocked at her door and called to her, but was not admitted. At this his anger broke out again and he began to shout and make a great to-do, and at last forced the door open and burst into the room. When she saw him Eminé was utterly terrified and thought her last moment had come. She gazed at him with a curious fixity, and suddenly had a stroke. Before morning she was dead.

It was not only to Ali that her death caused regret. The gentleness of her nature was well known and she was said to have been able at times to restrain him from acts of violence. Certainly she had often been kind and generous to the unfortunate, whatever their creed. She had probably been the best influence in Ali's life, and he was perhaps fonder of her than of anybody else. He never got over her death, and it left him with a feeling of guilt. For ten years at least it haunted him, and he felt fear as well as remorse, at times was afraid to be alone at night or even to put his arms outside the bedclothes, and sometimes he woke up crying out her name and asking to be saved from her.

In September Ali launched his grand final attack on Suli. Veli was in command, and by treachery managed to get 200 of his men into Suli at night. The Suliots suffered great losses, and only had two forts left, Kako-Suli and Kunghi, which 'Last Judgment' Samuel had built. Photo, who had managed to escape from Jannina, led an attack from Kunghi. The fighting went on for seven hours, and stones were used as well as sabres and muskets. Seven hundred of the enemy were killed, while the Suliot losses only amounted to eleven, including three women. But it was all in vain. There was no water left, and the Suliots agreed to enter into negotiations with Veli to determine the conditions of their surrender.

On December 12th, Veli gave them a written promise, signed by all the chief beys and agas as well as by himself, to let them go unmolested. The document was drawn up with the utmost formality, proclaiming the authority of Ali the Victorious, and of the Sultan himself, the King of Kings. The Suliots were to be free to leave Suli with all their possessions and settle in Albania or abroad as they pleased; Veli undertook to provide them with transport; the hostages still at Jannina would be returned; and those Suliots who wished to stay in Albania would be given free land and would be ever accorded honourable treatment, safety, and the protection of Ali and his family. The treaty was declared to be sacred and a guarantee that no Suliot should ever be made to suffer for anything

111

that had happened in the past, and it concluded with an invitation to the Almighty to strike Veli dead if he failed to keep his word.

Three days later Photo and Dimo Draku set out for Parga with two-thirds of the Suliots, while the rest went towards Preveza. But 'Last Judgment' Samuel refused to surrender; with five other men he stayed at Kunghi, and blew up the fort as the enemy approached. The poet Valaorites has a ballad on the subject which lends to the scene an element of magic, while heightening the drama. Samuel is represented as celebrating his last Communion on earth before his five companions:

> And as upon the Flesh Divine the priest in rapture gazes,
> Falls from his eye the cup within, one tear, like dew
>   transparent.
> My God and Father, buried here within Thy house, I
>   thirsted;
> Unmixed with water, incomplete would be Thy Holy
>   Supper;
> Accept, Creator, this sad tear, and do not Thou despise it,
> From my heart's leaves, all clean and pure, Thou seest
>   that forth it floweth;
> Accept it, my Creator, now; I have no other water.

> .   .   .   .   .

> The sacred cup he trembling held, and to his bosom
>   pressed it:
> And as he kissed, with reverent lips, he heard, like heart's
>   pulsation,
> That soft, with newly given life, the Sacred Blood was
>   throbbing.

His five companions are kneeling before him, and

Unmoved the priest approaches them, upon his face a
  glory,
As bright as snowy mountain-top, illumined by the
  moonbeams.
A barrel in his hand he bears, those hands so maimed and
  wounded;
Imprisoned in its staves are death, and fire, and desperation.

He prays, recalling the sufferings of Suli, and commends
his companions to God as martyrs for liberty, and as they listen
to him

Drop after drop, drop after drop, their bitter tears are
  falling,
Where they bedew the marble floor they crack and rend
  the pavement.
'Tis sorrow deep that tears their hearts, death has for
  them no terror.

He offers each of them the Sacrament, and by this time
the attackers have begun to hammer at the door:

His eyes he lifts as loud the blows upon the door are
  falling,
And from the Spoon within his hand lets fall upon the
  barrel
Of Christ's pure Blood one flaming drop, one drop alone
  has fallen.
'Tis struck as with a lightning-flash, and the whole earth
  is thund'ring.
One moment shines the unsullied church, one moment
  glitters Kunghi,

and then the building and the six men inside it are blown to
glory. But

The monk's black cassock, floating still, towards the sky
   ascended,
And spread, and spread upon the wind in wide and fearful
   darkness,
And rising with the smoke it soared, and with it on was
   sailing.
And sailing, floating on it went, and still like death was
   poising;
And where its flaming shadow fell, upon the hills and
   valleys,
Like mystic fire it burnt the groves, and scorched the
   wooded hillsides,
But with the first rain-storms of spring, and with the
   showers of summer.
Shall spring again the freshest grass, with laurels, olives,
   myrtles;
With slaughters, victories and hopes shall spring fresh
   joys and Freedom!

Fresh joys and freedom, however, had not yet been
attained by the departing Suliots, for Veli's solemn and
sacred promises proved to be not worth the paper they were
written on. He sent a force of 4000 men to attack the con-
tingent of refugees on their way to Parga, but the Suliots beat
them off and reached Parga safely. There Veli was afraid to
pursue them, for the town was still under Russian protection,
and Count Mocenigo, the Russian plenipotentiary in the
Septinsular Republic, allowed them to cross over in safety to
the Ionian Islands.

The other party, about 1000 in all, had reached a
monastery on a mountain called Zalongo when they were
attacked by another division of Ali's army. The gates of the
monastery were forced open and a massacre began. About

sixty women and children managed to escape up the moun-
tainside, and when they reached the top the women, working
themselves up into a frenzy of defiance, began to sing the old
Suliot songs and dance the old Suliot dances, ever increasing
in pace and fervour as they gradually drew nearer to the edge
of a precipice: then with a final cry of triumph they threw
themselves over. It was perhaps the most sensational act in
the whole history of Suli.

A number of other Suliots had managed to escape from
the monastery and force their way through the enemy lines.
The women were in the middle, some with babies at their
breasts, while some of the men carried a child in one hand and
a sabre in the other. Twenty were killed and many captured,
but others were able to hack their way through and escape, in
a storm of wind and rain, into the woods and mountains,
while 150 got away in the direction of Parga.

It happened that about twenty Suliot families, consisting
mostly of widows and children, had been living, by Ali's
leave, at a village called Riniassa, and early in 1804 Ali
decided to send troops to capture and enslave them. In the
village was a tower called Dimula where a widow named
Despo Botzi was living with ten other women and children.
She made them fire on the attackers till they had used up all
their ammunition, and then, emulating Samuel, she set a
light to a barrel of powder on which she was sitting and blew
up the whole place and all its occupants.

Nor was that the end. At Vurgareli, a village about
twenty-five miles from Arta, some Suliots had been joined by
some of the refugees from Zalongo. They were not unnaturally afraid of Ali's vengeance, and retired to a monastery
called Seltzo on a steep rocky height above the river Achelous.
There were about 1150 of them altogether. Ali sent 7000
troops to demand a surrender, but they were answered with a

volley of musket fire, so they surrounded and laid siege to the place. The siege lasted three months, and in order to encourage the besiegers Ali put in the front ranks men who had lost relations and friends in the Suliot war. They closed in at last on the monastery. Some Suliots made a sortie and fifty of them were killed. Among the survivors there were more women than men, and 100 of them faced the enemy with stones, sticks and knives. Three hundred Suliots were captured or killed, and 160 women, some with children, threw themselves into the Achelous. The rest of the women were captured, all but one, who with fifty-five men managed to escape to Parga. Ali and the Turkish commissioner for the coast towns brought pressure on the Parghiots to give them up, so they crossed over to the islands.

Most of the Suliots who had been taken to Jannina as prisoners during the final operations were tortured, and more than 200 were murdered. Some were flayed or burnt alive, some had their throats cut. For pregnant women a particularly monstrous fate was chosen. The conquest of Suli had taken some fifteen years of fighting, on and off, besides an immense expenditure of men and money, and Ali felt that he had a real triumph to celebrate. The conquest of the supposedly unconquerable brought him greater fame than ever, and the Porte began to regret having sanctioned and even encouraged the campaign. Having demolished the greatest obstacle in his way, Ali, it was feared, might aim now at independence.

The Suliot refugees in Corfu were not condemned to idleness. They were formed into six companies of light infantry under a Russian general named Anrep, combined with four from Khimara, under a Colonel Beckendorf, and then sent to Naples against the French, Photo being made a captain and his mother Moscho a major. But they did not understand European notions of discipline, or the enlistment of soldiers for daily pay instead of for the promise of glory and loot. They thought themselves ill-used, suffered from sickness and homesickness, and grew tired of exile. Some of them, led by Photo, went back to Jannina, submitted to Ali, and entered his service. Major Moscho went to Jannina, too, and found a new husband there. It was indeed the end of Suli.

CHAPTER XIII

PLUNDER AND TREACHERY

THE anxieties of the Porte after the collapse of Suli were
shared by the Russians, who began with the Porte's consent to
intrigue against Ali and lend help to his enemies, including
Mustapha Pasha of Delvino and the rulers of Paramythia and
Margariti. Some desultory fighting took place, but nothing
much came of it, and the Porte began to cast about for another
plan. They soon thought of one by which they could flatter
Ali, get him away from Jannina, and perhaps with luck get
him out of the way altogether.

At this time Macedonia, Thrace and Bulgaria were all
infested with swarms of brigands known as Kersales, and it
had become urgently necessary to put them out of action.
Who more suitable for the task than Ali, a specialist in the
suppression of brigandage? He was made commander-in-chief
and Viceroy of Rumelia as well, and off he went to Monastir
at the head of an army of 12,000 men to join forces with the
other troops that had been put at his disposal, troops so
numerous that by the time he arrived at Philippopolis he
found himself in command of no fewer than 80,000 men.
On his way he had levied huge sums on the towns he had
passed through, and had always stayed in them long enough
to squeeze the rich according to his usual custom. In camp outside Philippopolis he had the Kersale leaders who had already
been captured brought before him: some he kept as hostages,
others he beheaded.

His success alarmed the Porte more than ever. They did
not like the rapidity of his movements, the size of his army, or

118

his determined way of enriching himself, and they were afraid that he might be thinking of trying his strength against the Empire itself, though actually he was only concerned to make himself all-powerful in his native West, the master of an immense feudal domain which he could hand on to his sons. If only he could be induced to declare himself openly a rebel! *Agents provocateurs* were sent from Constantinople, and in the camp at Philippopolis men could soon be heard making seditious speeches, singing revolutionary songs, and talking boldly of raising a new flag. The army was divided by a confusion of languages and dialects, and by rivalries and jealousies as well, and every opportunity was taken to try and catch Ali in a trap. He knew he was in a tight corner, saw that a restlessness was breaking out which would be hard to control, and decided on a bold stratagem.

'I see that you're tired of waiting here and doing nothing,' he declared in a speech, 'and I can well understand your feelings. We shall accordingly strike camp and march to Sofia. Let everyone follow me.'

He knew quite well that the more discontented divisions would make this an occasion to desert, and he was right. Then, instead of marching to Sofia, he retired in the direction of Monastir, loaded with loot and treasure of all kinds. He had freed many of the captured Kersales in return for heavy ransoms, and had carried off all the artillery he could lay hands on, meaning to use it to fortify his own strongholds. From policy as well as avarice he had left Rumelia in a completely exhausted state, and almost as full of brigands as ever, for he knew that his successor, finding himself without either supplies or means of defence, would then be no danger to him. He was very relieved to be back in Epirus, and the Porte certainly preferred him at a distance. He asked for a free hand if it should be necessary for him to march again, but the

Porte, overwhelmed with complaints against his graspingness, wrote politely thanking him in the Sultan's name for his services, but hinted that they thought it no longer necessary for him to exercise his talents in Rumelia.

Veli was now appointed Pasha of the Morea, and the pashalik of Trikkala fell vacant. Ali asked that it should either be•left with Veli or else returned to himself. But the Russians, still in the Ionian Islands, were still anxious to prevent any increase in the power of their dangerous neighbour the Vizier of Jannina, so their ambassador at Constantinople protested against his being allowed to keep Trikkala. The Porte did not want to offend Ali, so they effected a compromise by giving the vacant pashalik to Elmas Bey, the son of Ali's sister Shainitza. Elmas, however, soon died of small-pox, and as by that time the Turks were no longer on good terms with the Russians Trikkala was given back to Veli, who sent a deputy there to govern in his name. It was said that Elmas had died as the result of being sent by his Uncle Ali, who wanted him out of the way, a magnificent coat of black fox skins infected with the germs of smallpox. Shainitza made an inordinate display of her grief at the death of her son, cursed the day she was born, and swore to have the life of the doctor who had attended him. In the midst of her lamentations there was a booming of cannon at Jannina to announce the birth of Ali's third son, Sali Bey, the offspring of a Georgian slave in his harem. It is said that when female infants were born to his wives he had them thrown into the lake because he was afraid that they might grow up to make marriages which would dim the lustre of his name.

There are one or two domestic occurrences which call for special notice as they were to be of consequence later on. Ali was particularly anxious (for a reason which will appear) to get rid of an individual in Jannina named Ismail Pasho Bey.

He therefore appointed him to act as sword-bearer to Veli in the Morea, but Ismail understood perfectly well that he was being sent into exile.

'Ah, he's banishing me, the old crook!' he exclaimed, catching sight of Ali sitting in a window of the palace. 'But I'll punish him for it one day, and I'll die happy, even if I have to buy the old monster's head with my own.'

Receiving orders to blot out a gang of coiners who were busy making Turkish piastres and Venetian sequins with great skill, Ali led an expedition against a village called Plichivitza, surrounded the place at night, caught the coiners red-handed among their moulds and melting-pots, and ordered a massacre. When it had begun, a ravishingly lovely young girl of twelve, named Vasiliki, managed to dodge the Skipetars and came and threw herself at Ali's feet and begged his protection for her mother and brothers. He was so taken with her that he ordered them to be spared, and carried her off to Jannina, where she became a special object of his attentions, and later his wife.

On the pretence of keeping order round Arta, Ali had managed to get hold of Acarnania, Aetolia, and the town of Salona, for which he showed his contempt by appointing a priest as governor there, sending word at the same time that if the citizens showed any dissatisfaction over this he would send along an old cook from his harem to govern instead. The rich landed proprietors were of course of special interest to him, and he decided to rob them on the pretext that they had been in secret alliance with the Suliots. For particular attention one Susman was singled out, a local grandee descended from the ancient kings of Serbia, and Veli was to be made his father's instrument in the matter.

In January 1805 Veli went to Missolonghi, pretending that he was setting out on an official tour of the Morea.

Susman sent him the presents which custom required, but did not come in person to pay his respects, and sent excuses for his absence, for he had already heard a rumour that Ali intended to victimize him. Veli replied urbanely, thanked him for the presents, accepted the apology, and said how sorry he was that false reports should perhaps have influenced Ali's opinion of Susman unfavourably. Any danger there might have been, he said, had now blown over, and he would himself reassure his father. Susman had been on the point of escaping to the mountains with his family, but Veli's letter quietened him down, and he stayed at home. A few months later Veli was at Arta and again wrote to Susman, saying that Ali had restored his favour towards him, and that he (Veli) would be pleased to receive Susman and his son at Arta, in order to convey to them personally an assurance of the Vizier's good-will. He even had the great condescension to add a postscript in his own handwriting.

'I am your friend, and shall always protect you. If this assurance is not enough, I turn it into an oath to defend you, and in the name of the Faith and by the heads of my children I swear to you eternal friendship.'

Susman had sense enough to take all this with a grain of salt, and he hoped that all would be well if he gave Veli some particularly handsome presents. His family did their best to prevent him going to Arta, but he went, taking his son with him. They were met by an escort and a guard of honour, and as soon as they arrived Veli sent a secretary from the arch-bishop's palace, where he was staying, to welcome them and invite them to a banquet on the following day. He also sent his gardener with flowers, and a band to play to them in the meantime. Next day horses were brought and Susman and his son were escorted to the palace. Veli received them very kindly and invited them to sit beside him on the divan. He graciously allowed them to stay there while he dined, and at the end of his meal, when musicians and dancers and boy-prostitutes were shown in, he asked his guests to go and enjoy their banquet in another room and then come back and join the party. What followed when they had gone out of the room is told in a contemporary account:

'Heated with wine, Veli threw off his turban and pelisse to join the lascivious dance, and at length, maddened by his passions, he disrobed himself of his remaining clothing, and plunged without restraint into the most revolting excesses that obscenity can inspire. While this disgusting revel was at its height, a cry of "Here they are!" was heard in the banqueting room. It was uttered by two executioners, who came forward with the blood-dripping heads of Susman and his son. Veli burst into a fiendish laugh as he looked on the two bleeding evidences of his baseness and ferocity . . . then commanded the dance to be resumed . . . and the whole of the night was spent in inebriety and licentious enjoyment.'

CHAPTER XIV

THE FRENCH CONSUL

THE whole of southern Greece, with the exception of Attica, Boeotia and Negropont, had now come under the rule of Ali and his sons, and with the exception of Mehmet Ali, the ruler of Egypt (who was also an Albanian by birth), he could regard himself as the strongest man in the Turkish Empire. But the position of a strong man is never a tranquil one, for his very nature prevents it. His existence depended on the use of force and cunning, and his authority was liable to be threatened or interfered with from abroad as well as from Constantinople. The successes and ambitions of Napoleon made the Vizier uneasy, and he felt he needed an ally, so he turned to the English and carried on a correspondence with that excellent man Collingwood, as a result of which Major William Leake, who was both young and capable, was sent on a mission to Ali and instructed to stay in Albania and make a military survey of the country in order to determine how it might best be defended against an invader. While Leake was surveying Albania, Ali was busy building forts.

After Austerlitz, when Napoleon had obtained Dalmatia, Ali changed his tune and thought it best to make up to the French. His overtures were well received by Napoleon, who saw that it was to his interest to win Ali over from any Russian or English entanglements and that Ali might well be useful to him as an ally in the Near East. A report was sent to Napoleon by two French officers who reminded him that before the Revolution France had obtained timber from Albania, that this timber was better than any from the Baltic, and that it had been used at Toulon to build the finest French frigates. More important still, they had something to say about Ali. He showed no signs of a premature old age; he was brave in the extreme, and his arms and breast were covered with honourable scars; whenever circumstances obliged him to deviate from a plan, he would return to it again and again and never rest till he had got his way; he was powerful and astute, and never lulled into a false security; in short, he was somebody to be reckoned with.

One reason why Ali made up to the French was that he wanted them on his side against the Russians, who had backed his enemies against him and often tried to thwart him – especially in his incessant attempts to get permission to take over the coveted coast towns – for they were never without large ambitions of their own in European Turkey. Napoleon had already thought of sending an agent to Jannina who would be able to keep an eye on affairs in the Ionian Islands, and who, residing between Corfu and Constantinople, between the Adriatic and the Aegean, would be in a very good observation post. Now that he was in control of Dalmatia, it was obviously vital to have agents in the neighbouring countries. He decided to send to Jannina Julien Bessières – one of those passengers on the *Madonna di Montenegro* who had been pressed into Ali's service and had later escaped – on a mission to promote an alliance, and he decided also that Bessières should take with him François Pouqueville, who could remain at Jannina, if Ali agreed, as consul.

Pouqueville, then aged thirty-five, was a doctor of Norman extraction, who had been with Napoleon in Egypt on a commission of arts and sciences. He, too, had been a passenger on the *Madonna di Montenegro*, but was one of those who had been landed at Navarino and had therefore not yet seen either Ali or Jannina. He had been a prisoner for seven months at

Tripolitza, the seat of government in the Morea, and had then been sent to Constantinople and imprisoned with various other Frenchmen, including some of the survivors of Preveza. After two years, during which he had learnt Greek, he had returned to France, where he published an account of his adventures, dedicated to Napoleon.

In September 1805 he received orders to go with Bessières.

'I felt little inclined,' he afterwards wrote, 'to undertake the job as I knew the reputation of the Satrap of Epirus. I had experienced so many unpleasantnesses in my travels in Turkey that the idea of the man to whom I was being sent and the still fresh memory of a three years' captivity made me weigh up whether I would accept a mission which I should otherwise have been thrilled to undertake.'

He decided to go, left Paris in October, and met Bessières at Milan. Owing to the difficulties of travel in those days and at that time of year the journey took a long time. They got as far as Ragusa and were kept there two months, and it was not until February 1st that they reached Epirus. At six in the evening they appeared off Porto Panormo, on the wild coast of Khimara, where Ali's garrison of Skipetars greeted them with such a hearty salvo that the captain of their boat was alarmed and would have opened fire had it not been for reassuring shouts from the shore. An officer of Ali's, who had been waiting for them for a month, came forward to welcome them in the name of his master, and at once invited them to a meal, which consisted of a sheep roasted whole, maize bread, and resinated wine that had to be drunk from a common cup. After this they retired to sleep on straw mats full of fleas.

On their way to Jannina they passed through Delvino, which was in the occupation of Ali's troops, who had looted the shops and set fire to the bazaar. The Frenchmen were put up at the very uncomfortable house of a bey who was a supporter of Ali's, and the next day they went on to Dzidza – half-way between Delvino and Jannina – where Ali was staying in one of his country houses and awaiting their arrival. They were lodged in a monastery, and had hardly entered it when Ali sent for them.

'We arrived,' says Pouqueville, 'at the gates of the house, which groaned on their hinges when opened; we passed through a silent court, climbed a dark staircase, a trap door was raised, a curtain was lifted, and we found ourselves in the audience room where Ali stood waiting for us.'

Unfortunately, although Ali embraced Bessières, who was a former acquaintance if not an old friend, he did not take the slightest notice of Pouqueville, and with an erratic movement stepped backwards and subsided on the divan without even glancing at him. However, 'a white-bearded spectre, dressed in black, honoured me with a slight movement of the head, to show that I was welcome. This scene, in which there also figured a Greek secretary who knelt as if in terror, was lighted by the wavering gleam of a yellow candle stuck on the floor, which just enabled one to make out who was who and what was what.' With the aid of an interpreter a conversation was carried on between Ali and Bessières. 'In the gloom I could see his eyes flashing and his convulsive movements, as I listened to his apparently vague talk, which was really full of astuteness. He was lively and laughing, and although he spoke very quickly not one word was without point. Occasionally he looked penetratingly at me, and at last dismissed the Greek secretary, who was stealthily watching the proceedings, and the black spectre. The interpreter remained, and after two hours we left his Highness wavering between doubts and hopes.'

Gordon says of Pouqueville that he was 'unfortunately wedded to violent prejudices'. There is no record of a divorce.

'Pouqueville,' said Byron, who disagreed with his opinions, 'is always out,' and it must be admitted that the Frenchman, though goodness knows he was in for a hard time and faced it with courage, had his deficiencies. With regard to this first meeting with Ali he tries to make out, in the rhetoric of the period, that he had expected 'a Theseus, a Pyrrhus', and that his illusions were shattered at a blow. But this was absurd, for he had already admitted his distaste for a duty which would bring him in touch with the 'Satrap of Epirus', whose reputation he had learnt during his previous sojourn in Turkey. No, the truth was that Ali had ignored and slighted him, that there had probably been from the first moment a mutual, instinctive dislike and distrust, that the surroundings were gloomy, and that all this, combined with the fatigue and discomfort of the journey, the wintry weather, and the very doubtful prospect for the future, was too much for him. 'Ali's manners', he frankly admits, 'had disgusted me, and though I was far from foreseeing all the vexations which he was to cause me, I could not but secretly grieve over the fate that had sent me to live at the court of such a man.'

Back at the monastery, he found the Greek monks very kind and hospitable. Father Gregory, the prior, a good old soul, was a champion boozer and boasted that he had once outdrunk Mukhtar himself. Dzidza, it may be said, was famous for its fragrant white wine, made from grapes left for three days in the sun and flavoured with absinth. While he sat drinking and now and then bursting into song, the prior bewailed the loss of a group of trees under which he had been fond of sitting, like his father before him. They were a couple of hundred years old and people used to dance under them on fête days, but he had to allow them to be cut down, as Ali required the wood to build his house in the neighbourhood.

Next morning there was a second interview with the

Vizier. The courtyard of his house was swarming with petitioners. In the middle were two human heads, freshly cut off and planted on stakes, but nobody took any notice of them. Ushers with long sticks parted the crowd to open a gangway for the Frenchmen, and for the second time they came before Ali. Pouqueville now noticed that Ali was very fat, that his face was lined but mobile, that there was a twinkle in his wicked little blue eyes, and that when he was not indulging in his famous guttural laugh he knew how to say things not without a certain charm: evidently a good night's rest at the monastery and the hospitality of Father Gregory had put Pouqueville in a better humour. Ali accepted the presents brought by Bessières with some alacrity, and grew quite affable, calling the two Frenchmen his children, his brothers, his good friends, and so definitely acknowledging the existence of Pouqueville – 'as if he had seen me for the first time, he condescended to promise me his protection over my consulship.'

The next day they reached Jannina. As it was likely to take some time to get the papers from Constantinople accrediting Pouqueville to his post, they lived incognito at the palace in the Castro, wearing Albanian dress, and making a few excursions to pass the time. On March 4th Bessières had to depart, and Pouqueville was naturally depressed: 'I saw myself abandoned in a land of barbarians . . . and found myself at the mercy of a man of whom, in spite of his apparent kindness, we had already had cause to complain . . . The general aspect of the country and its inhabitants terrified me, and filled me with forebodings of trouble.'

Two days after Bessières' departure Pouqueville's papers arrived and were ceremoniously read out in public. He then left the Castro for the house which Ali had assigned to him in the town, and was established as French consul.

CHAPTER XV

THE CONSUL'S FEARS COME TRUE

AT first the new alliance seemed to promise well. Bessières went back to Napoleon with the presents and messages sent to him by Ali, and Napoleon replied with thanks, saying he was pleased to think that Ali would be keeping an eye on the intrigues of the Russians, and adding that if Corfu were to fall into his power he was sure that he could not entrust it to better care than Ali's. (Only a couple of years later he was to call it 'the key of the Adriatic' and to say that the loss of it would be the greatest misfortune that could happen to him.) Ali was delighted at Napoleon's friendly attitude and behaved very nicely to Pouqueville, who had made a good start by alleviating the Vizier's rheumatism. This has been called 'the period of mutual illusions' between Ali and the French: as Napoleon once wrote to the King of Naples, 'Things are never so plain as they seem'. Pouqueville had quite changed his opening tune, and wrote to the French *chargé d'affaires* at Constantinople to say that the Vizier was a very remarkable man, full of *esprit* and integrity and so on, astonishingly apt and quick in his affairs, and delightfully pro-French. ('O wise and upright judge!') He even went so far as to suggest that Ali should be given possession of the coast towns in order to counteract Russian intrigues: it is not hard to guess with whom the suggestion originated.

In the summer of 1806 the French general Sébastiani arrived at Constantinople to intrigue on behalf of his country, and other French agents were busy at the same time in various parts of the Balkans. Ali wrote to Sébastiani about Pouqueville, praising the consul's talents and personal qualities, and speaking of the spontaneous friendship he had felt towards him from the first! Ever a master of the effusive diplomatic lie, Ali was not lickspittling the French for nothing, and before long he began to nag at Pouqueville about those desirable towns on the coast. He was having some trouble with rebellious beys who, he said, were getting Russian support through Preveza, and Vonitza, therefore those two towns at least ought to be ceded to him. A little later he heard that the Russians had invaded the Danubian provinces of Turkey, so he made up his mind to wait no longer, took possession of Preveza, turned out the commissioner appointed by the Porte, took lands and houses from the owners and gave them to his followers, destroyed part of the town, including the churches, and laid the foundations of a palace and a mosque. His idea was to act swiftly and present his enemies with a *fait accompli*: he knew that the Porte would rather see him in occupation of the town than that it should fall to an infidel power. He did not neglect Vonitza and Butrinto, but the Russians put a strong garrison into Parga to thwart him there. He replied to this by arresting the Russian consul at Jannina, and decided to make an attack on the Russians in the Ionian Islands. He accordingly asked for help from the French army in Dalmatia and from Joseph, the King of Naples, and got it. Lauriston, the French general commanding in Dalmatia, sent him a battery of artillery and Colonel de Vaudoncourt arrived as well to help him to manage it, and to advise and be generally useful to him. Ali was very pleased, and Vaudoncourt fortified the palace at Litharitza, strengthened the defences round Jannina and Preveza, and began to make preparations for an attack on the island of Santa Maura, a project for which Ali was prepared to lend an army of 4000 men under the command of his foster brother, Yusuf Arab the Blood-Drinker. Meanwhile

131

Ali sent Guerini (now known, it will be recalled, as the Reverend Mr. Mehmet) to Napoleon to find out definitely what reward he could expect for helping the French against the Russians in the Ionian Islands. He hoped for Santa Maura and possibly Corfu as well.

It was April 1807 when Guerini left, and to find Napoleon he had to go to Tilsit. He could not have arrived at a more unsuitable moment, for Napoleon was making peace with the Czar and planning to occupy the Ionian Islands. *'J'ai l'honneur de vous offrir,'* wrote Talleyrand to Ali from Tilsit in July, enclosing a brief and rather cool letter from Napoleon, *'très haut, très excellent et magnifique seigneur, l'assurance de ma plus haute estime,'* but Ali's little games had been checkmated; Santa Maura no longer seemed almost within his grasp; in August the Septinsular Republic came under French protection; Napoleon was soon talking openly of a proposed partition of Turkey; the French officers who had been helping Ali went back to Dalmatia; and he felt himself deserted and cheated. But he had not quite lost hope. No sooner had General Berthier occupied Corfu with 3000 men than Ali sent a deputation, including the schoolmaster Psalida, with presents and a request for the cession of Parga. Berthier seemed fairly willing to oblige him, but as soon as the Parghiots heard what was going on they implored Berthier to be firm, saying they would prefer death to the rule of Ali. Berthier therefore occupied Parga himself, and issued a reassuring proclamation to the inhabitants. Ali's patience with the French was now at an end. He was exasperated, and when Pouqueville made proposals for the raising of a loan for the Ionian Islands Ali refused point blank, saying that only if Parga were ceded to him would he even consider the matter. Every time he received Pouqueville in audience, he spoke of nothing but Parga.

Thoroughly disappointed with the French, Ali turned nasty towards them, and since Pouqueville was the representative of that nation and near at hand he had to bear the brunt of the Lion's displeasure. The flow of compliments had suddenly dried up, and Pouqueville found that he was being watched by spies and that his letters were being opened. Feeling that the French had failed him, Ali set himself to pay them back in their own coin. He did everything he could to hinder their trade and to prevent or delay the export of corn and cattle to Corfu: he also instructed Veli to close the ports in the south to any ships flying the French flag. At Constantinople Sébastiani kept complaining of these things, and Ali turned secretly to the English again. He was ordered by the Porte to keep in with the French, and lied to Pouqueville to try and keep him quiet while he played a double game. In November an English brig appeared off Preveza, and Ali had a conference with William Leake in secret on the seashore at midnight. Leake, who as we have seen had already spent some time in Albania on a military mission, was a raiser of exotic regiments, a sort of minor precursor of T. E. Lawrence, had been sent to Constantinople in 1799 to teach the Turkish troops artillery practice, had later travelled through Asia Minor disguised as a Tartar courier, and was altogether well fitted for this clandestine meeting, at which Ali promised to help the English if they would attack the Ionian Islands.

Meanwhile Ali kept Pouqueville shut up in his consulate, cut off his local communications, intercepted all his letters, stopped the export of provisions to Corfu, and wrote some hostile letters to Berthier. The French ambassador at Constantinople protested vigorously, and when the Porte remonstrated with Ali he replied abusing the French in general and Pouqueville in particular:

'He behaves in an intolerably arrogant way to the people

133

of Jannina: armed with a sword-stick, he goes through the street hitting dervishes and other Mohammedans on his way, putting out the eyes of some and cracking the heads of others: not content with ill-treating Mohammedans and insulting them, he demands satisfaction, asking that so-and-so shall be hanged: he permits himself to do in public things that are formally forbidden by the law. For instance, he went for no reason at all to the house of the Chief of Police, forced his way in, and struck him with his stick.'

After this surely exaggerated and perhaps largely fabricated appeal to religious and patriotic prejudice, he ended by asking that Pouqueville should be recalled and replaced by another consul who would know how to mind his own business, but all he got from Constantinople in reply was an order to change his behaviour towards the French, to break off all relations with the English (who were at this time at war with Turkey) and to come and give an account of himself. This threw him into a fit of anger, and he shut himself up for several days and would hardly see anyone, though Pouqueville's brother did manage to obtain an interview, which was unpleasant.

One morning Pouqueville learnt that a supply of 1500 blankets and 250 head of cattle that had been bought for Corfu was being detained outside Jannina, so he at once sent his brother (who was on better terms with the Vizier than he was himself) to ask why this had been done. Ali said he knew nothing about it, and at once signed two passes providing for the free transit of both goods and cattle. But in spite of this, the head of the customs in Jannina, a Greek named Samanioti, refused to let the convoy go. Pouqueville went to see him and asked the reason, but was answered only with insults, so he took him forcibly before Ali. As they were going into the palace a mad dervish, armed with a club round which a live snake was coiled, rushed at Pouqueville who managed to dodge out of the way. He found Ali in a towering rage.

'If your customs officer won't obey you,' said Pouqueville, 'why don't you hang him?'

Ali stormed, and cursed the name of Napoleon, and Pouqueville withdrew, saying he would complain to his government. When he got home he found some Jews waiting for him: they were the merchants who had sold the blankets, and they had taken refuge at the consulate because they were afraid they were going to be hanged. A hostile crowd soon collected round the house and threatened to burn it down. Pouqueville and his brother put on their uniforms and got ready to destroy their codes and correspondence directly there was any direct attack on the house. He then sent a formal protest in writing to Ali, which was ignored. At dusk one of his servants was nearly beaten to death by one of Ali's officials armed with a stick: 'You dog of a Frenchman, you work for the consul, don't you! Just you tell me who has been going to his house and who's hiding there, or I'll do you in!' The servant was left bleeding on the ground. During the night, a Mohammedan who had made the contract at Corfu for the sale of the blankets came to join the refugees at the consulate, as he had heard that his life was in danger.

The next day Samanioti put the blankets up for sale. Pouqueville waited four days, and then, wishing to get the matter settled, sent his brother to the palace.

'What do you want?' cried Ali in an angry voice.

'To know your last word on the prevention of the convoy for Corfu.'

'Get out of it! Go home and stay there, and don't go out at all. Do you hear me? I don't want to hear any more complaints!'

In the evening Pouqueville sent to tell Ali that he was

going to send his brother to Corfu, and to ask if he himself might leave Jannina. The next day at dawn, the consulate and adjoining streets were guarded by Skipetars who had orders to stop the Pouquevilles if they made any attempt to leave. Ali had forbidden, on pain of death, that anyone should let them have horses. But he felt that he had gone too far, and some days later tried to bribe the consul to say nothing about the way he had behaved. Pouqueville's worst fears had come true, but how richly he was able to work off his feelings against Ali in later years, in those voluminous writings that contain many a pointed passage! Here is a single example:

'His guard is composed of assassins; his pages are the depraved children of victims of his ferocity; his emissaries, blackguardly Vlachs, ready to commit any crime, and his confidential agents poisoners who glory in their wickedness. Sacrilegious priests of the living God are let into the dark secrets of his council chamber, to reveal to him the thoughts of innocence and the secrets of the confessional. Spies, disguised in all sorts of ways, seek out and search the places where the widow has buried her mite, and the orphan his pennies. The timid virgin, hidden in the obscurity of the harem, cannot escape their piercing eyes. She is snatched from her mother's bosom, so is the son, hope of a worthy family; and honour, beauty, decency, are sacrificed to the most shameful passions.'

CHAPTER XVI

CAPITAL PUNISHMENT

'As I have dedicated myself entirely to your nation,' wrote Ali to Collingwood in the summer of 1808, 'I hope that it will feel a pride in protecting me.'

The correspondence was conducted in a somewhat elevated tone: Collingwood would appeal to Ali's humanity and Ali, with his wicked old tongue in his cheek, would let fall a pious allusion to God's mercy and the hopes to be placed in it. As a result, twenty-seven English ships arrived at Preveza from Malta, bringing goods, subsidies, ten cannons, and munitions. It became impossible for Ali to conceal his relations with the English, and in order to try and save face he spread a rumour that peace had been made between England and Turkey. The English, on their part, had assured him that if he got into trouble for helping them against the French, they would lend him at least their moral support against Constantinople.

While Pouqueville was helpless at Jannina, Corfu (that 'phrontisterion of political speculators', as a contemporary called it) was seething with anxieties and intrigues. Berthier had been succeeded by General Donzelot, who made it his policy to offer sanctuary to refugees from the mainland, to unite Ali's enemies, and to offer every possible convenience for rebellion against the 'Satrap'. A regiment was formed of some Suliot and other refugees and disaffected priests, agas, beys, and obscurer persons were offered a sympathetic ear. Amongst them was the Reverend Mr. Mehmet (Guerini) who pretended that he was being persecuted by Ali (perhaps in connection with his lack of success at Tilsit?) though it seemed more likely that he was acting as a spy. Donzelot had no doubt reached the same rather temperate conclusions as Collingwood: 'A great deal of caution is necessary in treating with the Pacha, from what I have collected of his character. He possesses consummate art and subtilty, is powerful, and has a thirst for power.'

The endeavours of the French to promote an alliance on the mainland against Ali received a sudden encouragement, for war broke out again between Russia and Turkey, and Ali had to send an army under Mukhtar to headquarters: as it consisted of 8000 men he found himself somewhat vulnerable, so he went on making up to the English. He had sent an agent to England, via Malta, to ask for help in driving the French out of Parga and the Ionian Islands, and the results were gratifying, for the English sent another shipload of war material to Preveza and in Sicily General Oswald was soon preparing an expeditionary force. Ali himself, at the head of 4000 men, set out for Preveza, having announced that, with the help of his allies, he was about to attack Santa Maura.

Like so many of Ali's public announcements, that was a lie, and he was as usual perfectly ready to fool everybody he could. He certainly went to Preveza and collected the war material, but it was not against the French that he meant to use it. This, he felt, was the moment to strike against nearer and older enemies, always unforgivable and still in league against him, notably Mustapha Pasha of Delvino and Ibrahim Pasha of Berat. Certainly two of Ibrahim's daughters had married two of Ali's sons and a third his nephew, but how could Ali ever forget that it was Ibrahim who had married the Wolf's daughter and come into the pashalik of Berat, besides helping the Suliots? To revengeful feelings was added envy, for Ibrahim's land was rich, fertile and well-watered, and included the port of Vallona. And to envy was added contempt, for Ibrahim, though much respected in his own country and at Constantinople as well, was weak, easygoing, and ever nervous at the thought of Ali's overwhelming ambition and utter unscrupulousness. Always well informed about the private affairs of his neighbours, especially when they were hostile to him, Ali knew through his spies that Ibrahim had obtained promises of help from the French, and that, heartened by the absence of Mukhtar and his troops, he had been plotting rebellion with his allies of Argyro Castro and Delvino. The Vizier went to work in the usual way – with money. One by one he bought over Ibrahim's allies and supporters, and he greatly reduced the size of Ibrahim's army by bribing some of his regiments into disloyalty. He knew that the Pasha of Berat was highly thought of at Constantinople not only for his personal qualities but as a most useful thorn in Ali's side, and spread exaggerated reports of Ibrahim's dealings with the French, saying that Ibrahim meant to cede some of his land to them. Having weakened and isolated Ibrahim as much as he could, he tried without success to have him assassinated, then offered him unacceptable terms of peace, and finally determined to reduce him by force.

His choice of a general was good. The son of a man who had been persecuted by the old Wolf, Omer Bey Vrioni had himself been persecuted in turn by Ibrahim, and had had to leave Berat. He had had an adventurous and successful career, serving first with Pasvan Oglou of Vidin and later in Egypt, where he rose to the rank of general and greatly enriched himself; later still returning to Albania to settle at Jannina, and taking care to curry favour with Ali by presenting him with a camel, some Arab horses, and a handsome sword. So now Ali sent this Omer Bey Vrioni against Berat, at the head of a considerable army, and equipped with all the artillery, the howitzers, mortars and Congreve rockets, which the English had provided for use against the French in the Ionian Islands. Pouqueville, penned up in his consulate and something of an anglophobe, was not altogether sorry to hear how the Vizier had diddled the English and was misusing the guns. 'He won't give them up and he won't pay for them,' wrote the consul, 'it's the finest bit of cheating he has ever done.'

Jannina at this time was disturbed by the most fearful shrieks proceeding from the palace, and emanating, it was discovered, from Shainitza and her women. The news at once spread that she had lost her only surviving son, Aden Bey. A promising young man of twenty, he had just died of consumption. General alarm was felt in Jannina at the possible consequences of Shainitza's emotion, and all the shopkeepers hurriedly put up their shutters. It was the custom in that part of the world in those days for women to show the most excessive signs of grief for their dead menfolk; they did not mourn, they howled and bellowed, and it was not thought at all odd for them to howl daily at the tops of their voices for five and ten years. Shainitza, bereaved of her last male child, was not satisfied to be a blubbering and cater-wauling Niobe. Foaming at the mouth, she demanded that the doctors who had failed to save her son's life should be delivered up to her so that she might drink their blood. Not being obeyed, she threatened to kill herself. She wanted to throw herself into the lake, but seeing that she was being watched tried to take an inglorious header into the sewer which led from the harem. Stopped, she called on heaven, swore not to utter the name of the Prophet for a year, forbade her women to observe the fast of Ramazan, had some dervishes beaten and kicked out of doors, and ordered that the manes and tails of Aden Bey's horses and mules should be cut off. She had to be watched closely for it was feared that she might set fire to the palace and so kindle the powder magazine and blow up half the town, and the advice of Ali, who was away in the country, was hurriedly sought.

'Let her leave at once for Liboövo,' he said. 'Let the order be carried out by force if necessary.'

Liboövo was a village where Shainitza had a palace. When she returned there she gave further vent to her feelings, went into the deepest mourning, obliged all her attendants to do likewise, and forced Aden's widow (who was a daughter of Ibrahim) to sleep on a thin straw mat on the hard ground; she burnt her fine clothes and her furs, broke her jewels to dust with hammers, smashed every looking glass in the palace, and had all the windows covered with black paint. She refused to see any visitors and shut herself up to brood over her sorrows, her chief occupation being to cultivate hatred and bitterness and revengeful feelings, and to ponder over ways and means of ruining or annihilating those whom she regarded as her enemies, an occupation to which her brother was always devoted.

Ali had just had news of a Klepht leader named Katzantoni who had long been a source of vexation to him. A very small man, Katzantoni went about very splendidly dressed and haughty, pushful, and energetic as if to make up in impressiveness what he lacked in inches. He had lately had smallpox, from which he failed to make much of a recovery. He took refuge at a monastery in the fastnesses of Pindus, but was afraid that Ali might find him there, so, still weak, he retired to a cave where he was nursed by his brother George, food being brought to them by an old woman. Either by the woman or the monks he was betrayed to Ali, who promptly sent sixty Skipetars with orders to take the two brothers alive. George, sauntering out of the cave one morning, found himself face to face with the Skipetars. He darted in again, put

Katzantoni on his back, and holding his sabre in his teeth and his musket in his hand, rushed out, shot a Skipetar, and made a dash for escape into the forest. The Skipetars closed in on him, he put his brother down, and killed a second Skipetar with his sabre, but in a few moments he was overpowered. The brothers were taken to Jannina and condemned to have their legs crushed with blows from a mallet. The sentence was carried out in public before a large crowd. Katzantoni, still weak from illness, cried out under the torture. 'Katzantoni,' said his brother George, 'will you cry like a woman?' and himself died without having uttered a sound. Such a silence is more powerful than all the resources of a dictator.

While Omer Bey Vrioni was advancing on Berat a rebellion had broken out in Thessaly, the fruit of an old project formed some years earlier by two remarkable men, Niko Tzaras and Evthymio Vlachavas. One a Klepht and one an Armatole chieftain, they had in mind not highway robbery, but nothing less than the ultimate liberation of Greece from the Turks, and as a first step they meant to overthrow Ali.

Of all the Klephtic heroes none was more famous than Tzaras. His beauty, strength, courage and agility were all superlative; it was even said that he could jump over seven horses standing abreast; besieged once in a house he had escaped by lowering on a rope at dusk a stuffed figure dressed and made up to resemble him and then dashing away while the attackers ran forward to cut off what was thought to be his head; another time with a band of 300 followers he had defeated an army of 3000 Turks; and was eventually killed on the seashore in 1807 by a shot in the hip from an enemy sniper hidden behind a tree. It was left to Vlachavas to carry on the good work, so now with a thousand insurgents he appeared in the neighbourhood of Arta, where he was joined by some Suliots and other malcontents. Whatever success he might have had was prevented, for his plans were given away by a traitor, and he found himself surrounded by 4000 Skipetars under Mukhtar, who had returned to Epirus. Vlachavas fought and lost, and was taken alive. Mukhtar sent him to Ali, together with a trophy of sixty-eight of the heads of his companions. Ali condemned him to death, he was bound to a stake in one of the courtyards of the palace, and the French consul was a witness of his last moments. Once, in the course of a journey in Thessaly, Pouqueville had been Evthymio's guest at a nocturnal feast in the mountains, all in true Klephtic style, with lambs roasted whole, bumpers of wine drunk in honour of the patron saints of the guests, music, singing, dancing, joyful salvos of musket fire, and a general hubbub and jollification. And now he saw the hero bound and facing the Vizier's torturers. The rays of a burning sun shone full upon Evthymio's bronzed head, and glittering drops of sweat ran off his thick beard. Faced with an appalling fate he was calmer than the tyrant who was gloating over him, and Pouqueville seemed to detect in the serenity of his eyes a consciousness that this was not only his most frightful but his greatest and most exalted moment. Without flinching or uttering a sound he endured the slow cruelties of the torturers. In the end he was torn to pieces, and the pieces were exposed in various parts of the city as an example to the seditiously inclined. A few days later a monk named Dimitrios, who had been his friend and constant companion, was taken prisoner and tortured: sharp laths were driven under his nails, a chaplet of knucklebones was drawn tight round his head, he was hung upside down over a slow fire, covered with a board which was jumped on in order to break his bones, and at last walled up in a cell with only his head free. He took ten days to die.

A fanciful ballad by Valaorites declares that the parentage

of Vlachavas was never known, and that he was the offspring of a union between the mountains Olympus and Ossa. It goes on to tell how, when his head had been cut off and set up on a stone pillar in Jannina, his faithful dog was waiting unnoticed in the crowd. After night had fallen, the dog alone remained on the scene, and stretched himself on the ground, moaning and howling incessantly. At midnight he leapt up and tried to seize the head in his mouth, but it was too high, and again and again he fell back, maimed and bleeding and his claws broken on the stone. At last, with one wild leap, he managed to seize the head, and ran away with it over the mountains and valleys. The trees recognized the head as it was carried past, and at dawn the faithful dog reached the summit of Ossa, dug a deep hole in the snow, buried the head, and lay down near it to die. So Ossa, 'the mother who bore the hero, again opened her womb, and received him to rest like a babe in the cradle . . .'

CHAPTER XVII

BYRON AT TEBELENI

An Englishman described Preveza under the rule of Ali in the following terms: 'The town consists chiefly of miserable little huts, divided by narrow streets crowded with the Pacha's soldiers, who, from the variety of costume, exhibit motley groups indeed. Yet the personal appearance of the men is fine. No women are to be seen and the rest of the inhabitants are generally squatted at their doors and windows, their usual employment being smoking or expurgating their persons, with all that apathy, and indifference to strangers, which is so peculiar to the Turks.' Scarcely an attractive picture, yet something of the sort presented itself, on a rainy evening at the end of September 1809, to no less a person than Byron and his Cambridge friend John Cam Hobhouse, who had landed there on their way to Jannina.

Fortunately the weather cleared up before they reached the capital, and after a long ride they came to the top of a slope and enjoyed their first view of it. In a burst of sunshine they saw before them the houses, domes and minarets of Jannina, brilliant among gardens and groves of orange and lemon trees and cypresses, the lake beside the city and the mountains precipitous beyond it, all as beautiful as the Elysian Fields with which the scene was sometimes identified by over-enterprising scholars. Shortly, however, they passed a tree, in which was hanging, by a bit of string tied round one of the fingers, a man's arm and part of the side torn from the body: other joints from the same individual, they were told, could be seen prominently displayed in other parts of the town. It was the arm of Evthymio Vlachavas, pointing, one might say, to Missolonghi.

Ali was away at Tebeleni, which he had made his head-quarters for the campaign against Ibrahim, now being be-sieged in Berat, only a day's journey further off. But he had left orders for the visitors to be given a flattering welcome: he was most anxious to please the English just now, and the two travellers could not have arrived at a more suitable moment. At the Vizier's expense they were put up at the house of Nicolo Argyri (the same whom Ali had defrauded of his patri-mony) and had scarcely arrived when one of Ali's secretaries came to call, accompanied by the archbishop. The secretary, whose hat was large, spoke French and was extremely polite; the archbishop, whose hat was enormous, said nothing but bowed again and again. When the two callers felt it time to withdraw they rashly resolved to attempt the European cere-mony of taking off their hats, but only managed it with 'extreme awkwardness' and had no little trouble in getting the hats to go back on their heads again.

As the two Englishmen were unable to see the Vizier in Jannina, they were received at the palace by one of his grand-sons, a son of Mukhtar's named Hussein. The boy was only ten, but very polite and ceremonious. Though highly delighted by Byron's sword, he managed to maintain his dignity and gravity. After coffee and sweets, the visitors said they would like to see the palace, so word was sent to the women to retire to the inner apartments of the harem, and then Hussein offered to guide them. They noticed in the bearing of the attendants towards him a delightful mixture of familiarity and respect, and as he walked sedately out of the room (it was according to etiquette that his guests should follow him) a shabbily dressed Skipetar in waiting embraced him very tenderly. They passed down the long gallery decorated with naive mural paintings by some local Douanier Rousseau or Niko Pirosmanishvili, and thought some of the rooms both handsome and comfortable, pausing to admire the divans covered with richly embroidered silks, the fine Turkey carpets, and the clear Venetian glass in the windows. They noticed that no rooms were set aside for sleeping, each, according to Oriental custom, containing a cupboard for the mats and quilts that served as beds: but there was a marble bathroom with a fountain. The little Hussein Bey enjoyed taking his guests round, showed them his watch and two or three other little ornaments, and bade them a polite good-bye.

They also called on another of Ali's grandsons, Mehmet, son of Veli, a lively boy thought to have something of the genius of his grandfather, and although only twelve already in possession of a pashalik. He proposed a visit to his younger brother Ismail, who was living in a palace belonging to their father Veli. So they set out in state, on horses with gold trappings, and preceded by officials with silver wands. As the boy passed, all the shop-keepers rose, and people who were walking stood where they were, everybody bending very low, touching the ground with their right hands, and then raising them to their mouths and foreheads. Mehmet returned the salute by laying his right hand on his breast and gently inclining his head. His brother Ismail, then only seven, was standing on the steps of Veli's palace to receive him. They embraced with ceremony, bowing their heads over each other's shoulders. The Englishmen were given the usual pipes and coffee, and were then shown the house, but the younger boy was merry and skipped about a little, so Mehmet said, 'Brother, recollect you are in the presence of strangers; walk more quietly'.

After a few days Byron and Hobhouse set out for Tebeleni. Owing to the appallingly wet and stormy weather they had a trying and dangerous journey, but they were both

young and adventurous and excited by the prospect of meeting
Ali. On the way they stopped at Dzidza, where Father
Gregory's place had been taken by a 'humble, meek-mannered
man'. They thought there was perhaps no view in the world
more romantic than the one to be seen from the monastery,
but had time to notice that the village people, although tilling
a rich soil that produced wine and corn and tending flocks that
provided meat, wool and milk, were yet 'starving in the midst
of abundance; their labour was without reward, their rest
without recreation'. After nine days they came in sight of
Tebeleni.

> The sun had sunk behind vast Tomerit,
> And Laos wide and fierce came roaring by;
> The shades of wonted night were gathering yet,
> When, down the steep banks winding warily,
> Childe Harold saw, like meteors in the sky,
> The glittering minarets of Tepalen,
> Whose walls o'erlook the stream; and drawing nigh,
> He heard the busy hum of warrior-men
> Swelling the breeze that sighed along the lengthening glen.

The streets of Tebeleni were dirty, but they soon entered
the courtyard of Ali's palace through a gateway in a tower.
They felt, justly enough, that they had entered the castle yard
of a great feudal lord: there were soldiers and horses everywhere, and cooks preparing kids and sheep for roasting. The
scene made an immense impression on Byron, and he has left
brilliant descriptions of it in prose and verse. 'Our journey,'
he wrote to his mother, 'was much prolonged by the torrents
that had fallen from the mountains, and intersected the roads.
I shall never forget the singular scene on entering Tebeleni
at five in the afternoon, as the sun was going down . . . The
Albanians, in their dresses (the most magnificent in the world,

consisting of a long *white kilt*, gold worked cloak, crimson velvet gold-laced jacket and waistcoat, silver-mounted pistols and daggers), the Tartars with their high caps, the Turks in their vast pelisses and turbans, the soldiers and black slaves with the horses, the former in groups in an immense large open gallery in front of the palace, the latter placed in a kind of cloister below it, two hundred steeds ready caparisoned to move in a moment, couriers entering or passing out with the dispatches, the kettle-drums beating, boys calling the hour from the minaret of the mosque, altogether with the singular appearance of the building itself, formed a new and delightful spectacle to a stranger . . .'

The visitors were given rooms opening on to a gallery, from which they continued to have an excellent view of the 'new and delightful spectacle'. Ali sent to congratulate them on their arrival, and later in the evening they were visited by two of his secretaries.

About noon the next day a palace official carrying a white wand came to tell them that the Vizier would see them, so they set out with a dragoman and a secretary, who had put on his worst cloak in order that he might not appear too rich, and so provoke his master to extortion! They were led along a gallery crowded with Skipetars, to another wing of the palace, over some rubbish where a room had fallen in, then through some shabby rooms, then into the room where Ali himself was waiting, and two of the most remarkable men of that age stood face to face.

Ali received them standing, looking short and fat, with a cheerful expression on his face instead of anything like 'Turkish gravity', on his head a high turban formed of many small rolls of fine gold muslin and in his girdle a dagger studded with diamonds. As for Byron: 'I was dressed in a full suit of staff uniform, with a very magnificent sabre, etc. The Vizier received me in a large room paved with marble; a fountain was playing in the centre; the apartment was surrounded by scarlet ottomans. He received me standing, a wonderful compliment from a Mussulman, and made me sit down on his right hand. . . .'

Meanwhile Hobhouse had noticed that Ali's face was very pleasing, his eyes blue and quick, and his beard long and white: unlike most of his countrymen he did not keep looking proudly at his beard and smelling and stroking it, and Hobhouse interpreted this as a sign that he was more taken up with his guests than with himself. Certainly he was 'mighty civil' and said he looked upon them as his children. Instead of having his room crowded with officials as was the custom of most pashas, he was attended only by four or five pages or Ganymedes (or, as Hobhouse discreetly describes them, 'young persons with very magnificent clothes and long hair flowing half-way down their backs') who brought the coffee, sweets and pipes; he offered these refreshments without any fuss, and was in such a good temper that he now and then laughed aloud, which was very unusual behaviour for a Turkish grandee. In fact, he was altogether lively and easy, in spite of the language difficulty. He showed his guests a mountain howitzer which was in the room and told them he had several large cannon, though he omitted to add that he had obtained them from the English on false pretences. He turned away two or three times to look through an English telescope, and at last handed it to his guests so that they might look at a party of men on horseback riding along the bank of the Voiussa towards Tebeleni. He turned with a smile to the secretary who was acting as interpreter and said:

'That's the chief minister of my enemy Ibrahim Pasha, and he is now coming over to me, having deserted his master to take the stronger side.'

No wonder he was in a good temper, and no wonder he was a little exuberant in his behaviour towards Byron:

'His first question was, why, at so early an age, I left my country (the Turks have no idea of travelling for amusement). He then said . . . Leake had told him I was of a great family, and desired his respects to my mother . . . He said he was certain I was a man of birth, because I had small ears, curling hair, and little white hands, and expressed himself pleased with my appearance and garb. He told me to consider him as a father whilst I was in Turkey, and said he looked on me as his son. Indeed, he treated me like a child, sending me almonds and sugared sherbet, fruit and sweetmeats, twenty times a day. He begged me to visit him often, and at night when he was at leisure.'

There is no doubt that Ali was in a good temper, since his affairs were going well; that he was very pleased with Byron; and that he wished, from both personal as well as political motives, to please him in return, but, even allowing for Oriental effusiveness, it seems doubtful whether his interest in Byron was exactly as paternal as he pretended, for a father does not give his son sweets twenty times a day and beg him to visit him at night. It is worth remarking that Ali was a judge of character and a connoisseur of beauty, whether male or female, and that the like of Byron, and Byron at twenty-one, is not often seen.

On the following evening the Englishmen paid their second call on Ali. They found him this time in a room more elegant than the one with the fountain, and while they were with him a messenger came with good news from Berat. Nor was this all. The English had just made a successful attack on the Ionian Islands, and Zante, Cephalonia, Cerigo and Ithaca had been taken without any loss. The old man was already imagining what it would be like to have Parga

and perhaps even Santa Maura in his clutches. He congratulated his guests on the feat of the British squadron, said that
he would be happy to have the English as his neighbours, that
he was sure they would not serve him as the Russians and the
French had done, and that he had always been a friend to our
nation.

'And why are you travelling in Albania?' he asked suddenly, with a suspicion of some sort, it may be, at the back of
his mind.

'To see so great a man as yourself,' they replied.

'Yes,' he said. 'But do you ever hear of me in England?'

'Oh, but indeed, your Highness is a very frequent subject
of conversation in our country.'

This gratified him still more, and he showed them some
pistols and a sabre, and then took down a gun that was hanging
in a bag above his head, and told them it was a present from the
Emperor of the French. (He did not, however, tell them that
in return for it he pretended to have sent to the French in
Corfu a shipload of provisions that had been unfortunately
lost at sea, or that, in order to repair the imaginary loss of this
imaginary cargo he had levied a special tax on his subjects.)
The gun proved to be a short rifle, with the stock inlaid with
silver and set with diamonds, which made it appear to have
been a handsome present, but the secretary explained in an
aside that when it came from Napoleon it had only a common
stock, and that the ornaments had been added by Ali himself,
to make it look more like a royal gift.

They paid a third and final visit to Ali, when he gave
them minute instructions as to the course of their intended
journey into the Morea and the state of the country. He gave
them a letter to his son Veli, Pasha of the Morea, and was
generally obliging, giving some instructions to their Albanian
servant, whom he jokingly warned not to let any accident

happen or he would have his head cut off. And so they left him.

Before leaving his dominions they spent a week in Jannina. The return journey only took them four days, and when they got back, they managed to pass their time pleasantly, sailing on the lake, riding into the country, strolling through the bazaar in the morning, and in the evenings paying calls. They were not a success with Pouqueville, nor he with them. They found him wanting in urbanity, which is not surprising, considering the wretched time he had been through and the news from the Ionian Islands. Besides, it must have been galling to Pouqueville to see them being made much of by the Satrap who disliked him so plainly and had treated him with such contempt. He was jealous, and wrote of them as 'soi-disants mylords', adding a sneer at 'these arrogant Englishmen, these fops at the feet of a savage for their bread and butter' – a somewhat rhetorical allusion to Ali's hospitality. Byron took occasion to score off Pouqueville in the notes to *Childe Harold* and Pouqueville hit back in one of his books with a reference to 'the noble Timon of Great Britain', saying that he would set no more store by his approval than his condemnation. With some reason to be embittered, he seems to have taken them more seriously than they took him.

They continued to enjoy themselves before they left Jannina, though Hobhouse thought it tiresome that in a city where so many people were good at embroidery there was nobody capable of mending an umbrella: the complaint comes very naturally from a man who was to become a cabinet minister and a peer under Queen Victoria. One evening he and Byron saw a wedding procession. A Christian Albanian officer in Ali's service was marrying a slave of the harem. First, the bridegroom passed through the streets, attended by a large party of men, some with fiddles and some with coloured paper lanterns, on his way to fetch the bride from the palace. Half an hour later the whole party went to the house of the bridegroom, who led the procession with his musicians and lantern-bearers and a crowd of other men. Next came six young girls dressed in gold and silver stuffs; then a woman with a red box containing the dowry which Ali had given the bride as a member of his harem; then the bride herself, looking like a doll or wax figure, moving very stiffly, her face daubed with red and white paint, and on her head a high cap studded with pieces of gold money. Her left hand was held by an armed Skipetar, magnificently dressed, and her right by a Greek priest. Behind her came a vast crowd of women with music and lanterns.

Another diversion was a marionette shadow-show, of the kind that are still to be seen in Greece. It was the only thing in Jannina in the nature of a theatre, took place in a café, and was attended mostly by boys. The hero, Karagyozi, a kind of ribald Punch, was supported by a buffoon, and other characters were a man, a woman, and a devil. The dialogue was in Turkish and enlivened with topical allusions that caused loud laughter, and the action so grossly indecent that the Englishmen could find nothing to compare it with except 'the morrice-dancing in some counties of England' – a curious sidelight on Merrie Epirus.

CHAPTER XVIII

THE ENGLISH CONSUL AND THE
COLLAPSE OF IBRAHIM

HEARING that the English, having taken four of the Ionian Islands, were going to attack Santa Maura, Ali spoke of helping them, but the Porte ordered him to remain neutral and told him to take care to keep on good terms with Pouqueville and the French in general. His main interest for the time being was to reduce Berat, where Ibrahim Pasha had taken refuge in the citadel, which stood on the top of a hill and was strongly fortified. Poor Ibrahim, never a powerful nature, now deserted by most of his followers and continually bombarded by the English guns of Omer Bey Vrioni, to say nothing of the Congreve rockets, became something of a defeatist. After a siege lasting three months, during which the attackers had lost only two men who blew themselves up by mistake, he decided to abandon Berat and retire to Vallona. Ali was of course jubilant. Berat, the fortress which Scanderbeg himself had failed to take with 15,000 men, was of great strategic value to him and the centre of a district that has been called 'the very granary of the country', a beautiful and important and altogether desirable place to capture from an enemy of long standing.

About this time (it was the spring of 1810) there arrived in Jannina a rival to Pouqueville in the shape of an English consul. This was a man named George Foresti. A man of education and character, he was a Greek by birth, which gave him an advantage over the Frenchman; also, he was more imaginative and more tactful than Pouqueville, which enabled him to obtain a considerable influence over the Vizier. Ali seems to have respected the firmness and constancy in Foresti's nature and in his policy, which has been well described as 'general forbearance, and inflexibility when necessary' – a better policy than that of Pouqueville, who was always nettled and generally exasperated. An example of Foresti's strength and humanity is to be found in an episode which took place soon after he had established his influence over Ali. A citizen of Jannina named Michelachi, who was one of Ali's friends, had died, leaving his son Michael under Ali's guardianship. Ali had treated the boy well, given him a good education, kept his fortune intact for him, put him in an important official post, and had finally arranged for him to marry a local heiress. Whether the lucky Michael became a victim of jealousy and suspicion or whether the Vizier suddenly decided, as was sometimes his capricious way with people who owed their position and success to his favour, to make an example of him, the young man was arrested without a word of warning and charged with hiding a treasure which had belonged to a previous Pasha of Jannina. He was confronted with false witnesses and ordered to give up the treasure. Being perfectly innocent, he managed to deny the charge with calmness and dignity, but Ali had him put in chains in the Buldrun. While he was there his house was looted and his furniture thrown out into the street. Foresti had been spending the day in the country with an official who had been on a mission to Jannina and was just returning to Constantinople. When he got home he found a deputation of Greeks waiting to tell him what had happened to Michael Michelachi. The first thing next morning Foresti called on Ali, and started an ordinary quiet conversation before coming to the point.

'I notice there are a lot of people hanging about the palace to-day,' he remarked, 'and the city's in quite a turmoil. I asked what was the matter, but nobody would tell me till my cook, who's a foreigner, said that you've killed my friend Michael Michelachi. I'm very sorry to hear it, because I know he was a good man, and innocent as well. What a good thing that you didn't kill him while that official was here – he would certainly have told them all about it in Constantinople, and I'm afraid it would have made rather a bad impression.'

'But I haven't killed him!' Ali protested. 'He's still alive!'

'Ah, God be praised for that! I'm very glad to hear it.'

'Yes, but you know, my boy, he's treated me very badly,' said Ali. 'He has cheated me. If you only knew how shamefully he has behaved! Considering that I've brought him up so generously ever since he was a child and I don't know how he could make me such a bad return.'

'If that were true,' said Foresti, 'I should be the first to condemn him. But have you given him a chance to prove his innocence? And who, I should like to know, are his accusers?'

'Oh, a lot of people came here and took solemn oaths before the archbishop, and kissed holy ikons, swearing that the whole thing is true.'

'That may be,' said Foresti. 'But are these accusers trustworthy people? Can you take their words against the word of a man like Michael Michelachi? After all, what will people say in Constantinople and what will the English government think, when they hear that you've murdered or at least ruined one of your best friends on such questionable evidence?'

'But my boy,' Ali weakened a little, 'what on earth can I do, now that I've gone so far in this business?'

'You can order a proper inquiry to be held.'

'Well, yes. And supposing I were to put *you* in charge of the inquiry, would you undertake it?'

'Indeed I would,' said Foresti. 'But first of all you must release him on bail, or he may die before he can be proved innocent.'

'All right, then. Go ahead, and do it in your own way.'

Armed with this authority, Foresti at once had Michelachi released from the Buldrun, then went to the young man's house to reassure his wife and children, pretending at the same time to search for the alleged treasure. In his court of inquiry he questioned Michelachi and his accusers, who he found could prove nothing, and then declared the young man innocent. As a result of this, Ali pretended to be furious with the false witnesses he had himself caused to be suborned, and declared that they should be tortured to death, but owing to the intercession of Foresti and Michelachi consented that they should only be imprisoned for a few months so that he might save face.

Soon after Foresti's arrival at Jannina the English went on with their attack on the remaining Ionian Islands and proceeded to bombard Santa Maura. Ali was uncertain whether they would succeed in taking the island which he so much coveted and in which he so much wanted to obtain a footing. He was determined to be on the winning side, and therefore played a double game. While entertaining the English commanding officer, General Oswald, to supper at Preveza and professing his devotion he was secretly intriguing with Pouqueville to get provisions into Santa Maura for the besieged and even to take over the citadel himself, intending no doubt that once he had got in no power on earth should get him out. The English had told an envoy of Ali's that there was some likelihood of their ceding the island to him, but now, on Foresti's advice, they decided to do no such thing. In April Santa Maura surrendered; the garrison, mostly Italians, were taken prisoners; and the place was occupied by a regiment known as the Duke of York's Greek Light Infantry, which had been raised and commanded by Richard Church.

The Vizier at once sent a secretary to congratulate

General Oswald, to whom, in spite of the neutrality he had been ordered to maintain, he had lent material aid: he received in return a boatload of sugar and coffee. Later he received Oswald in person at Preveza, and made him some presents of arms and horses. The English wanted to keep Ali sweet in case they should need help from him in their projected attack on Corfu, so they decided to send him a subsidy, and twelve horses duly arrived at Jannina loaded with silver. The indignant Pouqueville knew very well what was going on, and kept complaining to Latour-Maubourg, the French minister at Constantinople, with the result that the Porte sent a commissioner to Jannina to inquire into Ali's alleged breaches of neutrality. Ali received the commissioner with open arms and dismissed him with bulging pockets, with the convenient result that the Porte were assured that Ali's behaviour was exemplary and that Pouqueville had been spreading false reports and ought to be replaced: it was also hinted that the inquiry might be taken as rather an affront to the dignity of the Vizier.

Ibrahim at Vallona, between Ali and the deep sea, was busy intriguing with the French, and Ali, always the master of a perfect intelligence service, heard of it through his spies and saw his chance of grabbing Vallona from a traitor to the Faith and the Empire. First he got the English to send a couple of ships to anchor off Vallona to keep the French away and prevent Ibrahim from escaping to Corfu; then he frightened Ibrahim with unpleasant rumours and seduced his few remaining allies with bribes; then he went to Berat to prepare an attack on Vallona. The French in Corfu were unable or unwilling to help Ibrahim, and finding himself completely cornered he decided to agree to Ali's terms, sent him hostages, formally made over to him all his territory except Vallona and also his niece, the daughter of Sefer Bey, whom Ali had had poisoned twelve years before.

But Ali was not yet satisfied. Hearing of further French intrigues with Ibrahim's ally, Mustapha Pasha of Delvino, he decided to get rid of Ibrahim at once and for all. Early in 1811 he had some beys of Vallona arrested and brought to Jannina, where he had them strangled for being supporters of Ibrahim. He then tried to get leave from the Porte to kill Mustapha Pasha and send his head to the Sultan, and failing in that, did all in his power tó weaken him, so that Mustapha soon found himself left with only 300 men, and in desperation sent his only son to Ali as a hostage and himself retired to the mountains. His brother, with a few companions, did likewise, and Ali promptly gave orders that they were to be blown up in their house with a charge of gunpowder.

At the beginning of August Ali's troops entered Vallona and Ibrahim fled to Gardiki, whose inhabitants (ancient enemies, it will be remembered, of the Vizier and his mother) had offered him their protection. Ali was so pleased to hear of Ibrahim's flight that he rewarded the messengers who brought him the news and at once turned his attention to Gardiki. He sent for the Gardikiots living in Jannina, flattered them, bribed them, promised them rewards, and sent some of them off to their home town with a forged order from the Porte to deprive Ibrahim of his rank and dignity – about all that was now left to him. At the same time he sent ten horses loaded with silver, arms and embroidered stuff as a present to the leading citizens of Gardiki, and in due course Ibrahim was delivered up to him, and at once imprisoned, together with his wife, in a castle near Jannina. To the new master of Vallona and Berat, whose latest campaign had been fought more with money than arms, the chieftains of Northern Albania now thought it advisable to come and pay their respects.

CHAPTER XIX

THE VIZIER'S GREEN SPECTACLES

ALI's seizure of Berat and Vallona and his treatment of Ibrahim were against the express wishes of the Sultan, and it was becoming ever clearer that sooner or later something drastic would have to be done to curb him. He was a dangerous viceroy, as good as independent, treating privately with foreign powers, making war as he chose, immensely rich, with a large army, endlessly cunning, contemptuous of the Porte, disloyal to the Empire in whose name he pretended to act, a backer of its enemies, all-powerful in a country that it would be very difficult to invade, lord over corn-growing Thessaly, the crags and forests of middle Albania, the orange and olive groves of the Gulf of Arta, and the upland pastures of Pindus. Owing to the agitations of Pouqueville, the French minister at Constantinople was continually complaining of Ali, and had even said that Napoleon himself could not put up much longer with the fact that the safety of Corfu was continually endangered by Ali's whims and would if necessary declare war on him. A sore point with the Porte was Ali's refusal to march against the Russians when ordered to do so. He had excused himself on account of his age and infirmity, but had actually been shamming sickness with as little subtlety as a schoolboy, having himself carried in a litter, only appearing in public attended by all the doctors he could muster, and wearing a large pair of green spectacles as if his eyesight were failing. He sent his sons instead, but they went very reluctantly, and once when Pouqueville – let us hope at an opportune moment – congratulated the Vizier on looking so well, saying that he would probably outlive his children, Ali replied, 'May God hear you! For if they outlive me they'll waste my fortune and get themselves hanged like the idiots they are. My poor Ali, you've hatched out nothing but chickens!'

Veli, like his father, was in bad odour with the Porte. The inhabitants of the Morea were continually presenting petitions and complaints against his government. They said that he was ruining them by his monstrous extortions and was altogether behaving exactly like his father; that no parents felt safe about their children, for whenever Veli heard of any beautiful boys or girls he had them seized at once and shut them up in his palace to serve his pleasures; that a great many people had taken refuge elsewhere to avoid oppression and ruin; and that he was completely spoiling the country. The Sultan (Mahmud II) decided to act. He deprived Veli of his command of an army corps in the Danubian provinces and gave it to somebody else, and then sent an old personal enemy of Veli's as a commissioner to report on the state of the Morea. At the same time he again brought pressure to bear on Ali to try and make him march against the Russians, but Ali would not budge, said he was obliged to stay where he was to keep his dominions in order and was in any case old and ill. In May 1811 two special officials of rank came to press him to do his duty, but he promptly called his doctors and clapped on his green spectacles again. He was absolutely firm in his refusal, for Mukhtar and Veli, who were still at the front, had sent word to warn him to stay where he was whatever happened, for they had heard that the French had been urging the Sultan to try and do away with him altogether. He sent the two envoys back with large sums of money and a promise to send an army of 4000 men to the front, but he felt for the time being extremely anxious and insecure. Afraid of treachery, he could not sleep, and even felt it necessary to appeal to the better natures of the Ganymedes who slept with him: 'Boys, don't forget that I'm a father to you. I'm in your hands, and I count on you not to betray me.' Considering that, in his own words, there was not one of them 'whose father, brother, uncle or some other relation I haven't had murdered', it is surprising that he had survived so long, but the domination of a dictator, especially that of one who is 'more mild, but yet more harmful, kind in hatred', is apt to have a hypnotic effect on his subjects. One remembers how, at the wedding of one of Ali's sons, a dervish had thrown himself from the top of the palace, crying out, 'I invoke on my own head all the misfortunes which may threaten the young bridegroom!'

Having failed to get the Vizier to go and fight the Russians, the Porte decided in their shilly-shallying way that he must at least be forced to behave properly towards the French, so later in the year a special commissioner was appointed to see to the matter. When Ali received the news of his coming he remarked rather grimly, 'There have never been two bosses in Jannina'. The commissioner's name was Djelal Effendi. On arriving in Jannina he assured Pouqueville that he would compel the Vizier to do his duty towards the French. Two days later Pouqueville went to the palace and found Djelal and Ali together ready to discuss in his presence the charges brought against the latter. One of the orders had to do with the fate of a French barque. This ship, chased by the English, had taken refuge at a place called Murtus, where it had been attacked and its cargo looted by the local inhabitants, who were subjects of Ali's. By some mistake, instead of Murtus the name of the place had been put down in Djelal's papers as Loroux.

'Loroux,' said Ali, who saw the mistake at once, 'is a river running into the Gulf of Arta, which the English never enter. Isn't that so, consul?'

'Yes,' said Pouqueville, 'but they've muddled the name. Of course they meant to put Murtus, where this affair happened.'

'Oh well, I've got nothing to do with what they *meant*. What they've *written* is Loroux.'

'But evidently,' Djelal put in, 'they did mean to write Murtus.'

'Oh, but as they've written Loroux,' said Ali, disingenuous as ever, 'I shall go by that. If they choose to write all askew at Constantinople, that's their business.' He turned to a secretary. 'Write that there's no port called Loroux. The charge is false.'

'Vizier,' protested Pouqueville, 'you can see there's been a mistake. Surely you're not going to quibble over a mis-spelling?'

Passing on to the other charges, Ali answered them all, either by denying facts, bluffing, or evading leading questions asked by Pouqueville, and refused to make any amends. When he turned to confer with his attendant ministers and secretaries he spoke in Albanian, which neither Pouqueville nor Djelal could understand, and naturally Djelal, who remained kneeling before Ali, missed a good many points, to say nothing of contemptuous personal remarks, because they were not translated to him. Bringing the meeting to an end, Ali turned to Pouqueville and said:

'Yes, just fancy, they really are a funny lot at Constan-tinople, aren't they? Fancy writing all askew!'

Before long Pouqueville realized that he could not count on Djelal to carry out the Imperial commands, for Ali had obviously bought him over. Ali even said to Pouqueville's secretary:

'Oh, the Porte has sent me a lot of these tiresome crea-tures at one time or another, but I know how to shut their mouths. The Porte really ought to have had the sense to learn by now what sort of notice I take of their orders.'

And to one of his own secretaries, Spiridion Colovo, he said:

'I can't think where they dug up this individual.'

Then one day when the question of trade with Corfu was being discussed, Pouqueville said:

'You must admit, Vizier, that you've imposed the most frightful duties on grain exports.'

'I want a monopoly,' replied Ali. 'I've had all the available supplies bought in on my account and I mean to make a profit out of them. I like to make the most of my position. So now you know.'

Djelal spoke in support of him, and in fact he only opened his mouth now to agree with whatever Ali said.

'I shall obey the commands of the Sublime Porte,' Ali concluded, 'if I choose and if it happens to suit me to do so.'

Some days later, he suddenly grew very civil to Pouqueville, pretended to be seeking the goodwill of the French, and made some complimentary remarks about Napoleon.

'May I remind you, Vizier,' said Pouqueville, 'that I'm only asking you to be just and to do something perfectly easy. I'm not asking you to drive the English away. I'm simply asking you to be neutral.'

'My dear Consul, a man can't possibly carry two melons under one arm, can he? The English have led me a dance, and I mean to get my own back on them – you may be sure of that. They have made me feel bitter towards them, and I won't go on eating their bread.'

The reason for this outburst was that although he still looked forward to enjoying English protection, and perhaps counted on it, he was at the moment annoyed with the English for having refused to hand over fifty bandits who had eluded his patrols, stolen a ship, and taken refuge in Santa Maura. But for some time Pouqueville thought his relations with the Vizier much improved, and it may be that Ali thought it advisable to keep in with the French after all: he liked to have eggs in every basket.

During these proceedings there had been other matters to attend to. The beys of Vallona who had betrayed Ibrahim came to Jannina to pay homage to their new overlord. Ali received them in state, then had them seized, bound and shoved into the Buldrun, and sent orders to Vallona that their goods and families should be confiscated. It was not a new thing for him to turn like this on traitors who had sought his favour by betraying their masters.

Under the command of Omer Bey Vrioni and the ever-faithful Athanasi Vaya he sent several thousand men against Argyro Castro and Delvino. They suffered considerable reverses. However, the people of Argyro Castro, under the joint influence of bombardment and bribery, and running short of flour and water owing to the smashing of their aqueducts and windmills, surrendered to Omer, and the three sons of Caplan Pasha and some local dignitaries were sent as prisoners to Jannina. Delvino also fell, and Mustapha Pasha fled to Gardiki, the last stronghold of some of Ali's most determined enemies.

CHAPTER XX

VENGEANCE ON GARDIKI

THE town of Gardiki, a little self-governing republic, stood on a conical hill in a wide natural amphitheatre at the head of a valley surrounded by the huge peaks of the Acroceraunian mountains. Few cities, observed a traveller, could boast of so superb a site. It was prosperous and well fortified, and Mustapha Pasha joining forces with Demir Dost, the governor of the place, was determined to put up a stout resistance. It is said that he was encouraged in this by the Sultan, who hoped that a failure on Ali's part to take Gardiki might provoke armed risings against him in other parts of the country. At all events, enough supplies and munitions were laid in to last for a year, and when the siege began it seemed likely that it would go on for a long time. But the people were not as resolute as their leaders against the power and prestige of the Vizier. Those who were farmers and shepherds looked longingly towards their pastures, now occupied by the enemy, and after some sharp fighting had taken place, with many casualties, they grew disheartened and yearned for peace. So the siege only lasted two months, and at the end of February 1812 Gardiki prepared to surrender.

Mustapha Pasha and Demir Dost, supported by sixty of the leading citizens, agreed to give themselves up as hostages to Ali on condition that they should be allowed to proceed freely to Jannina, that they should be received and treated there with the honour due to their rank, and that their families and property should be respected. Ali for his part engaged to take Gardiki and its people under his protection and to forgive all offences they had caused him in the past.

167

Why at this stage anybody in his senses should have believed for one moment that Ali was likely to keep a promise, heaven alone knows. Led by Mustapha and Demir Dost, the sixty Gardikiots proceeded in safety to Jannina, where they were met by a band, received in state, given comfortable quarters in the Castro Palace, allowed to keep their arms and their servants, and altogether treated with great consideration. But one night, less than a week after their arrival, sleeping Jannina was disturbed by the sound of a lot of shooting in the palace, and all kinds of rumours at once got about. Some people said that Mustapha and the others had tried to escape, and that only after two hours' fighting had the Skipetars succeeded in disarming them. Others believed that Ali had tried to catch the prisoners unawares and massacre the lot, but that, being on their guard, they had managed to resist till daybreak, only then being compelled to give up their arms. It was known for certain that two Skipetars had been killed, and six of the prisoners, and that the rest had been sent under a strong guard to prison on the island in the lake, that concentration camp of long standing.

A few days later Ali gave out that he would soon be leaving for Argyro Castro, and this was taken to imply a visit to his sister Shaïnitza at Liboövo. With the passing of the years, Shaïnitza had grown more eccentric and even more ferocious than her mother Khamco, and since the death of Aden Bey she had gone from bad to worse. She had often written to Ali of late to excite him against the Gardikiots, ceaselessly reminding him how they had maltreated and outraged Khamco half a century before. 'You will never have any real right to call yourself Vizier,' she wrote, 'unless you keep your oath and destroy Gardiki, and I count on you to present me with a set of mattresses stuffed with the hair of the Gardikiot women.'

168

Before Ali left Jannina, Pouqueville went to call on him. There was much ado, and troops and baggage trains had been on the move all the morning. Just before entering the palace, the consul had to pass a few freshly severed heads stuck on posts, and although he was quite used to sights of that sort he now trembled, as if with foreboding. He found Ali seated in a huge room, with his legs dangling over the edge of the divan. Wearing a scarlet cloak and boots of crimson velvet, the Vizier was leaning on a poleaxe and looking thoughtful.

'I'm just off to Gardiki,' he remarked, 'to see that order is set up again there, and I want to appoint new officials.'

'I hope, Vizier, that although you have old grudges against Gardiki you're not going to be too hard on the people.'

'Ah, yes, I know. I've shed so much blood in my time that it seems to follow me like a wave, and I daren't look behind me. Of course when I was young I was violent and impetuous, and obeyed nothing but my passions. Well, I've got the chief citizens of Gardiki in chains, but I shall free them, you know, and I only hope they'll be loyal in future. Ah, well, I'll be seeing you, and when I get back we must take a little trip to Preveza together.'

Never had he made a falser speech. Less than a week later he arrived at Liboövo to spend a couple of days with his sister, who at once set herself to work upon his feelings and excite as much as she could the revengeful cruelty he was already planning. Realizing that he meant to act in the way she wished him to, she at once gave up her howlings and broodings, and rushed to the opposite extreme. Delirious with joy, she had all the rooms brightened up with carpets and precious furniture that had been put away since Aden's death, ordered her entourage to dress themselves in festival clothes, and gave Ali a banquet with wine, women and song.

The next day he left for Schindriada, a fort built on a

169

height commanding the approaches to Gardiki. From there he issued a proclamation summoning the whole male population above seven years of age to come and pay homage to him and hear from his own lips a decree pardoning them for having opposed him and restoring peace and happiness to their town. At the same time he circulated an order amongst the neighbouring villages that no sanctuary was to be given to any Gardikiot, and that death should be the penalty for disobedience.

The weather at Schindriada was thundery, and since electrical disturbances in the atmosphere always affected him strongly, one may say that it was under a threatening sky and with a threatening heart that he prepared to receive the Gardikiots. In obedience to his order nearly 800 came before him unarmed, and he received them in the presence of his Skipetars and some auxiliary troops, about 3000 in all, under the command of Athanasi Vaya. They offered him their formal submission, and he welcomed them with a geniality that amounted to warmth, with all his old ingratiating kindness and cordial falsehood, 'throwing honey', softly calling them his friends, his brothers, his children, and charming them with promises broken before even uttered. He then said that he would like to speak to many of them individually, but that Schindriada was not very convenient for the purpose, so he had himself carried down in a palanquin on the shoulders of his men to a khan, or inn, in the valley below. There man after man was brought before him and closely questioned, and the 'royal memory' was brought into play. A few score of them he ordered to be taken aside to a safe place: they were probably members of families that had settled in Gardiki since the time of Khamco. All the rest, to whom he continued to speak kindly enough (as a spider might speak to a fly, or a cat to a mouse), were told to await his pleasure in the court-yard of the inn. Herded together in there, the Gardikiots suddenly realized what they had let themselves in for, and when Ali ordered his troops to advance and surround the inn, they began to expect the worst. The troops, ferocious as most of them were, found it hard to believe the orders they now received. The Mohammedans refused to attack their co-religionists in the courtyard, and the Mirdites (Albanians who were Roman Catholics) refused to fire on unarmed men.

'We are in your service,' said their leader to the Vizier, 'and always ready to fight for you. Give these Gardikiots back their arms and we'll fight them. We're soldiers, not butchers.'

Ali was not to be turned from his purpose or baulked of his revenge. He turned to some of his Greek troops – they surely would have no objection to killing Mohammedans.

'Those men are my enemies,' he declared, pointing towards the inn. 'What are you going to do about it?'

'We're at your service,' replied the Greeks.

'Then we'll shoot the lot!' cried Ali.

Led by Athanasi Vaya, the Greeks rushed towards the inn and many of them climbed up the high walls round the courtyard. The Gardikiots saw them and uttered loud cries of terror; a panic broke out; some tried to climb up the inside of the walls as if to escape, some tried to defend themselves by throwing stones, some screamed for mercy. But Ali took a musket from the hands of a soldier, and having ordered the gates of the courtyard to be opened, raised it deliberately to his shoulder and fired the first shot into the crowd: it was the signal for a general massacre. The soldiers went in, drove out the prisoners in batches of fifteen at a time, and shot them down before Ali, finishing off the wounded with knives. Some retreated into the inn, which Ali's men set fire to, and they were either burned alive or shot down as they ran out again. In an hour and a half the courtyard was empty: over seven hundred men lay butchered on the ground.

But Ali's blood-lust was not yet glutted. With that prodigious memory of his, he recollected that in one of his Mohammedan regiments there were three Gardikiots. He had them seized and brought before him.

'Have mercy, Vizier!' cried one of them. 'I've served you these seventeen years.'

'But I've been longing for this day,' said Ali, 'for forty years.'

The three were killed, and then Ali mounted his horse and rode triumphantly over the mangled and slippery corpses of his victims, and as he trampled on them cried aloud:

'At last my mother is avenged! Mother, here's the blood I promised you! Ach, I feel young again!'

And with that he withdrew, ordering that the bodies should remain unburied so that his sister might come and feast her eyes on the sight.

In the evening, Ali's troops went up to Gardiki, where the mothers, wives, and daughters of his victims were waiting. For two days these women were subjected to outrage by the soldiers, and on the third morning Ali had a thousand of them taken to the place where their men lay slaughtered and then marched off to Liboövo and brought before Shainitza, who was waiting for them, all agog. Mad with excitement, she ordered their hair to be cut off, stamped it under foot like a fury and shrieked that she would use it to stuff her divans. Then she had their veils and ornaments snatched from them, and as a final insult ordered that their clothes should be cut off just below the waist so that they should be indecently exposed in the sight of everybody. Then she had them turned out and driven to the mountains, threatening the death penalty to anybody who would shelter them or give them food. And at last, hearing that one of her own women was said to be pregnant by a Gardikiot, she hacked her open with a razor.

172

The bodies of the Gardikiots were left unburied to rot where they had fallen, and their town was set on fire. Ali had naturally stolen all their movable property first, and had even kept a careful account of all the debts owing to them from outside: he was careful to exact payment as it fell due. He ordered that Gardiki should never be inhabited again so long as his dynasty lasted, so 'it became a dwelling place for owls, and the coiled serpent basked within its desolated courts'. The gateway of the inn in the valley was walled up, and over it was set an inscription: THUS PERISH ALL THE ENEMIES OF THE HOUSE OF ALI. Soon afterwards an Albanian poet wrote a longer inscription in Ali's honour, and that was also put up, in gold letters, both Turkish and Greek, on a tablet of marble.

From Gardiki Ali went to Tebeleni, where he had the throats of twelve Gardikiots cut on his mother's tomb, after which he gave himself up to orgiastic rejoicings in his palace. Stimulated by that, he wrote to Mukhtar at Jannina, ordering him to kill the Gardikiots still held prisoners there. On the night of Easter Sunday 1812 Mukhtar went to the monastery prison on the island, taking with him some gipsy executioners, and another slaughter began. Demir Dost was the first victim. He was tortured, his limbs were dislocated, his loins broken, and his head crushed in a spiked chaplet of iron. After killing seventeen men the executioners were tired and had to stop. The next day, a bey and his son, only twelve years old, were publicly hanged. The day after that, twenty-two others were strangled. Altogether sixty-four people perished. Mukhtar had the bodies thrown into a well: it was long known as the Well of the Gardikiots. Revenge, filial piety, despotic vanity, and lustful cruelty were all satisfied, and Ali returned to Jannina in the best of tempers.

CHAPTER XXI

THREE BRIDES

A MORE gradual death was reserved for Mustapha Pasha.
He was shut up on the island and slowly starved to death on
the most meagre allowance of bread and water. Ali had a
report put about that Mustapha had died a natural death, but
nobody believed it.

And then Ibrahim disappeared. His daughters used to
send a messenger every morning to ask after his health and
bring back an answer, but one morning the messenger came
back and said that Ibrahim was missing and that nobody
seemed to know anything about it. His daughters, naturally
enough, believed that the old man had been secretly assassinated, and began to mourn and howl with their women.
Rumour at once flew round Jannina, and reached the ears
of a venerable dervish named Yusuf who had been a friend of
Ibrahim's and held him in great respect. Yusuf lived in a
hut near the great mosque in the Castro, and had a high
reputation for holiness and asceticism. He had in his keeping
an alleged hair from the beard of the Prophet, never accepted
money or bribes, observed his religion strictly, and lived
mostly on bread and olives. Directly he heard of the death of
Ibrahim he went straight to the palace, where all doors were
open to him. Without the slightest hesitation he came
straight into the presence of the Vizier, who invited him to sit
down beside him on the divan. But instead of sitting down
Yusuf launched out into a fiery denunciation of Ali and all his
works.

'The divan you ask me to sit down on,' he cried, 'is

soaked in blood! Every carpet, every stick of your furniture is wet with the tears of your victims! The swords that hang on your walls have been blunted on Suliot heads, and from here I can see the lake, where you had those women drowned, though their wombs were chaster than your lecherous tongue. Your evil sister, egging you on to crime, has profaned our most sacred laws by having the veils torn off the Mohammedan women of Gardiki, and with her own hands she cut open one of her women with a razor, so as to destroy an unborn innocent, because its father was supposed to be a Gardikiot. You wretch, listen to the truth for once! Everywhere there are signs of your crimes, and you can't take a step without walking on the grave of someone you've murdered. Why, even from where I stand I can see the grave of Eminé, the good wife you killed. You live in state and luxury, among supple flatterers, but time's passing, and one day you'll find you're mortal, and you'll have to reckon with . . .'

'Stop! Enough!' cried Ali, visibly agitated by the mention of Eminé.

After looking straight at him in silence Yusuf turned and stalked slowly out.

Pouqueville had sent a messenger to Constantinople with the news of Ibrahim's death. It provoked great anger, for Ibrahim had always been highly thought of, both for his personal qualities and as a bulwark against Ali. A commissioner was at once sent off to Jannina to investigate the circumstances.

'What!' cried Ali, pretending great surprise, when he heard what the commissioner had come for. 'Dead? Ibrahim, my father, dead? What an extraordinary idea!'

All his attendants expressed incredulity, and looked at each other and at the commissioner in apparent bewilderment. Turning to two of his ministers, Ali said:

'Go with this officer to Ibrahim Pasha's room, so that he may see for himself what lies have been told about us.'

The commissioner was led to a very comfortable room, where he found Ibrahim alive and looking well.

Ibrahim had been told by Ali what to say, and now sent a message to the Sultan, declaring that he kissed the ground on which his sovereign stood.

'As you see, I'm perfectly well and quite happy. The Vizier is most kind, and allows me to see my daughters and my grandchildren. Of course I'm too old now for the cares of government, so it's a comfort to me to know that everything is being looked after so well by my dear friend Ali Pasha.'

'There! You see,' said Ali, turning to the commissioner, 'I'm simply surrounded by enemies, suspected and lied about. Just the same sort of thing happened the other day, when people tried to make out that Mustapha Pasha hadn't died a natural death. So go back to the Sultan, tell him what you've seen and heard and say that I shouldn't dream of acting in opposition to the wishes of my lord and master.'

The departing commissioner was loaded with presents, and Ibrahim was at once shut up again under guard. In April he heard sounds of festivity, for three of his grandchildren, the daughters of Veli, were married in one day. Ayesha, the youngest, was paired off with Mustai Pasha of Scutari, an impoverished young man whom Ali hoped to ruin completely. A curious policy, one might say, to ally one's progeny to an intended victim, but it had been his policy towards Ibrahim and had seemingly paid him in the long run, and he no doubt felt that pressure could be more easily brought to bear on relations than on outsiders. (He later sent Mustai a letter, but it was opened by Ayesha, when it exploded and mortally injured her.)

The wedding festivities were on a tremendous scale, and

lasted for nearly three weeks. Presents poured in, and the secretaries were kept busy listing them. Ali had a vast number of guests, and the whole town let itself go in riotous enjoyment, so much so that the rejoicing seemed to the French consul the noisy abandon of a population of slaves diverting themselves in order not to hear the rattling of their chains. Flocks of rams with leaves of gilt paper twined round their horns were driven into the town, and whole flocks of sheep with their fleeces stained red. Everywhere goats and sheep were being roasted whole on spits to satisfy the swarms of hungry Skipetars, and wine flowed like water. Bonfires blazed, bands were playing, tightrope dancers were greeted with loud applause, *djerid* or jousting tournaments were held, even the priests joined in the drinking and dancing, and in the streets behaviour grew openly licentious. Bands of gipsies burst into the houses singing at the tops of their voices, and stealing whatever they could lay hands on: these 'harpies' even invaded that sacred preserve the French consulate, and the perennially indignant Pouqueville had to drive them out by a method 'more energetic than words'.

Although Ali joined in the merrymaking he soon had affairs of state to attend to. In the early part of the year he had been feeling a little chilly towards the English, partly owing to their refusal to return to him fugitives from his dominions, but in May General Airey, who was in command of the English army of occupation in the Ionian Islands, sent a friendly mission to Jannina. The party included a Major Monk and his wife, the Governor of Zante, Airey's own wife carrying wedding presents for Veli's daughters, three officers, and a suite. The general no doubt thought it a graceful attention to send his wife, but this big idea was contrary to Eastern custom and could only have seemed ludicrous to a Mohammedan. Ali, however, found it easy enough to overlook this silly breach of etiquette, for Major Monk presented him with a sum of money and some fine diamonds, bringing him at the same time a promise of regular subsidies. Naturally enough he turned abruptly against the French again, for with Ali money talked.

'Vizier,' said Pouqueville, 'isn't the goodwill of the Emperor Napoleon worth more to you than a few bags of gold?'

'The Emperor took Parga away,' said Ali, and went on to complain of some of his enemies being sheltered at Corfu, where there was now a regiment of chasseurs largely made up of Suliot refugees, besides some near relations of Mustapha Pasha. 'I want my land,' he said, 'and I want my enemies to be delivered up to me.'

To show that he meant what he said, he put new embargoes on the sending of convoys to Corfu, and when Pouqueville complained, threatened to stop any supplies being sent at all, and as far as Parga was concerned, carried out the threat. He was pleased with the money the English were sending him, and undertook to help them if they decided to attack Corfu, on condition now that Parga should be his reward.

In September a sinister thing happened. A new Grand Vizier was appointed at Constantinople who was a personal enemy of the Pasha of Jannina. His name was Khurschid Pasha. Ali at once took steps to restore his credit with the Porte, sent more presents to the capital, and more spies, including a clever Greek doctor who was able to eavesdrop in exalted circles and repeat pertinent conversations. At the same time he kept a closer watch than ever on Ibrahim, who was kept shut up at Litharitza. He knew that the Sultan and the Porte would like to restore Ibrahim to his former dignities, and he feared that they might subsequently try to use the old man as a centre of hostile agitation and rebellion against Jannina.

CHAPTER XXII

'GENIAL CONVERSATION'

TOWARDS the end of 1812 there arrived in Jannina an English
doctor, Henry Holland, a thin young man of 24, who was a
cousin of Mrs. Gaskell, a great-nephew of Josiah Wedgwood,
and afterwards the father of the first Lord Knutsford. He
brought with him letters of introduction to Ali and to the
secretary Colovo, and was put up at the house of a rich Greek.
Colovo, then in his fifties, seemed dignified and agreeable,
spoke French, German and Italian, and offered his services as
interpreter. The day after his arrival Holland was escorted
to the Litharitza Palace for an audience with Ali. He had to
pass through the usual crowd of lounging and splendidly
dressed Skipetars, and on his way in noticed one of Ali's
carriages, an old lumbering German thing that looked as if
it had crossed Europe a dozen times. At the top of a stone
staircase he passed through a wide gallery with many windows and a fine view of the lake and mountains. It was
crowded with people – Skipetars, Turkish and Moorish soldiers,
Turkish officers of the household, Greek and Jewish secretaries, Greek merchants, Tartar couriers, pages, black slaves,
and petitioners seeking audience. Then he was led through
a great and gaudily-decorated hall to the audience room.
A curtain was drawn, and he found himself in a lofty saloon
with richly decorated pillars, large windows giving on to the
lake, walls painted in crimson and blue and gold, a ceiling
divided into squares of carved wood stained crimson with gold
borders, and pilasters between which hung trophies of arms
encrusted with gold and jewels. The floor was carpeted, and

179

there were wide divans nearly all round the room: they stood about fifteen inches from the floor and had crimson cushions and deep borders of gold lace.

Near a wood fire which was blazing under a carved canopy Ali was sitting on a slightly raised divan with his legs crossed under him. Bedizened like an old-fashioned political hostess, he had a high round cap on his head of deep mazarin blue edged with gold lace, and was wearing a yellow embroidered robe over two striped inner garments, with an embroidered belt, in which were stuck a pistol and dagger, their hilts covered with diamonds, pearls and large emeralds. He was wearing diamonds on his fingers as well, and even the mouthpiece of his hookah was jewelled. His manner was gracious as ever, and his expression 'open, placid and alluring', but of course under the smooth and polished surface there was 'the fire of a stove burning fiercely'.

As Byron put it, Ali was

'a man of war and woes;
Yet in his lineaments he cannot trace,
While gentleness her milder radiance throws,
Along that aged venerable face,
The deeds that lurk beneath, and stain him with disgrace.'

Of Byron and Hobhouse, Holland took an early chance to make some mention. Ali seemed pleased to speak of them but was even more anxious to discuss politics and the latest news of the French in Russia and the English in Spain. Holland gave him a more detailed account than he had yet heard of the battle of Salamanca and of Wellington's entry into Madrid. There then arose a rather awkward question about one of Ali's corvettes which had on board a cargo of grain and had been seized by an English frigate and detained near Corfu. Holland made a tactful and non-committal comment, at which Ali gave a loud laugh and said he would change the subject. He inquired if Holland was being properly looked after and said he would like to consult him professionally before he left Jannina. The audience had lasted half an hour, and during that time Colovo had remained standing, and so had Ali's richly dressed attendants – four handsome young Albanians, and two negroes in white turbans.

A day or two later Ali sent for Holland in his professional capacity. Through Colovo he described his symptoms and said he thought he had dropsy of the abdomen, though this was a mere fancy. Holland's professional discretion was such that he left no printed record of Ali's health beyond saying that at this time he was suffering from no acute disorder and that his symptoms were the result partly of his age and partly of his manner of life.

Reassured by Holland, Ali grew more and more affable. He could never resist a doctor, especially an intelligent one, and he found this one very interesting to talk to. He spoke of politics again, and then of longevity, a subject always dear to him, and asked how it could be attained. Holland said the idea of finding the elixir of life had been quite given up in scientific circles. Ali then touched on alchemy, and said he wondered if one could not perhaps discover some secret way of making gold. Holland replied that there was no way of making either gold or silver, and added rather pompously that 'the advantage of philosophy was in being able to employ the best means of raising them from mines, and purifying them for use'. As they went on talking about telescopes, arms, the power of various nations, the art of war, the making of roads and bridges, the improvement of agriculture – Holland found his host free from Turkish prejudices, ready to admit his inferiority to Europeans, constantly anxious for information, and indifferent to matters of education and literature. Ali was

181

so pleaséd with Holland that he presented him, before he continued on his travels, with a splendid sabre from Damascus, and insisted that he must see him again.

In the course of his travels Holland paid a visit to Veli, who was now nearly forty. He found him sitting on a divan, wearing a large blue turban with a white linen border, and a red robe edged with fur. Veli had regular features and a pleasant smile, was handsome, seemed polite and refined, invited Holland to stay as long as he could and offered to lend him his carriage. He was said to be more of a statesman and less of a soldier than his brother Mukhtar, and even to have some leanings towards culture – it was known that he had once turned aside from a journey to visit the ruins of Athens, which was thought extraordinary for a Turk. Always a hedonist, Veli had had translated for him the most pornographic books to be found in Europe. Like his father he was a sadist, and it was said that he could not kiss without biting or fondle without scratching, and a woman in Jannina known as Earless Kate was said to have been mutilated by him for pleasure. In attendance on him was Lucas Vaya, the brother of Athanasi, who had finished his medical education at Ali's expense in Vienna and Leipsic and was now engaged to the daughter of Psalida the schoolmaster, Jannina's leading intellectual.

In February Holland arrived at Preveza, where he found Ali stopping with an immense concourse of Skipetars. The Vizier was very pleased to see him again, asked him about his travels, and expressed a wish that he would settle down in Jannina. Holland said he wanted to make an excursion in the Gulf of Arta to look at some ruins, so Ali detailed two Skipetars to escort him. Their names were Kapsamuni and Fissuki, but although handsome in appearance their pleasures were primitive, for their chief amusement while sailing along with Holland was to fire at the fishermen's boats they passed, taking deliberate aim at the fishermen. A day or two later Holland met the Vizier amongst the ruins of Nicopolis. He found the old man sitting on a cushion of crimson velvet and wondering if there was any buried treasure to be found. Reaching no conclusion on the subject, Ali rattled off to Preveza in his carriage, with a swarm of his dressy, smelly, wasp-waisted, flea-bitten Skipetars riding and running with the greatest of ease beside him.

Back in Jannina again, Holland paid a call on Mukhtar, whom he did not find very interesting, and met Coletti, Mukhtar's doctor, a man of some culture, who had translated *Rasselas*. While waiting in an anteroom for his audience he saw an amusing scene between two dervishes, who were quarrelling as to which had the more power to influence heaven by prayer – gesticulations turned to menaces, and protests and assertions to angry shouts and yells. A verbatim report of the quarrel would have made a piquant addition to religious literature.

At Argyro Castro, where work was proceeding on the fortress, Holland saw Ali's youngest son Sali Bey, at this time only twelve years old, but nominally governing the place. He was a bright boy, fair, with light hair and eyes like his father when young, and had quite an air of manly independence as he sat there in a red cap and a purple pelisse, with a dagger and pistols made specially small for him. He was being taught Turkish, Albanian, and Greek, and physical exercises as well.

At Tebeleni, where the bridge had again been washed away, Yusuf Arab the Blood Drinker was in command, now a very old man, over ninety in fact. Old age had not made him less formidable, and only a few days before Holland's visit he had stabbed a man to death with his own hand. Holland found him sitting in a small and dirty room surrounded by a crowd of richly dressed guards. His face with age had contracted into a fixed expression of ferocity, and his complexion had darkened so that he now seemed a Moor rather than a mulatto. His general air of uncouthness was somehow intensified by the presence of seven or eight dogs and cats, some of them wearing little jackets. Holland was given rooms in the palace, where Sali's mother, the favoured Georgian slave, was living in the harem with sixty attendants. Everything was on as sumptuous a scale as the bedclothes – a purple velvet counterpane with gold embroidery, and muslin sheets with long fringes and knots of flowers worked here and there in various colours, embellishments which unfortunately tended to catch the toe-nails as well as the eye.

At Jannina once more, Holland stayed a fortnight and often saw Ali, who asked him many more questions about the possibility of finding gold and silver mines, and told him that he intended Sali Bey, when 16, to travel for four or five years, beginning with a year in Morocco, then seeing England, France, Germany, Russia, Constantinople, and Asia Minor: he hoped Holland would be kind to the boy when he came to England. At his last interview Ali's manner, which had always been not merely courteous but genuinely friendly, was marked now by a particular warmth.

'I hope,' he said, 'that you won't forget me, that you'll come back some day, and that you'll sometimes write to me.'

Holland says that when he got up to go it was 'certainly not without a sentiment of regret in leaving a man, who, whatever be his habits as the despotic ruler of a half-civilized people, had interested me greatly by his talents, by his conversation, and by the uniform courtesy and kindness with which he had treated me, during my several visits to his court. . . .

'When I rose from my couch to make my adieu, the

Vizier rose also, and advancing towards the middle of the apartment with me, kissed each cheek in bidding me farewell.'

The tone of this reminiscence is especially remarkable coming from a highly civilized man who had seen in Ali's courtyard bleeding heads newly cut off, and mangled limbs – but Holland was, of course, a doctor – who must have known something of his history and reputation, and who met him only a few months after the butchery at Gardiki. It is a notable example of that strange thing, the kindness of the cruel, and suggests that the honey which Ali threw was not always poisoned. And Holland, who afterwards became a fashionable doctor in Mayfair and physician-in-ordinary to Queen Victoria, had in his intercourse with Ali been able to dose himself with what later became one of his favourite prescriptions, and a wise one, namely, 'the frequent half-hour of genial conversation'.

CHAPTER XXIII

PANIC

VELI was in trouble again. Returning from the army in the Danubian provinces he found his subjects in the Morea completely out of hand, and even with the help of troops sent by Ali was unable to restore order. The Porte accordingly turned him out and gave him the government of Thessaly instead. Ali was furious with him for losing the Morea, and cursed him for putting his private pleasures before his duties as governor. He particularly blamed him for leaving the administration to Ismail Pasho Bey, whom, it may be recalled, he had banished from Jannina. Ismail, he said, was responsible for the gross mismanagement that had cost Veli a kingdom and Veli must get rid of him at once. This Veli refused to do, for Ismail had been his friend since childhood, and he was very fond of him, so when he transferred himself to Thessaly Ismail went with him. Ismail was a kinsman of Ali's, having married one of his cousins, and before incurring the Vizier's hatred had been held in favour. The hatred which had caused Ali to banish him was not unmixed with fear, and this fear was not altogether groundless. A dervish had foretold Ali's downfall, saying that a man named Ismail would be not only the cause of it but would succeed him as Pasha of Jannina. It was in the belief that the Ismail in question must be Ismail Pasho Bey that Ali had sent him into exile. Ismail's friendship with Veli and his enmity with Ali were suddenly stimulated by the discovery of an appalling truth which set the son irreconcilably against the father.

Ali had forbidden Veli's wife Zobeidé to leave Jannina,

saying that he wished to keep her as a hostage for her husband's good behaviour. It seems, however, that he had an ulterior motive, and that his feelings towards her were not those generally considered becoming to a father-in-law. He was not given, it is hardly necessary to say, to self-restraint, but although she was in his power he had not the face to declare himself to her. In the end he had her doped, and took advantage of her while she was comatose. In due course she found herself pregnant, and a frightful suspicion grew in her mind. Some confused memories of her own, some veiled hints and half-reluctant admissions from her women, whom she closely questioned, and whom Ali had threatened with death unless they acted as his accomplices and kept his secret, convinced her that it was none other than her father-in-law who had had her. She accordingly sent him an urgent note asking if she might see him. Whether Ali had been driven to the act by sexual passion alone is doubtful: most likely he derived a peculiar pleasure from outraging the daughter of the hated and despised Ibrahim, and from making at the same time a cuckold of his son, whom he also despised. When he came to the harem, in answer to Zobeidé's note, she fell weeping at his feet and told him what was on her mind. He admitted that it was he who was responsible for her condition, ordered her to say nothing to anybody about it, and promised that the fruit of his embrace should be destroyed either before or after birth.

This was the story which Ismail got to hear, and which he told Veli, who joined him in swearing vengeance against Ali. As for Ali, when he learned that his secret was known to Ismail, he determined to kill him, and accordingly sent eight Skipetars in secret to Larissa, where Ismail and Veli were now living, to carry out his wishes. The men hid themselves in a Mohammedan monastery near Ismail's house,

and in the evening, just as he was returning home and had
reached his front door, he suddenly came under a volley of
musket fire. Every shot missed him, and his escort fired back,
while an alarm was given all over the town. One Skipetar was
killed, six were taken and either hanged or quartered by Veli's
orders, and only one got back to Jannina with the news.

'But he won't escape me!' cried Ali when he heard what
had happened, and at once began to hatch a new plot. Some
days later he sent for his aged foster-brother, Yusuf Arab the
Blood Drinker, and told him to go to Larissa and ask Veli to
send Ismail to Jannina, in return for which Yusuf and his
suite were to remain as hostages at Larissa. Veli refused, and
Ismail, feeling thoroughly unsafe, went away and attached
himself for a time to the Pasha of Negropont. But even there
he was pursued by hired agents of Ali's, so he crossed over to
Asia Minor and led a wandering life there and in Egypt until
the time came for him to fulfil his destiny. Meanwhile Ali
set about trying to cover the traces of his rape of Zobeidé.
The odalisques who had helped him by drugging her were
seized, sewn up in sacks, and thrown into the lake by some
gipsies, and as soon as that was done the heads of the gipsies
were cut off by a negro deaf-mute. The services of a Thes-
salian abortionist were obtained for Zobeidé, and Ali then
wrote to Veli to say he understood that a scandalous story had
been spread to the effect that Zobeidé was pregnant by him
but that there was no truth in it and no reason why she should
not now take her children and join her husband at Larissa,
when Veli would be able to see for himself that there was
nothing wrong.

From these complications Ali turned to foreign affairs.
The successes of the French in their advance against the
Russians in 1812 swung the Vizier's inclinations over towards
them once more.

'I already have powerful enemies,' he remarked to Pouqueville, 'and I'm going to reckon the English among them.'

He went on to express a hope that Napoleon would give
him a personal assurance of permanent protection against all
those who might seek to injure him. In return, he would
undertake to close his ports to the English, would lend
help to any attempt to re-take Santa Maura and the other
islands, and would do his best, through his influence in
Constantinople, to provoke bad relations between Turkey
and England.

Hardly were the words out of his mouth than he began
to try and tone them down, for he was afraid that the English
might bombard his forts on the coast. But very soon there
came the news of the burning of Moscow (causing great
agitation amongst some of the rich Janninot merchants who
had interests there) and of the retreat of the Grand Army,
news so momentous that even rumour could hardly over-
estimate its significance. Naturally Ali, with his acute
sensitiveness to the variations in European politics, was
immediately an implacable enemy of the French once more!

It was soon being said on good authority that he was
shortly going to attack Aya, a district near Parga then occupied
by the French, and it was known that he had sent Colovo off to
Malta *en route* for London on a special mission well equipped
with money and clothes in order that he might cut a dash.
Colovo was to ask for English protection, further subsidies,
and munitions, and to offer in return Ali's help if an attack
were made on Corfu; in case of war between England and
Turkey, Ali would put all his resources at England's disposal;
and as a reward he asked for Parga, Santa Maura, and some
small islets off the coast – rather on the principle of a man
borrowing money who tries to count on getting at least half
of what he asks for.

This continual bargaining sometimes for a French and sometimes for an English alliance was due not only to greed for more territory but to an ever-growing anxiety about the intentions of Khurschid and the Porte. He knew he was hated, feared and distrusted, and thought some sudden blow might be aimed at him, so he went off to Preveza for a time, thinking he might feel easier there. He had a conference with the English general Airey and our consul Foresti, and as a result of it the English sent him some artillery, after which he returned in state to Jannina. Pouqueville saw him the next day, and found him in a very bad temper because some of his prisoners (including a son of Mustapha Pasha) had escaped from Delvino and been given sanctuary by the French at Corfu: by way of reprisal everybody suspected of helping the prisoners to escape was condemned to death by drowning, and fresh regulations were made to handicap trade with the French.

Shortly afterwards General Airey arrived in state at Jannina, bringing with him his wife and two daughters, his son, his aides-de-camp, and several officers. He was welcomed by a troop of cavalry, a battalion of Skipetars, a band, and salvos of musket fire, and then Ali received him, with all his suite, in audience. He handed Ali a magnificent solitaire diamond ring as a present from his government, and when later Ali showed it proudly to Pouqueville he said, 'There, look at that! The French have never given me anything like that!' Airey was lodged at the house of a Greek notability, and Ali did him the rare honour of coming to dine with him there, while Airey's women were received in the harem by the wife of Mukhtar: forty freshly severed heads had just been put up over the gate of the palace, by way of decoration. Banquets and festivities went on for a week, but business was not neglected. Promises of mutual aid were exchanged between the general and the Vizier, and Ali was promised Parga, and perhaps more.

An order now came to Ali from the Porte that he must march against the Serbs, who were in open and successful rebellion. His answer was to send an envoy with excuses, supported by thirty horses loaded with money and valuable presents, to Khurschid Pasha, now at Adrianople. The envoy stayed there for a month and a half but was not even given a single audience. He reported that the Sultan wished to see Ibrahim restored to Berat and the family of Mustapha Pasha to Delvino, and that Ali was either to come at once to Adrianople or else retire to Tebeleni. This had no effect, and the order was repeated. The idea that any sort of compulsion should be brought to bear on him by his enemy and superior Khurschid was more than Ali could stand. Furious and frightened, he wandered about in his apartments all day long, raving with anger and vituperation, and unable to bear anybody near him. He was beginning to realize that the unpleasant realities of the world could no longer be lent an agreeable tinge by being regarded through green spectacles, so he had affidavits sworn that he was old, blind, ill, unable to mount a horse, and confined to bed.

'Very well,' the Sultan most reasonably replied, 'if he's in such a state he'd better give up trying to govern Epirus and go home to Tebeleni. I'll give him a pension. But I want to see a new Pasha at Jannina and put an end to this rebellious dictatorship once and for all.'

Ali was panic-stricken, and kept consulting dervishes and astrologers about his future. At the same time he gave orders that the fortifying of Argyro Castro was to be continued on a grand scale and the place prepared as if for a long siege. He spoke of retiring there.

'I'm getting sick of Jannina,' he said. 'I want to go back

to the mountains where I was born . . . for my health's sake,'
he added.

He still cherished aggressive designs against Parga, and
although he did not dare to attack the town itself he decided
to proceed against Aya, a small outlying dependency. Colonel
Nicole, commanding the French garrison at Parga – his full
name was Hadji Nicolas Papas Oglu, he was a Greek who had
served with Napoleon in Egypt – at once wrote to Ali to
remind him that Aya belonged to France by virtue of rights
transferred from the Venetian Republic to the Emperor
Napoleon, who alone ruled it. But this did nothing to deter
Ali, who gave orders for an attack. A whole day's fighting took
place in which twenty-four Skipetars were killed and many
more wounded before they retired from the scene, a reverse
which kept Ali from doing anything further in that direction
for the time being.

The Serbian revolt was by now in full swing, and a
peremptory order came to Ali to bring an army to the Imperial
headquarters at Sofia. He naturally did not obey, but retired
instead to Argyro Castro, taking his wives with him, besides
a son of Veli's and a son of Ismail's as hostages. After inspecting the fortifications he went on to Tebeleni, where, he said,
he meant to spend three or four months. He was afraid that
at any moment the Sultan might issue a decree proclaiming
him a rebel, so he sent large sums of money to the Grand
Vizier and the other ministers, and at the same time concentrated on his plans for Argyro Castro, packing that place with
munitions, supplies of grain, money and cattle, including a
thousand carcasses of salt beef, and having his treasures moved
there from Tebeleni, in case he should have to use the place
as a bolt-hole. In September, as the result of an immense
contribution to the Imperial treasury, he received a decree
confirming him in the government of Jannina. Evidently

the Sultan's attention was so fully taken up with the Serbs that he did not want to chance just yet having to subdue a powerful rebel Pasha as well, but he sent an envoy with an order to Ali to free Ibrahim and send him back to Berat. The old man was still shut up at Litharitza, where his daughters, though forbidden to see him, managed to send him food which they had prepared with their own hands for fear of his being poisoned. Ali was furious at the order and quite determined not to let Ibrahim go back to Berat, but he knew how great was the esteem in which the old man was held at Constantinople, on account of his distinguished origins and quiet character, and he felt obliged to show him a little more consideration, so he allowed Ibrahim to see his children.

While the envoy was at Jannina Ali stayed shut up in a room that looked like a chemist's shop. He was surrounded by a whole squad of doctors, wore a large poultice on his chest, and restored the indispensable green spectacles to his nose. The envoy left on Christmas Day and in the evening Ali said he was feeling much better, took off his plaster and his spectacles and got up and dressed. On December 27th and 28th he was as fit as a fiddle, but he heard a rumour that another envoy was on the way and all his anxiety returned. He therefore staged a relapse, all the doctors were routed out in the middle of the night, and the Vizier put on his spectacles again and withdrew to the harem.

CHAPTER XXIV

MORE ENGLISH VISITORS

AT about noon, on a December day in 1813, a small boat was
stuck on a sandbank at the entrance to the harbour of Preveza.
It contained three young Englishmen, all in their twenties.
One was Richard Townley Parker, the only son of a rich
county family in Lancashire, now on his travels. With him
was his tutor, the Rev. Thomas Smart Hughes, who had been
at Shrewsbury under Dr. Butler and later a master at Harrow
and had found time to publish some polite literary exercises,
including a poem in Latin on the death of William Pitt and
another in Greek on the death of Nelson. To say that Hughes
was a Christian, a scholar and a gentleman is to speak of him
with some admiration for a polished product of a particular
phase of civilization, not forgetting that he had a certain
insularity and was free neither from pedantry nor the pom-
pousness and self-righteousness sometimes displayed by the
educated in those days, when they were doing their best to
set an example of stateliness and virtue. The third member
of the party, C. R. Cockerell, was a son of Samuel Pepys
Cockerell, architect to the East India Company. After leaving
Westminster, the son had followed his father's profession, and
was now travelling to examine classical examples of architec-
ture. An idea of his appearance, which was pleasant, can be
gathered from a beautiful drawing of him by Ingres. In later
life Cockerell was to become a Royal Academician and Parker
a member of parliament, while Hughes accepted a fellowship
at Cambridge, produced some theological works, and was an
unsuccessful candidate for the headmastership of Rugby.

Goodness knows how long the boat might have stayed

where it was, had it not been shifted by the exertions of a Greek sailor of remarkable muscular development, which not only gave the travellers a much-needed impetus towards Preveza but enabled Hughes, whose mind was a perfect encyclopaedia of classical allusions, to compare him to an ancient athlete. The boat shot forward over the clear calm water (through which could be seen, in exquisite detail, the coloured fields of seaweed) towards a landscape of somewhat theatrical splendour. The sun was shining on Preveza, on its dingy hovels and on the gaudily-painted walls of the palace which Ali had lately completed, and which stood out in bright relief against the sombre and stormy background of the Acroceraunian mountains and the more remote and snowy peaks of Pindus.

Apart from the new palace, the town was perhaps even more squalid than at the time of Byron's visit. In the old days it had been prosperous, with fisheries and olive groves and vineyards and a population of 16,000, but now, under Ali's rule, it contained no more than 3000, and these seemed to be worn out with poverty and famine and disease. Most of the houses and every church but one had been destroyed, and the people lived in wretched shacks and sheds half open to the weather. It was plain what sort of man was master here, for the Greeks were obviously melancholy and dejected in contrast with the leisurely, dignified Turks and the haughty, strutting Skipetars. Ali's triumphant-looking new palace had a superstructure of wood on a basement of stone, and was built on a pretentious scale, with a great hall 200 feet long and 40 feet broad, having galleries 60 feet long beside it. The interior was showily decorated, with much carving and gilding and naive or primitive mural paintings of landscape.

There was nothing to detain the travellers in Preveza, so they rode off towards Jannina. The keen air of the mountains and their youthful energy enabled them to enjoy a breakfast of black bread and resinated wine, and galloping along in the frosty morning air they came to the top of a slope and suddenly saw Jannina before them, the mosques and palaces glittering in the sun, and the snowy mountains reflected in the lake, over which boats were gliding, carrying sportsmen out after wild duck. Like Byron and Hobhouse before them, they were billeted at the house of Nicolo Argyri, who, having been so heavily defrauded by Ali, was not too pleased to have to receive Ali's guests, until he realized that perhaps he could make some money out of them.

Ali did not receive them at once, and they spent their first evening as guests of Foresti, the English consul, at whose house they found a distinguished agent of the English government, Colonel (later Sir Richard) Church, and also Psalida the schoolmaster and leading light of the local intelligentsia. Psalida when young had lived in St. Petersburg and had been given some slight patronage by the Empress Catherine, to whom he had dedicated *True Happiness*, a little book he had written, somewhat sceptical in tone. Whether on account of his scepticism, or his conceit, or his rudeness, or all three, he made no conquest of the Englishmen. Hughes, differing from him in matters of scholarship and general opinion, thought his learning over-rated and his manners bad. 'As far as manners go he is a mere barbarian,' was Cockerell's opinion, and that was scarcely surprising, for on hearing that Cockerell had done some excavating in Aegina, Psalida called him a 'tomb-breaker and a sacrilegious wretch'.

The next day Colovo called with Ali's compliments, and in the afternoon, accompanied by Church and Foresti, they went to Litharitza. There they passed through the usual turmoil of the courtyard, a confusion of kilts and beards, turbans and skull-caps, pistols and daggers, smells and embroidery, with petitioners waving their petitions about on long sticks like the antennae of unhappy insects – saw the unwieldy German carriage, and were led into the great barbaric saloon with its plate-glass windows looking on to the lake. Ali kept them waiting half an hour, during which they were thoroughly stared at by officials, pages, slaves and eunuchs; pestered by a black man who had been in London and was determined to air his small and dubious English vocabulary; and annoyed by a mad dervish, who kept muttering at them what sounded remarkably like a curse.

When it was time to see Ali they went down a great staircase, and Hughes' heart, for one, began to palpitate rather quickly at the thought of coming into the presence of the ogre of Epirus. Several Skipetars were standing about at the entrance to the audience room and amongst them Odysseus, a favourite of Ali's and later a hero of the Greek revolution, together with his friend Gourra, who eventually murdered him. (Odysseus, whose personal appearance is said to have suggested that of some Homeric hero, is supposed to have once challenged a favourite horse of Ali's to a race, on condition that if he did not tire it out and win the race, he should forfeit his head: the course was prepared, and so were the instruments of execution, but Odysseus ran till 'the noble animal fell down and breathed his last'.)

And now the door of the audience room was opened, and there was Ali sitting on a lion's skin on the divan. He was wearing a scarlet cap with gold lace, and sparkled discreetly with diamonds: a hookah stood near him. He nodded amiably and said how pleased he was to welcome the visitors. Whatever they had expected they were almost taken aback, like others before them, by his gentleness and charm. His beard, now quite white, gave him a mild Santa Claus-like benevolence, his expression was frank and open, his voice honeyed.

He seemed almost too good to be true, but they might have reminded themselves more strongly than they did that at this time he was out to please the English, always hoping that with the help or connivance of our nation he might one day get a footing in Parga and the Ionian Islands. He noticed that Hughes, who was nearest the fire, was finding it a little too hot, so he ordered a screen, remarking jovially that young men do not need fire, and recalling how as a young man he had been used to sleeping out in the wintry mountains with only his sheepskin capote to cover him. And now it was Cockerell's turn to be astonished, for Ali 'laughed with so much *bonhomie*, his manner was so mild and paternal and so charming in its air of kindness and perfect openness', that 'remembering the blood-curdling stories told of him' the young man 'could hardly believe his eyes'. Hughes did his best to detect 'a crafty gleam' in the twinkling blue eyes, to persuade himself that there was something terrible about the paternal laugh, and that 'a sarcastic smile' was lurking in the Father Christmas beard, but it was not easy, especially as at that moment hospitality appeared in a more tangible form, some of the Ganymedes arriving 'dressed in rich garments with their hair flowing over their shoulders' and bringing jewelled and amber-headed pipes for the guests, to say nothing of coffee in china cups with gold holders. The talk, however, proved rather desultory, perhaps because the Englishmen were shy. Ali asked about Byron and Hobhouse and paid a few compliments, and then it was time to go. His visitors left him feeling delighted and perhaps a little relieved. On the way out they saw Veli's two sons, Mehmet Pasha and Ismail Bey, and thought the 'little despots' very proud in their bearing.

At dinner that evening Psalida quite rightly attacked the absurd English pronunciation of Greek. Hughes retorted by showing him 'a copy of beautiful Iambics from the pen of the late Professor Porson', which was very coldly received, and when Hughes said quite justifiably that the modern Greeks sacrificed prosody to accent, Psalida grew quite hostile. It was perhaps scarcely tactful of Hughes to deplore, under Psalida's own roof, Mrs. Psalida's immediate withdrawal from the room after bringing in the food.

'It's a very injurious custom,' he said, 'to exclude women from society, and with them all the delicacy and refinement which their influence produces.'

Psalida was horrified.

'All women,' said he, 'are prone to evil, and if liberty were granted to them they'd only abuse it.'

'But nothing,' said Hughes, 'is so likely to produce honour and sincerity in the female sex as confidence placed in them by men. What about Englishwomen as an example?'

'Ah,' said Psalida, 'and what about the example of the ancient Greeks?'

Which put Hughes in the same hole as many a classical scholar professing to adore the ancients and yet trying to excuse, ignore, or hush up their ideas about sex and their sexual behaviour.

In the morning the Englishmen went for a walk, and were impressed by the number and richness of the shops in the bazaar (there were said to be more than two thousand) and by the bustle of business – the city had greatly increased and prospered under Ali, in spite of his extortions. It was not considered at all safe for foreigners to go near the bazaar, because ferocious watch-dogs were kept there, and indeed one of them took a fancy to Parker's greatcoat and nearly tore it off his back. Near the bazaar they saw the open space before the city guardhouse where Ali used to have people tortured or executed when he wanted to make public examples of them, and Foresti told them how once when he was on the way to Litharitza he had seen a man who had been the leader of some Klephts crucified on the outer wall of the palace. Away from the bazaar, they did not meet many people in the streets, though once or twice they saw a great lady, heavily veiled, followed by her maids as she was going to the public baths or to pay calls. And they noticed that owing to the benevolence of the rich Greeks there were no beggars to be seen.

In the evening Foresti took them to pay a visit to Mukhtar in his own palace. They had to wait half an hour for him, as he had just returned from a hawking expedition. He came in followed by a troop of beautiful Greek and Albanian boys with flowing hair, gold-embroidered clothes and bare feet. It was the presence of these attendants, perhaps, that caused Cockerell to regard Mukhtar's court as 'a sad blackguard affair'. The visitors had formed no very favourable idea of their host, having heard that he was brutal and debauched, had most of Ali's vices and none of his virtues but bravery, was avaricious like his father but much less generous, and had several beautiful Italian girls in his harem who had either been kidnapped or bought from their parents. However, he welcomed them cordially, and though rather rough seemed open and good-humoured. He certainly had none of his father's charm and little of his father's acuteness, but was very civil. His talk, as usual, was dull, but as he sat on his divan, with a number of snuff-boxes and mechanical singing-birds beside him, he kindly promised to take the visitors out for a shoot one day on the lake.

Their next call was at Veli's palace to meet his son Mehmet, who had so much interested Byron. They found him as dignified as ever: his face was charming, his voice was sweet, his manners were beautiful, and he showed good sense in conversation, for he said he would like to visit England. The next morning they went to see the Kiosk. At the entrance to the gardens some Skipetars were quartered and a leopard was kept in a cage, but it was so tame that it was often allowed loose in the yard. The sight of an Anglican clergyman, however, was too much for it, and the Skipetars had to give it a large piece of meat to calm it down. The visitors duly admired the Kiosk with its musical fountain, and were interested to learn that it had been the scene of a grand dinner given on gold plate by Ali to the Earl of Guilford.

The mention of Guilford compels a digression. That enthusiastic philhellene had founded a university at Corfu, and his predilection for professors and students, thought Captain Robert Spencer of the Royal Navy, was a mania, 'such as that of some men for horses, others for dogs, or others, again, for rare books . . .' 'Lord Guilford is here,' wrote Napier once from Corfu, 'a queer fish, but very pleasant. He dined with Sir Thomas (Maitland) and entered the room at the head of twelve little men, professors, in black, with powdered heads, bandy legs, cocked hats under their short arms, and snuff-boxes in hand. They "louted low", flinging and scraping their little crooked legs about with great formality; then waddling, each to a chair . . . . stuffed their dirty coloured handkerchiefs into their pockets, and sat silent, though brimful of snuff and Greek, and hoping to be full of dinner and claret. Ogling the door they remained until grub was announced, and then such scraping, such bowing, such Greek, Italian, French and German compliments! All the Greeks would speak Italian, the Italians English, the English French and Italian mixed, and the French all the five languages together. The twelve waiters were of different nations, and each endeavoured to speak every tongue but his own. Babel and the confusion of tongues. Lord

Guilford was very pleasant, addressing every person in a different language, and always in that which the person addressed did not understand.' Then rather later, 'Lord Guilford . . . goes about dressed up like Plato, with a gold band round his mad pate and flowing drapery of a purple hue. His students' dress is very pretty, and said to be taken from ancient statues'. 'It consisted of a tunic and chlamys.' (I quote the late Mr. Ferriman.) 'The students were coifed with the petasos of Hermes and shod with . . . buskins of red leather reaching to mid-leg. It was the garb of the *epheboi* of ancient Athens. The professors bound fillets round their heads. The Faculties were distinguished by the colour of their garments. Medicine had the tunic citron and the chlamys orange; Law, the tunic light green and chlamys violet; Philosophy, tunic green and chlamys blue.' Naturally enough, gossip about Guilford and his fancy dress university caused a good deal of merriment in London: Byron had yet to die to make philhellenism generally acceptable. 'It was the normal and obvious view throughout Europe,' says Mr. Mavrocordato, 'to regard the Greeks simply as rebellious subjects of the Sultan', and the philhellenes as 'cranks in advance of their time'. Hearing of his eccentricities, Guilford's sister, Lady Lindsay, wrote to say she feared for his health in a garb to which he was not accustomed. He replied that he was never in better health, and the dress was so comfortable that if he were younger he would sleep in it. . . .

It is not to be supposed that Hughes and his companions omitted to go and see Pouqueville, who still had his brother living with him. Poor Pouqueville, he had nothing to do, for French interests at Jannina had for some time been non-existent, and there was nothing to keep him there except the fact that the French were still in occupation of Corfu. He cultivated his garden, getting flowers from Paris, and was, let us hope, consoled to some extent by his housekeeper, a young widow who had been turned into the street when her husband died, leaving no heir and consequently forfeiting his estate to the Vizier. Since Ali had forbidden Pouqueville all intercourse with his subjects the Frenchman's existence was pretty secluded, and he may well have been at times bored and irritable, but Hughes (unlike Byron and Hobhouse) found him very polite, generous and humane, and thought him a scholar and man of the world, 'nor did that contest in which our respective countries were engaged, in the slightest degree repress his hospitality and attentions' – an instance of good manners which would be surprising in the hate-ridden world of to-day. On Cockerell the brothers Pouqueville made a much less pleasing impression. Perhaps he thought they did not take enough notice of him, or perhaps because he was a little too English, or perhaps because it was true, he thought them both 'the worst type of Frenchmen – vulgar, bragging, genuine children of the Revolution', and as for their conversation, 'nothing worth remembering was said'.

The visitors wanted to see something of the surrounding country and went to pay a second call on Ali before setting out. This time he received them in the Castro, which they entered over a drawbridge, noticing the entrance to the Buldrun and passing through the miserable ghetto. Ali received them in a large saloon. He was sitting on the divan and smoking a hookah, and an open book lay face down beside him. His welcome was as gracious as ever. He expressed great surprise, perhaps not untinged with irony, that Parker, an only son, should leave his home and friends and pleasures to wander in such desolate uncivilized countries, and blamed his mother for allowing him to leave England. He next gave his attention to the hat that Hughes was holding, asked if he might handle it, and said what a good hat it was. When a troop of Gany-medes came in with pipes and coffee, he ordered them to fire off from the balcony a brace of pistols which the travellers had given him, and was very pleased with the loud report they made. 'A most agreeable old man he is,' thought Cockerell, who was 'more than ever struck with the easy familiarity and perfect good humour of his manners.'

CHAPTER XXV

A WILD PARTY

MUKHTAR did not forget that he had promised the visitors a little sport on the lake, and a shoot was duly organized. When the morning came, the guns set off in no less than a hundred boats (called for some reason *monoxyla* though they were not made of one piece of wood) and there was a great deal of excitement as the birds rose in clouds, with hundreds of eagles and vultures soaring over them and screaming with delight at the sight of so much prey. The sun was shining brightly, there was snow on the mountains, the villages with their white houses and cypresses were reflected in the water, and the air was full of the rush of wings and the echo and re-echo of the shooting. Mukhtar enjoyed himself as much as anybody: he was a very good shot, and it was said that when on horseback at full gallop he could hit a hare. Ali came out in his state barge to watch the sport but took no part in it, and soon afterwards the wind rose and the water grew choppy, so Mukhtar took his guests off to the island, where he had ordered dinner. Everything was very neat and clean, and everybody ate from the same dish, using their fingers. There were pilaffs and stews, boiled and fried fish, fowls and pastry, amounting to about thirty dishes in all, and the wine was poured out by a long-haired young Ganymede. Afterwards, while Mukhtar had a siesta, the Englishmen strolled about the village, and were pleased to find it all clean and tidy and the people cheerful. The evening was fine and clear, and they returned to the city in the best of humours, listening to the songs of the boatmen and watching the reflections of the lights of the Castro in the water.

After this it rained for several days, and they spent a good deal of time with Pouqueville and Foresti, but when the weather cleared up again Mukhtar gave them leave to go and shoot in a specially preserved part of the lake, and Parker had the luck to bag a *thalassopouli*, or bird of the sea: it was twice as big as a duck, had a superb tuft of scarlet feathers on its head, and its wings were mottled with purple and white. In the evening, when they were returning to Jannina by moonlight, Hughes thought he would like to row round the Castro, and while his boat was passing it he heard a sudden splash, as if something heavy had fallen into the water.

'What was that?' he asked Nicolo, who was with him.

'Oh, I suppose some incontinent lady tied up in a sack and chucked away.'

Hughes at once had the boat turned and made chivalrously for the spot where the splash seemed to have been, but the water was very deep just there and nothing could be done.

Another evening, as it was the carnival season, they got into fancy dress – Nicolo as an English officer, Parker as a Turk and Hughes as an old Greek lady, and made a round of visits. In one house Hughes was sitting with a large party of women, when a fine young girl called Alexandra, who had been staring at him for some time, suddenly called out 'It's a man!' and the whole party 'scampered off as if they had been stung by a gad-fly'.

The capital was full of troops. They had been pouring in for the last month, and were billeted everywhere on the citizens, who found them a considerable nuisance, but had no choice in the matter. An old Turkish gentleman, with whom Parker had played some games of chess, had had no fewer than fifty Skipetars to support, and they had broken every window in his house, smashed all his furniture, chopped up his portico for firewood, and obliged him to stay bottled up in his harem. One morning Ali reviewed his troops: that is to say, the soldiers stood or strolled about chatting, or lay on the ground; there was no drilling or attempt at a march past, but the men's names were called over, and anybody who had a grievance was allowed to bring it to Ali, who sat in a small room with large heaps of money by him and a secretary to dole it out.

About the middle of the month he paid the English visitors a tremendous compliment. They were just finishing dinner one evening when a messenger came with an invitation from Ali for them to go to a party which he was giving immediately at the house of a Signor Alexi and to dine with him at his own table. They could hardly believe their ears, for no foreigner but Lord Guilford had ever been honoured by the Vizier in this way before – not even Sir John Stuart, the hero of Maida, or General Airey, the governor of the Ionian Islands – and although the prospect of having to eat a second dinner might well have alarmed them, they were so excited by the invitation that they were quite ready to eat till they burst. As soon as they were dressed, they followed the messengers.

All the approaches to Alexi's house were crowded with Skipetars and all sorts of people in the Vizier's retinue. The rooms were brilliantly lighted, and a great clashing of cymbals and banging of drums was taken to mean that the potentate was already present. In the anteroom a band was playing, and a troop of dancing-boys, very effeminately dressed in flowing petticoats of crimson silk with silver girdles round their waist, were busy performing, and 'twisting their pliant bodies into the most contorted figures and lascivious gestures' they waved their arms and sometimes bent right back till their long hair swept the ground.

207

The guests were ushered into the banqueting room, and the first person they saw was Ali, who was sitting on the silk cushions of the divan. Next to him was an old Turkish nobleman of the most venerable appearance, with a white beard six inches longer than Ali's, and near him the archbishop of Jannina and two other church dignitaries. Signor Alexi, the owner of the house, then advanced with the Englishmen, and Ali invited them to sit on the divan at his right: he was very gay and kept making jokes, which were received with peals of laughter.

'And do people in England wear beards?' he asked, turning to Hughes, and stroking his own.

'Only the Jews,' replied Hughes, and at that Ali did not know whether to smile or frown.

The old white-bearded Turk, however, sat very dignified and silent, without the vestige of a smile on his face. His name was Mazout Effendi, and he lived in Constantinople, but usually came to spend a few months every year with Ali, with whom he was a great favourite, for this reason, that there was a very striking contrast between his extreme gravity when sober and his extraordinary gaiety when drunk, so that when he was in Jannina Ali would not go to any entertainment without him.

The proceedings began with a ceremonious washing in warm water poured from a silver pitcher by the lady of the house. Then rich scarves were put over the shoulders of the guests and they were given napkins so stiff with embroidery as to be perfectly useless. A fine silk shawl was spread over Ali's knees, which he graciously stretched out till it also covered the knees of Messrs. Hughes and Parker. After hors d'œuvres consisting of fruit and sweets, a thick soup appeared, into which Ali was the first to dip his spoon, a wooden one. Next came a roast lamb, eaten with the fingers, and then some partridges. With an air of great condescension, Ali with his own hands deposited one of them on Parker's plate and one on Hughes's, but before they could get their teeth into them the birds were snatched up by the far from clean fingers of the Skipetars in attendance who pulled them to pieces and very carefully and politely put them back on the plates. Dish followed dish – there were eighty-six altogether – and many of them were highly seasoned, the ragouts and piquant sauces being particularly appreciated. Perhaps the plainest was a baklava of pastry mixed with honey and pistachio nuts. In any case, every dish had to be at least tasted.

The Ganymedes had been taking the wine round, with special attention to old Mazout, and after a while he began to show the first faint signs of animation. He turned round and opened a window behind him, which gave on the anteroom, and joined in a chorus with the band that had been playing and singing there all the time. Ali ordered that he should be given a lot more to drink, and encouraged the others to drink as well – perhaps he even hoped to get the Englishmen to let themselves go a little, though he drank little himself.

And then old Mazout came to life. He suddenly let out a shout at the top of his voice, and began to sing doubtful songs in Turkish; he rolled on the divan and wrenched off his turban, and the sight of his bald head caused shouts of laughter, in which all the attendants joined. Then he called the dancing-boys to come in from the anteroom, and snatching a tambourine from them jumped and capered about like an old Silenus. Then he tried to catch one of the boys, but the boy was very supple and quick and eluded him, so the old nobleman fell flat on the floor amid shouts of joy. Then he got up again and rushed up to Ali, put his arm round the Vizier's neck and half suffocated him as he kissed him all over the face and chest, calling him by the most affectionate names. Then he rushed back to the boys, and seizing hold of their leader nearly stifled him too with kisses, then dragged him up to the divan, and wheedling a handful of small gold coins from Ali wetted them with spittle and stuck them like spangles all over the boy's face.

Ali felt that the moment had come to propose the health of the Regent and all the English Royal Family, which was duly honoured, and Hughes and Parker then drank to Ali's prosperity and (with their tongues in their cheeks) to the memory of Pyrrhus. Hughes then tactfully proposed the toast, not of Mukhtar or Veli, but of Sali Bey, Ali's youngest son, then much in favour. He followed this with a conversational opening, but Mazout got up just then to sing a comic song: before he could finish it his old legs failed him, he over-balanced, fell off the divan, and rolled under the table. However he managed to struggle to his feet, and pushed his arm through a pane of glass behind him. This was received with great applause, and with loud laughter from Ali, whom Mazout again rushed to embrace. He then broke every single remaining pane in turn with either his hands or his feet, pausing each time to embrace Ali before smashing the next one.

When Ali felt inclined to declare the party over, several Skipetars preceded him with long wax tapers to the head of the stairs, where he paused for a few moments to say good-bye to his guests. At the outer door several hundreds of Skipetars were waiting with a fine Arab horse: Ali vaulted into the saddle and rode off at a gallop towards the Litharitza Palace followed by the whole crowd, some on horses and some on foot, rushing along, shouting, and waving torches. No wonder that Hughes remarked to Parker, as they turned home in the sudden silence of the night, that it all seemed like a dream.

It is amusing to think that the evening may have afforded Hughes some inspiration for a prize poem that he wrote later at Cambridge. The subject was Belshazzar's Feast, and the poem inspired that picture by Martin which, in steel engraving, was a familiar ornament in many a Victorian home.

CHAPTER XXVI

'I WANT PARGA'

THE wild party was not the last of Hughes's adventures, nor did he see Ali there for the last time. He paid a visit to the ruins of Gardiki, where 'no living beings disturbed the solitude, but serpents, owls and bats. A chilly kind of sensation, like the fascination of some deadly spell, benumbs the senses, and almost stops the respiration of him who treads, as it were, upon the prostrate corpse of a great city . . . and while the deep silence is broken only by the breeze sighing in the ruins and the funereal cypresses which here and there wave over them, he almost expects to meet a spectre at every step'. In Jannina a night or two later there was anything but a deep silence: in fact he had great trouble in getting to sleep, for the carnival season was not yet over and drunken gaieties went on almost till daybreak. Just as Hughes was beginning to doze off, the most fearful shrieks were heard in the house, as if a pig were being killed. Hughes and everybody else rushed to see what was the matter, and it was found that the shrieks were proceeding from Nicolo's mother. When she saw Hughes and Parker she ran to them howling and crossing herself and begged them to interfere on her behalf with Ali. They asked why. The Vizier, she said, had sent her a present of ten kilos of wheat. They looked at each other in bewilderment, thinking she must be either mad or oddly ungrateful, but it was at once explained to them that the old lady was only too reasonable, for the *present* had to be paid for at double the market price, and the messenger who had brought it was waiting below for the cash. This was an example of a common custom of Ali's, especially at times when he wanted to raise funds for a campaign.

There was only one campaign that interested him at present: a second attack had already been made on Aya and had been repulsed, and now he was busy making preparations on a large scale to try and seize Parga. He had assembled 7000 men at Margariti under Omer Bey Vrioni, and Jannina itself was swarming with Skipetars.

When Hughes got up on the morning of February 21st, 1814, he noticed a great commotion in the city, and it was obvious that the Vizier was mobilizing his forces. In every open space could be seen multitudes of Skipetars dashing about in the keen morning air 'like wolves in search of prey', looking 'wildly picturesque' in their fleecy capotes and brilliant costume, and 'strutting in martial pride, as if they disdained to touch the earth'. It is clear that Ali meant business, for presently he himself went by on his way out of the city, riding in his old German carriage and escorted by a bodyguard of five hundred Skipetars. His harem followed soon after – in 'hen-coops on wheels' – and it was thought highly advisable to keep out of its way, for anybody who tried to get a peep at the hens was liable to be cut down where he stood by the sabres of the guards . . . At dinner that evening Pouqueville confirmed the rumour: Ali was off to Parga.

The Vizier did not go in person with his troops to the attack, but stayed at Preveza, awaiting news of its effect with the greatest eagerness, and planning a triumphal entry into the town he had so long coveted. The Skipetars marched on Aya, took it, and advanced on Parga, which was only defended by Colonel Nicole and a few hundred men. But how it was defended! The Skipetars, numerous, over-confident, ill disciplined and worse organized, were met not only by cannon fire from the citadel but by a tremendous fusilade of musket fire which the Parghiots kept up 'from the depths of clusters of orange trees, where the eye of the Turk could not discover them, and from gardens shaded by citrons entwined with garlands of roses and jasmine' – so says Pouqueville, forgetting perhaps that the month was February, when the garlands of roses and jasmine would hardly be at their best. That, however, is a trifling point beside the fact that the attacking Skipetars lost their nerve and retreated in disorder, leaving behind them more than a hundred dead.

When Ali heard the news he went off, as might have been expected, into one of his paroxysms of uncontrollable anger. He rolled on his divan, now sobbing with rage, now roaring like a wild beast.

'What!' he cried. 'Sixty Frenchmen have managed to hold Parga!'

Having calmed down a little, he sent for Foresti, who was with him in Preveza, and pleaded for English help. But Foresti was afraid that if Ali got hold of Parga he would not leave a single inhabitant alive, so he quietly arranged with General Campbell, now in command of the English army of occupation in the Ionian Islands, that if the French made any move towards abandoning Parga the English should immediately step in. The Parghiots, thoroughly frightened by their narrow escape, had immediately approached the English on their own account, and a conference was held on the island of Paxos between a deputation from Parga on the one hand and General Campbell's representative, supported by the commanding officers of the frigates *Bacchante* and *Savannah*, on the other, as a result of which it was arranged that Parga should come under English protection. The English did not agree to this out of pure charity for, as Captain Hoste of the *Bacchante* wrote on March 22nd, turning the French out of Parga 'would considerably distress Corfu'.

The Union Jack was now hoisted in the town of Parga, but Hoste sent word that unless it was flown as well from the citadel (still under the command of Nicole) he would consider the agreement broken and would set sail, leaving Parga to an unpleasant fate. Nicole was thinking of blowing up the citadel, and the Parghiots realized that if they were going to do anything they would have to do it quickly. Fortunately they got hold of a widow who was employed in the citadel as a servant, and when she was returning there from her evening out they made her hide a Union Jack under her skirt: it was duly hoisted, and the English approached at night and occupied the town. The French garrison in the citadel were taken by surprise and obliged to surrender, and the English took possession of the place in the name of King George. It may be imagined what effect this news had on Ali: the very first thing he did was to tell Pouqueville that he would be pleased to help the French at Corfu (now being blockaded by the English) by sending them supplies.

One afternoon, when the Vizier was back in Jannina, Pouqueville and his brother came to call on him in the Castro Palace. Admitted by the guards, who had so often let them in before, they walked slowly through the great reception hall, over the magnificent carpets. The blinds had been drawn, and in the dim light could be seen the gilding on the walls, the arabesques and trophies of arms. There was no one else in the room, but there were a number of nightingales in cages of green gauze, and they were all singing as if, said Pouqueville, 'they were in the depths of a moonlit forest. We walked carefully, hardly daring to breathe, for fear they might stop singing, and when we passed into another room there were nightingales singing there as well . . .' All at once they saw Ali reclining on a leopard skin in the corner of a divan covered with cashmeres. He smiled and held out his hand: the nightingales had put him in a soft and dreamy mood.

'Vizier, you seem happy,' said the younger Pouqueville.

'Yes, I am. It's so delightful to listen to these charming birds. Perhaps I should always be happy if I could only do what I like . . . Do you know, there's a peasant woman in my harem who sings the old songs that remind me of my young days. Her singing takes me back to my native mountains. My life was carefree enough once. What a time my friends and I used to have when we stole a kid from the shepherds and cooked and ate it on our own! Or when I went to my friends' weddings: I used to play the mandoline better than anybody. I could dance and wrestle with the best of them; but that time won't come back again, and at this other end of life I see nothing but family troubles and who knows what else . . . Perhaps I shan't have the happiness of dying on the mat that belonged to my ancestors. I keep it here always: it reminds me that I was born poor, and that I've suffered.' Then, getting up suddenly, he said, 'Ah well, if need be, I'll know how to face things out to the bitter end'.

Having reminded himself that he was getting old, he returned to his obsession and spoke of Parga.

Pouqueville grew diplomatic:

'Why worry so much about Parga? Perhaps even if you got it, it would only bring you bad luck.'

'Why should it? I defy it to do that. If I can only build a house on that bit of rock, that'll make up for everything. Every man carries on his forehead the irrevocable mark of his fate, and what is written must happen. I want Parga. What, do you think I ought to be frightened of being the master of Parga? *I want Parga!*'

Soon after this, Hughes had his last interview with the Vizier.

'Do tell me something,' said Ali, 'about the people who used to live in Epirus in ancient times. You English travellers are really extraordinarily well informed about things of that sort.'

Hughes did his best, at some length.

'You mentioned Pyrrhus just now,' said Ali. I should like to know more about him. Those elephants, now, that he used in war,' and here he laughed, 'do you imagine they'd be any good against my Skipetars?'

'Well,' said Hughes tactfully, 'of course warfare has rather altered since Pyrrhus's time. There are firearms now. But we use a lot of elephants in India, you know.'

He went on to speak of the Romans.

'And you mean to say,' Ali exclaimed, 'that the empire of the world has been twice fought for in my dominions? I've heard that there was once a great victory near Preveza, but I'd no idea it was as important as that . . . But now let's talk about your country. I suppose there's nothing to prevent your King having his own way in everything, cutting off people's heads and so on?'

'King George has no more power to cut off the head of one of his subjects than the subject has to cut off *his* – unless he has committed a capital crime.'

'Well, well, how odd!'

'And further, a member of the royal family or even the king himself can be sued in a court of law.'

Ali burst out laughing. No doubt he had never heard of Charles I, but it would scarcely have surprised him to learn that when this sovereign was tried by his subjects they cut his head off.

'But tell me,' he said. 'How does your king get his income? What does he live on?'

'His people vote as to how much he shall have, and then grant it to him of their own free will.'

217

At that the Vizier shook his head: perhaps he was wondering what his own income would be in similar circumstances. The whole story was almost incomprehensible to him, and he began to deplore his lack of education.

'You've done better,' said Hughes, making prudent and guileful use of parsonic soft soap, 'by studying mankind. In England we think more of your abilities than if you had been a philosopher. And that's why Mr. Parker and I came to Jannina instead of going to Constantinople.'

CHAPTER XXVII

1 8 1 6

WHEN the French general in command at Corfu heard of the entry of the Allies into Paris he found himself somewhat embarrassed. He was without instructions from home, short of money and hard put to it to pay his troops, most of whom were Italian or Albanian mercenaries, and at the same time trying to hold off the English, so he must have been very much relieved when a French squadron arrived from Toulon to take him and his garrison away, leaving the English to replace him. With the departure of the French from the Ionian Islands and from Dalmatia as well there was little point in their maintaining a consul at Jannina, so Pouqueville, after all his trying times, asked if he might be moved and was rewarded with a transfer to Patras.

Napoleon having met his Waterloo, and the Ionian Islands having come formally under English protection, the question of what was to happen to Parga again became acute. The Parghiots wrote to Sir Thomas Maitland, the new English High Commissioner at Corfu, complaining that the Treaty of Paris, which settled the new status of the Ionian Islands, made no mention at all of Parga; the Porte asked that in return for their consenting to that status Parga should be ceded to the Turkish Empire; and Ali naturally supported this claim to the utmost, sending an envoy to London, and to Maitland some handsome presents. Maitland in return sent him a young lion which he had been given and which he found a nuisance to keep. It was, he thought, a royal gift, particularly suitable for the Lion of Jannina, so he sent off the beast and a civil letter at the same time. Ali smiled when he got them, and is said to have dictated the following reply:

'The Vizier assures the Lord High Commissioner of his high consideration. He is in no want of lions, but will be pleased to accept this one, if Sir Thomas will be good enough to allow him to let it loose upon the inhabitants of Parga.'

In a report to Castlereagh at the Congress of Vienna, Sir Richard Church had suggested not only that the English should hold on to Parga, but that Vonitza, Preveza and Butrinto should be taken from Ali and put under English protection in order to ensure the safety of the Ionian Islands. 'Ali Pasha,' he wrote, knowing well what he was talking about, 'is now busy building forts along his coasts and strengthening his castles in the interior. In January 1814 he had 14,000 peasants at work on the castle of Argyro Castro and about 1500 erecting a fort . . . nearly opposite Corfu.' But it seems that the English, whether from indifference, or because they had made a promise, or because it was now part of their policy to support the Turkish Empire against the influence of Russia, had little intention of doing anything but agree to the cession of Parga. Perhaps if Maitland had been an enthusiastic philhellene like Church or Byron, to say nothing of Guilford, he could have taken a firm stand and stopped any such proceeding, but he had little or no sympathy with the Greeks. He said more than once that the Greeks were not worth all the trouble that was being taken over them, and that their state of subservience was probably the best thing for them.

Maitland was hardly a figure to inspire confidence and hope in the oppressed. Tall, and of an exceptional ugliness, his nickname at Corfu was The Abortion. He had brusque manners, a worried expression, and a raucous voice. Sir Charles Napier, who admittedly disliked him, said that he was 'narrow-minded, saw many things under false lights, was constantly drunk, and surrounded by sycophants', though amongst them were 'some good men' including Lord Sydney Osborne, who 'had no fault save that denounced by a witty Irishman, namely that he thought the sun rose and set in Sir Thomas Maitland's hinder disk!' The English called Maitland King Tom on account of his autocratic ways, and indeed he was an arrogant and domineering governor of a type not unknown in those days (Lord Charles Somerset was another example) but now happily rarer.

This, then, was the being on whom the Parghiots had mainly to rely, and it is not to be wondered at if they were martyrs to anxiety.

> 'On Suli's rock and Parga's shore, [wrote Byron]
> Exists the remnant of a line
> Such as the Doric mothers bore. . . .'

and a great many attempts were made by the liberally inclined to prove that Parga was an earthly paradise and its inhabitants the proper denizens of such a place. What is certain is that Parga had been free from the Turks ever since 1447, when it came under the Venetians; that it was the only place on the coast of Epirus to hold out against Ali; and that the people were full of the wilful independence natural to citizens of a tiny republic, especially one so situated. It was a pleasant and prosperous place, with olive trees as fine as those of Corfu, and groves of oranges and citrons, the fruit of the latter being gathered green and exported to Trieste or the Jews in Poland. The men tended to be well built, long lived and good tempered. The women, often handsome, wore jackets trimmed or embroidered with gold, and long pleated skirts; cords of red silk were twined in their hair, which they did up gracefully, and travellers particularly admired them as they went every day to draw water at the public fountain, carrying elegant vases on their heads (a proceeding which kept their backs straight and showed off their figures to advantage), and smiling and gossiping. Some of their customs were admirable. For instance, they had a very sensible system of what may be called companionate engagement. When two young people became closely attached and formally engaged to one another, the prospective bride went to stay in the paternal home of her lover. After a year, if all was well, the lovers still pleased with each other and the girl not too irritated by her relations-in-law-to-be, or vice versa, the engagement was ratified and the wedding soon celebrated: otherwise it was broken off.

While the fate of the Parghiots remained in doubt and the subject of long-drawn-out negotiations, there were a number of interesting happenings in Epirus. At the beginning of 1816 Ali was visited by Gustav Adolf, the dethroned king of Sweden, who was on his way to Palestine and had come to Preveza to get a passport for the journey. Ali, who had lately obtained six pearls said to have been the largest in Europe, bought some splendid diamonds from him and was given in return a sword that had belonged to Charles XII. With the jewels he formed a star to wear on his breast, in imitation of one worn by Maitland, and called it his 'order'.

The Vizier's policy in internal affairs continued as capricious and ruthless as ever. For some reason he decided to blot out the people of Khimara, but having no good excuse and hesitating to order a massacre, he decided to expatriate them instead, so they were driven out in winter and forced to go and live in a marshy and malarial district, and people were brought from Preveza and Thessaly to replace them. Then the district of Zagori, not far from Jannina, was turned into a feudal domain and its freeholders into serfs, as an inheritance for Ali's youngest son Sali.

In Jannina there was an odious display of religious prejudice. A Neapolitan engineer in charge of Ali's artillery, Carretto by name, had for some time been engaged in a secret love affair with a nineteen-year-old Turkish girl named Gelisem. They had been enabled to meet by the help of a Jew, who acted as go-between. Gelisem discovered that she was pregnant, and Carretto said he was willing to marry her, which could probably have been arranged if she had turned Christian or he Mohammedan. But before anything could be settled they were betrayed by the Jew. Gelisem was sentenced to death. She was insulted and led through the town with her face exposed to the public gaze, her hair was taken down and her clothes were torn off, she was made to enter a hole dug in the ground, and then slowly stoned to death. Carretto was flogged and sent to be imprisoned at Argyro Castro where the plague was raging. Some fanatical Mohammedans demanded his life, and in order to quieten them Ali spread a report that he had been executed.

Carretto's place as master of the ordnance was taken by a Strasbourg Jew named Samson Cerfbeer de Medelsheim, who had turned Mohammedan and entered Ali's service under the name of Ibrahim Mansur Effendi. Ali 'threw honey' at this individual and was altogether very flattering.

'I am called Ali Pasha,' he said, 'and I know how to make the fortune of anybody who serves me faithfully and well: nor will you be the first person that I've put in a position that would be envied by the grandees of Constantinople.'

The delighted Mansur was told to report for orders in four days' time. Strolling about in the bazaar he met a number of destitute European adventurers, each of whom told a disturbing tale about being held in the country against his will and cheated of what was due to him. Amongst them was Vincenzo Micarelli, a Neapolitan ex-priest who lived with two prostitutes, a mother and daughter. Then there was the French carpenter Michel, who remarked cheerfully that once in Jannina one could never escape.

'But,' protested Mansur, 'how can you prevent a man from travelling in a country where there are no passports, registers, prefectures, or hotels?'

'But there *are* passports,' said Michel. 'Nobody can get abroad without a passport sealed with Ali's own seal. You're liable to be asked for your papers at any time, and if you can't produce them you're dragged before Ali. If you happen to have lost your passport, you're accused of having sold it to somebody else who is trying to escape, and then you're tortured either to get a confession or money out of you. If you give neither, you get put in chains in the Buldrun, and if you're caught trying to escape they just cut your head off, and that's that.'

In order to make Mansur contented, Ali offered to find him a wife, a favour which he refused, and to provide him with a house, which he also refused, because a widow with two daughters would have had to be turned out of it to make room for him. However he accepted a pelisse, a horse, and various other things, and was well received by the Moslems in Ali's household, though the Greeks disliked and plotted against him.

One evening Ali asked him to supper. On his way into the palace he saw a very strange scene. It was the season of Ramazan, when small bags of paras were given as alms to the poor women of the town, who came to the gate of the palace to receive this charity. The proceedings were nothing but a cruel practical joke. The distribution of the money was in the hands of the Ganymedes, who kept the women, already weak from fasting, waiting at the gate, however bad the weather, as long as they chose. At last they came out with a retinue of Skipetars armed with long sticks. Then everything possible was done to provoke quarrels amongst the women, with the result that they soon began to fight, the strong trampling on the weak to try and get near the money, and some getting their veils and even their clothes torn off in the stampede. When the confusion was at its height the Skipetars charged in and began to beat the women with their sticks until they screamed and sometimes until they were severely hurt. The Ganymedes then threw out some of the money and keeping a good part of it for themselves went in laughing.

At supper Mansur ate very little, and excused his want of appetite by saying that he was upset by what he had just seen. He did not know that the whole proceeding was got up for Ali's own amusement, and that the Vizier had been sitting in a latticed window to watch it. Directly they were alone, Ali leaned over to him and said:

'Ibrahim Effendi, at present you're too unfamiliar with my court to know how to behave yourself, but as I love you as if you were my own son I'll give you a bit of advice, and that is, mind your own business, or you'll perhaps find that the Big Snake can bite.'

Another time, when Mansur ventured to make an allusion to Ali's severity towards his subjects, Ali said:

'You don't yet know the Greeks and Albanians. When I hang a man on the plane tree, brother robs brother under the very branches. If I burn a man alive, his son is ready to steal the father's ashes to sell them. It is their fate to be ruled by me, and no one but Ali can keep them in order.'

The day after the supper, Mansur was taken to see some powder mills recently built near the lake, and to give his opinion on some of the artillery and fortifications. Ali rode with him, and just when they were leaving an incident occurred which forms the subject of a poem by Victor Hugo.

As they rode out through the gate of the palace a large crowd of poor petitioners was driven back with sticks by the Skipetars. Only one, a dervish, was allowed to approach Ali. Being in a hurry, Ali asked the dervish to call in the evening and offered him a handful of small gold pieces, and asked him to pray for him. He then urged his horse forward, but the dervish had caught hold of the bridle and made Ali wait to hear his petition.

'Patience, my son,' cried Ali to Mansur, 'we shan't be kept waiting long.'

'Not long!' cried the dervish. 'How do you know that, you old sinner?'

And refusing the money and clinging on to the bridle he made a long speech. Ali looked up to heaven as was a trick of his when very annoyed.

'Oh, Ali, don't keep looking up like that! Look at the earth you came from, and to which you'll go back when Allah wills it.'

He then loosed the bridle, turned his back, and strolled away.

'My son,' said Ali, approaching Mansur, 'I may have my faults and I know they call me a tyrant, but I think I may really lay claim to one virtue which makes up for everything, and that is *patience*.'

Mansur remained in favour with Ali for some time, helping in military matters, drilling troops and so on, but the Greek secretaries worked against him and he fell out of favour, only being paid meanly and irregularly, so he asked for a passport to leave the country.

'No,' said Ali. 'I shan't let you go. Anybody who has once eaten my bread must stay with me for good. And I have the right to keep people in my dominions even against their will if I happen to need them, for all I do is for the benefit of

Islam and the injury of Christianity. If I commit crimes and
if I'm a tyrant, it's for the good of the Faith and the Empire.'

Mansur had been experimenting with the making of
explosives, and had evolved a powder consisting mostly of
chalk and gunpowder, which Colovo (who was jealous of him)
declared to contain arsenic and to be intended for poisoning the
Vizier: in making this accusation he was backed up by the ex-
priest Micarelli. Ali swore he would burn Mansur alive that
very evening, but Mansur was able to prove his innocence.

'All right,' said Ali. 'Then you can have any revenge
you like on Micarelli short of killing him. Sooner or later I'll
hang the dog, and nothing but one secret little reason keeps
me from burning him alive instead of you.'

The little reason, it appears, was that Micarelli, also a
dabbler in chemistry, was preparing a deadly but tasteless
poison for Ali to use against his enemies.

It may be recalled how Ali had spared the life of Vasiliki,
the coiner's daughter of Plichivitza. He had taken her into his
harem and made a great favourite of her, allowing her to
remain a Christian and to maintain a little oratory in the
palace where a Greek priest came to officiate. She had now
grown up to be, in the words of M. Remérand, 'a large and
beautiful woman with a white complexion, black eyes and
eyebrows, and a superb head of hair, and had succeeded in
retaining the Vizier's affections longer than any other member
of her sex, except Eminé, had succeeded in doing before. Ali
now decided to marry her, which he did with great circumstance, and Jannina was once more given over to wedding
festivities. The streets were choked with people and beasts of
burden carrying presents. Even the women of the poorest
villages brought a little honey or firewood: they were taken
into the palace and beaten to make them sing, while their
husbands waited for them outside. On the wedding day itself

two men announced that they had taken on their own heads all the misfortunes that fate might have in store for the Vizier, and threw themselves from a high tower into the courtyard below, both being severely injured. Ali graciously accorded them a minute pension and a daily ration of bread.

CHAPTER XXVIII

FIRE AT TEBELENI

As Ali grew older, richer and more experienced he did not become less cruel, less mean, or less superstitious. In 1817, when a Persian dervish who had been busy trying to find the elixir of life for him was prevented by death from bringing his attempt to a successful conclusion, Ali put up to him a fine mausoleum with a dome from which was hung a large silver lamp, and endowed in his memory an establishment of dervishes. Then a Greek from Salonica named Serio arrived to pursue the same line of inquiry. Among the ingredients he said he needed were large quantities of human blood and hair. The blood was easily obtained from the Ganymedes, but it was unthinkable that their crowning glory should be cut off, nor were the Skipetars more willing to part with theirs: a tyrant could cut off their heads if he liked, but not their hair. Before any hair could be obtained it was discerned that Serio was an impostor, and Ali had him hanged, with a list of his frauds nailed to his forehead. It is an ill wind that blows nobody any good, and very likely the bleeding did the Ganymedes no harm.

In the spring of 1818 Ali had a violent attack of 'the Lion's fever'. Whatever the precise medical significance of this complaint from which he suffered from season to season, it always brought him nearer than usual to madness, and he seemed only to find relief from it in frightful acts of sadism.

Blood follows blood, and through their mortal span,
In bloodier acts conclude those who with blood began.

This time his anger fell upon an Albanian who had robbed him of a large sum of money but had confessed and paid it all back: he had him thrown into a leopard's cage. The leopard showed no signs of ferocity, but fawned on the intruder, so Ali ordered that he should be taken out and hacked to pieces, the pieces to be thrown back into the cage. A Greek was thrown into a cauldron of boiling oil, and a Ganymede who had offended him was shot from the mouth of a cannon, his clothes having previously been soaked in inflammable spirit.

One morning, as the Vizier was leaving the palace, the dervish Yusuf barred his way, trembling with excitement, and cried out:

'Listen! Allah, who punished the wicked, has allowed your palace at Tebeleni to be burnt down! The world is perishable! Fire! Fire!'

Ali hurried off to Tebeleni as fast as he could to see if his treasures were safe, and fortunately for him the road between Jannina and his native place was one of the few in his dominions that were at all passable. Sali, it appeared, had been on a visit to his mother, the ex-slave, who lived at Tebeleni, and in the middle of the night there was a sudden alarm and the whole place seemed to be on fire. It was not known whether the outbreak was due to some carelessness or whether it had been caused by lightning, for there had been a storm on at the time. Ali's fury was so dreaded that everybody blamed the lightning. The women of the harem had tried to escape, but the eunuchs, armed with sabres, had driven them back, for they would rather have seen them burnt alive than exposed to the public gaze; however, the women had managed to get out of some windows and let themselves down to the ground. Ali found that his underground strong rooms and his tower were still intact, but a collection of furs and stuffs, watches and clocks, jewellery, furniture, arms and other objects had been destroyed. His first care was to try and think of a plan for rebuilding the palace without running into any expense, so he issued proclamations everywhere saying that the vengeance of heaven had fallen on him, and that he no longer had a home in the place of his ancestors, so he called on his 'loving' subjects to help him, and fixed a day for receiving their contributions.

On the appointed day Tebeleni was crowded with deputies from far and near, and at the outer gate of the palace Ali sat on a dirty mat, cross-legged and bareheaded, with a red Albanian cap in his hand, like any beggar waiting for alms. The old miser had hit on a cunning plan to squeeze his subjects. He had sent large sums of money beforehand to several of his poor retainers, and they now came forward and airily dropped them in the hat, as if they were giving presents. When therefore some important man came forward with a sum that Ali thought too small, the Vizier said:

'But look at these poor followers of mine. They've obviously made great sacrifices . . . And what good do you imagine this'll do me – me, a man afflicted by divine vengeance. No, no, take it back, you'd better stick to it and keep it for your own needs.'

This hint so alarmed the men of substance that they at once gave two or three times as much as they had first offered. And to the total thus collected Ali was soon able to add the wealth of the town of Arta, which had just been ravaged by the plague. He sent his representatives to catalogue and take over the possessions of the dead. The survivors were forced to wash the very bedclothes in the river and hand them over, and were even tortured to try and make them reveal where treasures were hidden. As a result of all this Ali was soon in a position to rebuild his palace at Tebeleni, and even after doing that found himself richer than before.

And he was now confident of Parga. Meetings had been held at Jannina between an English envoy sent by Maitland and a Turkish one by the Porte, and it had been settled that those of the Parghiots who wished to stay under English protection should be free to leave Parga and cross over to Corfu, and that they would be compensated for the loss of their homes and property. Naturally none of the Parghiots could forget what had happened at Suli, at Preveza, at Gardiki, and at Khimara, and they reluctantly agreed among themselves that they would be obliged to emigrate.

'What compensation,' they wrote, in a memorandum to the Anglo-Swiss Colonel de Bosset, temporarily in command of their town, 'could possibly make up to us for having to leave our native soil, to the independence of which our lives and families have been devoted: Where in the Ionian Islands can we find a place anything like so pleasant and prosperous? Nevertheless, obedient to our protectors, we resign ourselves, but with deep sorrow, to our fate, wishing thus to show our trust in our benefactors, the English nation, and we declare that we all wish to emigrate in order to escape the ferocities to which so many of our neighbours have fallen victims.'

An Anglo-Turkish commission was now appointed to value the real estate that was to be abandoned – more than 800 houses and the land attached to them, mostly planted with fine groves of olives, oranges, lemons and citrons. The Parghiots themselves made out that it was worth at least half a million pounds sterling, but Ali said he could not possibly pay so much. 'I hope,' he added, 'that many of the Parghiots will change their minds and decide to stay where they are. I think it would be a good thing if they were to be questioned individually.'

But the Parghiots had made up their minds, and the most that Ali could do was to arrange that a second valuation should be made by the Turkish and English commissioners acting independently. This revealed a great divergence of opinion. The English valuation, estimating the worth of the property as if it had been in Corfu, suggested £276,000 as a suitable sum; the Turkish valuation was only £57,000. In order to try and get the matter settled, Ali went down to Butrinto to confer with Maitland.

CHAPTER XXIX

ALI ENTERS PARGA

IT was now March 1819, and just before Ali left for Butrinto
there happened to arrive in Corfu a young French painter,
Louis Dupré, who had been a pupil of David: he had en-
countered in Italy three young Englishmen, Messrs. Hyett,
Hay and Vivian, who had asked him to go with them to
Greece. Dupré was delighted with Corfu, and thanks to his
companions and his own talents, social and otherwise, was
very civilly welcomed by some English officers of the garrison,
who entertained him to dinner, a meal which he found stylish
and gay, though long. His position as a guest made it difficult
for him to say that he would have preferrred the French occupation of the place to have continued, and he did not reveal
his real opinion of the English occupation, which seemed
beneficent enough, though in Corfu, 'as in all their colonies,
in Greece as elsewhere, the English do not hide their dislike
for everything which is not of their nation; their coldness
inspires constraint; their severity repulses affection; their
pride is offensive, their unsociability displeasing; but under
their authority the Corfiots have at least been able to resume
their customs, language and character . . . and this political
tolerance rarely fails to tell; for what men love best after
liberty is the semblance of it'. And had not a university been
started under *un homme vertueux, le lord comte de Guilford?*'
   There were some interesting types in the place, but none
more so than a number of picturesque Suliot refugees, who
were to be seen loafing about and gazing sadly over the sea
towards their distant mountains. Dupré very much wanted

to make some drawings of these people, and said so to a Greek servant who had been engaged as interpreter and factotum to his party. He rather feared, from the haughty and slightly *farouche* bearing of these exiled mountaineers that it might be difficult to get them to sit, but one morning the Greek servant brought two of them along. The first came somewhat abruptly into Dupré's room, but stood before him in a way at once so natural and so resolute that he asked him to keep still and began to draw him just as he stood. As soon as the drawing was done he showed it to the two Suliots. They were both very much struck by the likeness, and the model was very demonstrative and tried to convey by gestures his pleasure and astonishment. Then he suddenly took from his belt one of those little portable silver writing-sets which were often proudly carried by Albanians when just literate, and wrote his name at the side of his portrait, 'Photo of Suli'.

'What,' said Dupré, as soon as he saw the name, 'is he then some relation of the famous Photo Tzavellas and the heroine Moscho?'

Photo said he was, and while Dupré began drawing his companion he told some stories of the Suliot war. When he had finished, Dupré took Photo by the hand and wished him good luck and a happy return to his country, but perhaps Photo's feelings were too much for him, for he made no reply, and withdrew.

The two drawings were much admired by the English officers, and Maitland, getting to hear of them, asked to see them, and told Hay, who brought them, that he had better bring Dupré to Butrinto on the following day so that he could get a sight of Ali Pasha himself, Ali having chosen that place for the final conference on the subject of Parga. So next morning Dupré and his English companions set out in one of the light boats that followed in the wake of 'Sir Maitland', who was aboard the frigate *Glasgow*. Ismail, the son of Veli, came out in his barge, and was welcomed by Maitland with a salute of twenty-one guns. The frigate was gaily decked out with flags and bunting, and the yards were swarming with sailors who waved their caps in the air and cheered their guest probably without knowing exactly why – which caused Dupré to reflect rather pompously on the fact that 'the greatest maritime power in the world, one of the shining lights of civilization, was showing its respect and friendship for the family of an ex-bandit whom the oddness of fortune and the submissiveness of the Greeks had carried to the throne of Pyrrhus'.

Ismail, who was at this time barely twelve, behaved with the usual Turkish gravity and appeared remarkably indifferent to all the noise and circumstance, until somebody remarked to him that such a welcome was as a rule only given to royalties, when he condescended to smile faintly, and make a slight bow. When they had brought him up on to the quarter-deck, so that he could get a good view of the ship, he signed to an old functionary, the keeper of Ali's privy seal, and leaned his elbow nonchalantly on this individual's shoulder, while he puffed out clouds of smoke from a pipe. Dupré did not know which to admire most, 'the facility with which English arrogance lent itself to such a comedy' or 'the imperturbable bearing of the child', who was evidently not in the least upset by all the fuss. After further ceremony Ismail went off in his barge, and the foreigners soon followed, on their way to see the Vizier. To get to the fortress they had to pass through a large and undisciplined crowd of Skipetars, who were grouped here and there, without sentries, some eating, some smoking, and many asleep. The mixture of dirt and splendour and the confusion of ranks and costumes made a strong impression on Dupré, but most of all he was struck by the martial bearing and athletic build of the men, and by the bold, proud beauty of their heads which, he felt, needed only antique helmets to make them seem like the heads of the heroes in Homer.

Ali had no proper palace at Butrinto and the living rooms in the fortress lacked splendour. After ascending a narrow and rickety staircase his visitors were told that he was in a kind of kiosk in the middle of a long and clumsily built wooden gallery. In the first room they entered they saw Ismail again, sitting now with his elder brother Mehmet, both gravely smoking and taking very little notice of the new arrivals, who were now shown into the room where Ali was sitting. Like other foreigners, they had heard such fearful stories about him that they went in with some feeling of excitement.

Ali was sitting on a corner of the divan with Maitland and three Englishmen who had come out of curiosity. He replied to the bows of the extra guests by laying his hand on his breast, and asked them to sit down. The Ganymedes then brought coffee and pipes. Dupré, like others before him, had hardly expected this gentle and smiling face with the long white beard, and these simple and engaging manners, and he was astonished to find a man in his seventies so full of health and vigour, with such mobility of expression and such keen eyes. But alas, Ali had grown so fat that he could no longer cross his legs and sit in the orthodox Turkish way.

Maitland presented Dupré as a French painter travelling in Greece, and spoke of his drawings. Dupré had a portfolio with him, so he opened it and showed Ali the drawings of the two Suliots. When he saw the one of Photo, Ali uttered his characteristic guttural laugh and said, 'Oh, I know *him*! He's one of my enemies'. Maitland thought this a suitable moment to suggest to Ali that he, too, should let himself be drawn. But the only answer to this was an extremely wry smile, which could not be taken to mean anything like consent. Maitland therefore suggested that at any rate Dupré might be allowed to draw Ismail and Mehmet, and the Frenchman adjoined for that purpose. The boys were delighted, but while Dupré was at work a very cross old man kept giving him hostile looks and cursing him, and it was explained that he considered that by making images of the boys the foreigner was evidently out to bewitch or cast some spell over them. It was thought that some such reason had prevented Ali, so notoriously superstitious, from allowing his own portrait to be made. Mehmet was a charming and docile sitter, but Ismail less so. He had already some reputation for violence and was said to have chased one of his tutors with a loaded pistol for having attempted to correct him.

Dinner on the *Glasgow* enabled Dupré to get a good view of Maitland. Trained to admire classical models, he was unpleasantly affected by Maitland's ugliness, and indeed found him 'somewhat repulsive'.

A couple of days later Ali gave a grand shoot on the lake of Butrinto. Reclining on cushions in the stern of his barge he led the way, followed by Maitland, then by Dupré and his friends, then by several boats full of English officers, then by some containing musicians, then by a vast number of others full of Ali's retinue. They spread into an extended formation while five or six hundred beaters got busy in the undergrowth on the banks, screaming and making as much noise as they could to frighten the game. The scene was even more brilliant than Mukhtar's shoot on the lake at Jannina five years before. The sun shone brightly on the mountain sides and wooded hills, already touched with the fresh green of spring; the lake was full of reflections, and the boats came and went lightly over its surface, bearing all sorts of handsomely dressed people, while the air was full of music, and intermittent firing, and wandering echoes. Dupré's great moment was when he managed to get sufficiently near to Ali to make a drawing of him without the old man's knowledge. It was a little hurried, but Dupré considered that he had done well, and there seems no doubt that he succeeded in drawing the best portrait of Ali that exists. He noticed that Ali had by his side two richly dressed young men of the most perfect beauty; they were acting as loaders for their master, who was said to be a good shot, but did badly on this occasion.

Dupré had to have a second sitting in order to finish his very successful drawing of Ismail and Mehmet. Ismail was not at all pleased to observe that one side of his face had been made darker than the other. 'Can't you see,' he complained, 'that every part of my face is just as white as every other?'

As a result of the conference between Ali and Maitland the question of what the Parghiots should get for their property was finally settled. 'By the persevering exertions of the English,' says Finlay, 'the Porte paid to them £150,000, which was divided among them according to the valuation of their property. There is no doubt that the indemnity was most liberal, but many of the poorer classes, possessing no property, received no indemnity, and all who emigrated were loud in their complaints of the English policy, which had condemned them to exile.'

On March 15th Maitland issued a proclamation to signify that it was time for the Parghiots to get ready to depart. Now that the moment had come they were profoundly upset. They dug up the graves of their ancestors, burnt the bones on fires built of olive wood cut from their plantations, and declared that if any of Ali's troops were allowed to enter the town before they had left it they would with their own hands kill their women and children to save them from outrage. Maitland sent an officer to calm them down, and they were presently embarked for the Ionian Islands to the number of 4000.

When Ali's troops entered the town 'all was solitude and silence . . . nothing breathed, nothing moved; the houses were desolate, the nation was extinct, the bones of the dead were almost consumed to ashes, whilst the only sign that living creatures had been there was the smoke slowly ascending from the funereal piles'.

A few days later Ali himself arrived to enjoy the sensation of owning the place for which he had been intriguing for over twenty years. He had a country house built on a promontory which afforded a view all along the coast, and settled the town with Mohammedans.

It was expediency and not sentiment which had determined the English to act as they had done, but liberal opinion in England was outraged by what was considered, at the very least, a reactionary step, and continentals, particularly the French and the Greeks, lost no chance of raging against what they called this latest example of English perfidy, this betrayal of the weak to the strong and of the Cross to the Crescent.

CHAPTER XXX

THE AXE AT THE ROOT OF THE TREE

In 1820 Ali and his offspring held the pasahliks of Jannina, Trikkala, Elbassan, Lepanto, Delvino, Paramythia, Vallona, and Berat, where Mukhtar, not allowed the title of Pasha, still belonging to Ibrahim, was known as the Bey of Beys. Ibrahim was still alive, and Ali now kept him shut up in a dungeon beneath the grand staircase of the Castro Palace in order to have the pleasure of treading him underfoot, so to speak, every time he went up or down stairs. The Vizier's expenses were enormous, what with the maintenance of his army and his personal establishment, the sending of vast sums to Constantinople in the way of tribute, presents and bribes, and the building of forts, castle, country houses, mosques and even churches; but his wealth was even more enormous, consisting of accumulated cash (150 millions of piastres are said to have been moved from the strong rooms at Tebeleni at the time of the fire), besides jewellery, valuables, and landed property, with revenue pouring in from his hundreds of manors and domains, from taxes of all sorts, and the usual exactions and spoliations. But he was far from feeling secure. He could not be certain of keeping his wealth intact for his descendants, and he doubted in any case their ability to hold whatever he might leave them. Besides, he was growing old, and it was no doubt with a premonition of death and perhaps disaster that he remarked, 'Time has swung the axe into the root of the tree'. That was true, but it might be said that the wielder of the axe was none other than the predestined Ismail Pasho Bey, whom Ali had repeatedly tried to destroy.

In the course of his wanderings Ismail had arrived in Thrace, where he had attached himself to a local ruler, the Nazir of Drama. One day while a hunt was in progress and Ismail found himself separated from the rest of the party, a messenger arrived from the Sultan and asked him where he could find the Nazir. 'I am the Nazir,' said Ismail, and took him to an inn, where the messenger said he was carrying an order issued at the request of the Pasha of Jannina.

'Ah, from Ali!' exclaimed Ismail. 'Welcome, then! Ali's an old friend of mine. Now what can I do for him?'

'Your help is requested,' said the messenger, believing that he was speaking to the Nazir, 'in seeing that this order is carried out. There's a man supposed to be here in your service whose name is Ismail Pasho Bey. He's a disloyal subject, and his head must be cut off.'

'Ismail Pasho Bey? Yes, I know him well. But I must warn you that he'll be hard to catch. He's a brave, clever fellow and popular too. As a matter of fact, he may turn up here at any moment, and of course it wouldn't do for him to see you. And I don't think you'd better tell anybody who you are or what you're here for. We're only two hours' ride from Drama. Go and wait there. I shall be back this evening, and then we'll see what can be arranged.'

As soon as the messenger was out of sight Ismail went off as fast as he could in the opposite direction, fearing that the Nazir, who had not known him long, might have no scruples about cutting off his head. When he had gone a good way he sold his horse and arms to a Jew, disguised himself as a Bulgarian monk, and took refuge in a Serbian monastery in Macedonia, where he entertained the brothers with travellers' tales.

Directly Ali heard of Ismail's escape he accused the Nazir of having allowed it, but the Nazir easily exonerated himself by giving the Porte a true account of what had happened. Through his spies Ali was able to find out where Ismail was hiding, and at once hatched another plot against him, choosing Athanasi Vaya as his instrument this time. First of all he put Athanasi in disgrace, an act which astonished Jannina, for he was known to be one of Ali's oldest and best-tried favourites. There was a terrible scene in public, and shouting that he had a good mind to hang him Ali banished him with a flow of curses. Athanasi, pretending to be terrified and greatly distressed, begged Mukhtar to intercede for him, with the result that he was allowed to go into exile in Macedonia instead of being sent farther afield. After leaving Jannina he met one of the Serbian monks, grew very friendly and told him of his troubles, so the monk invited him to come and stay at the monastery for a time. The instant that Ismail heard of Athanasi's arrival he guessed why he had been sent, and fled at once to Constantinople. As if it were not enough to be persecuted by Ali, he had heard that his wife and children, held as hostages at Jannina, were being badly treated. Ali had tried to get the lady to agree to a divorce so that he might give her to Omer Bey Vrioni, and she now wrote to tell Ismail of her troubles:

'Your children are in prison and your wife is living in a hovel, living in misery, partly on charity and partly by sewing. My bed used to have a golden coverlet, but now I sleep on a straw mat under a threadbare saddle-cloth. I send you the last of my ornaments – my hair.'

At Constantinople, which seemed the safest place, Ismail fell in with a number of Albanian exiles, with some of whom he was connected, and together they began to plot against Ali. An energetic and fine-looking man, Ismail was lively and intelligent, travelled and experienced, and soon became a person of some influence. He made it his business to voice the grievances of all those who had cause for complaint against Ali and his sons, and found no difficulty in getting a hearing. Indeed, he won the friendship of the Sultan's powerful favourite Halet Effendi, and when the news came that his wife and daughter had died at Jannina as a result of Ali's persecution, he asked for and obtained an audience of the Sultan himself, who by this time was so ready to listen to complaints against Ali and so favourably impressed by Ismail that he made him one of his chamberlains.

When the news of this preferment reached Ali, he was both furious and frightened, and realizing that it would be useless to try and bribe Ismail, he decided to make another attempt to murder him and accordingly sent two assassins to Constantinople. They arrived there at the end of February 1820 and after prowling about for several days caught sight of Ismail sitting at a window and fired several shots at him, all of which missed him. One of the men was immediately arrested and confessed that he had been sent by Ali. He was tortured and hanged, and as soon as the news spread several of Ali's agents in the capital abruptly disappeared for fear of being implicated.

Angered beyond measure at an outrage that touched him so closely, the Sultan decided to take a step he must long have had in mind. He issued a decree deposing Ali from the pashalik of Jannina, depriving his sons Veli and Sali of Trik-kala and Lepanto, and ordering them all to go to Tebeleni and await his commands. As for Mukhtar, the Bey of Beys at Berat, he could not be deprived of a pashalik he had never been granted: it was officially understood that he only governed in the name of his father-in-law Ibrahim, whose title had been confirmed year after year. Ali was now ordered to come to Constantinople within forty days and give an account of himself, though it can hardly have been expected that he would obey. At the same time successors were appointed to the deposed pashas. Most insufferable of all, Jannina and Delvino were granted to none other than Ismail, it being understood that he would have to take them by force of arms.

Ali was not the man to yield to such a humiliation. He told his confidants that he had the men and the money to hold his own, and that a successor should only enter Jannina over his dead body. To the Porte, however, which he had for so many years defied and bamboozled, he sent from his new house at Parga (of which the harem stood on a spot formerly occupied by a church dedicated to the Virgin Mary) letters full of sham humility and gratitude. He tried bribery, his old resource, and failed; and then turned to ask for English help, but Maitland would guarantee him nothing more than a refuge in the Ionian Islands and safe custody for his treasures. The old Lion now heard that Ismail was to be put in command of an army and march against Jannina. All his old fighting spirit was aroused, and he began to make plans to resist such an invasion. He himself would take command at Jannina, and his sons and grandsons and trusty followers were to be put in charge of outlying places. Mukhtar should hold Berat, and Veli Preveza. Mukhtar's sons Mahmud and Hussein were to be entrusted with the defence of Tebeleni and Suli, and Veli's son Mehmet with that of Parga.

Since the decree by which Ali was deposed declared him a rebel and had all the force of an excommunication, he naturally turned for support rather to his Christian subjects than to his Moslem ones, who had always been jealous of the favour he had shown to the Greeks and were in any case not very willing to renounce their loyalty to the Sultan. He called together a conference of Albanian chieftains and Greek bishops and in an artful recruiting speech appealed to them for help against their common enemy the Turk. The speech was very well received, and seemed to produce satisfactory results, but if the Greeks were obliging it was not out of love for Ali, but because their heads at this time were full of ideas of revolution against the Turks. 'The social position of the mass of the Greek population,' says Finlay, speaking of the period when Ali was in power, 'explains the facility with which it was influenced by the revolutionary ideas of the French. The Ottoman government, though in some respects the most tyrannical in Europe, was in others the most tolerant. It fettered the body, but it left the mind free. The lower orders of its Christian subjects were in general possessed of more intellectual cultivation than the corresponding ranks of society in other parts of Europe. The Greeks were neither industrial slaves nor agricultural serfs; their labour was both more free and more valuable, and their civil rights were as great as those of the same class, even in France, before the Revolution . . . The cruelty and injustice of the Turks were irregularly exercised, and were more galling than oppressive. Towards the end of the eighteenth century . . . the Greeks possessed a numerous body of small peasant-proprietors of land, whom circumstances often enabled to better their condition; and in the towns an industrious population of labourers and traders was supported and protected by a body of wealthy merchants often enjoying foreign protection . . . The Greeks were superior in social and political civilization to the Turks. The fact was generally perceived, and a Greek Revolution was consequently regarded as an event which must occur at no very distant date.' The corruptness of the Turkish Empire naturally made things easier. So long as the pashas kept up a flow of tribute to Constantinople, they had been allowed to do pretty much as they liked, and not only Ali Pasha at Jannina, but the Deys of Tripoli, Tunis and Algiers, Pasvan Oglu 'at Vidin, Djezzar Pasha at Acre, and Ali Bey in Egypt, had been almost like absolute autocrats in their respective provinces. In Greece the Turkish domination 'had accomplished a task which neither the Roman power nor the Orthodox Church had effected; it had nationalized the Greeks . . . A great cycle in the history of Greece was completed. The tribe of Othman had fulfilled its mission in Hellas, and it was now to depart from the land, like the Romans, the Crusaders and the Venetians.'

The way had been prepared, and the movement foreshadowed, as in other revolutions, by literary men, and in 1814 there had been founded at Odessa the celebrated Friendly Society, a nucleus of advanced spirits who looked to the Russians as their deliverers, and who included among their original members, it is significant to notice, a native of Jannina and another of Arta. In April 1820, when Ali found himself in such a critical situation, the Friendly Society was holding a meeting at Preveza. He took care to keep in touch with it, and one of its leading members, Paparigopoulos, shortly left for St. Petersburg to discuss with the Russian government a plan for a joint rebellion of the Albanians and Greeks.

Ali now thought of letting loose the Armatoles, whom he had spent so many years in suppressing. He knew how much they hated the Turks and how they wished to play a part in the revolution that was being prepared; he knew also how easily they were allured by the hope of loot. There was no need to ask them twice to do their stuff. Experts in guerrilla warfare, and led by dashing figures like Odysseus, they promptly threw the countryside into confusion, robbing the mails, stopping convoys, destroying villages, forcing levies and demanding ransoms. Complaints poured into Constantinople, and suggestions that nobody but Ali could restore order. But the Porte took no notice: they had declared against Ali once and for all.

247

In May Charles Napier, who had been in Jannina privately the year before, returned on a secret mission to advise Ali on his defences. Here are some extracts from his diary:

'*May* 21*st*. Saw the Vizier, rode round his works and made a report of them: they would not resist half an hour.

'*May* 23*rd*. Proposed new works, traced the ground and again reported.

'*May* 25*th*. Began a sketch of the works: find the chief engineer, Mr. Carretto, a man of much intelligence, but no great engineer: he however appears to be a good artillery officer, and is the only person with a conception of engineering.

Napier was of course a very capable man and full of ideas, but Ali was not wise enough to make use of him. A fortnight later he was still trying to give Ali 'the works', so to speak, and the Vizier asked him to stay for another two months, but he would not, for he only met with obstinacy, lack of imagination, and excessive financial caution. 'The pacha might have a capital artillery,' he wrote, 'if he would allow Carretto to teach his men: he will not. I brought a bombardier, at Ali's own request, yet they would not let him work, though he could have formed a hundred good artillerymen for them. The pacha's natural genius is strong, but he has no idea of the details of war, or how to form troops. He has placed his troops well and he knows they want discipline and artillery; but with the means of having both in perfection he does not know how to go about the business.' The Englishman noted that Ali was 'hated more for his avarice than for his cruelty . . . His cruelty does not excite unusual horror, because all the pachas are cruel . . . With generosity and discipline he might indeed do much with his Greeks and maintain his ground, but he will give money only when forced, and then he tries to cheat . . .' Napier advanced plan after plan – even suggesting assembling 8000 British troops at Parga before February 1821, if Ali could hold his own until then – but Ali would have none of them, and at the beginning of July Napier was back in Corfu.

CHAPTER XXXI

ALI THE HUCKSTER

FULLY aware of his perilous situation, Ali did what he could to keep on the right side of his subjects. He showed himself often in public, riding on horseback, carried in a litter, or talking familiarly to the men working on the fortifications. He even announced that he would grant his subjects a constitution. 'And will that increase our pay?' the Skipetars asked drily. 'What!' exclaimed the Turks, 'a constitution? And what's wrong with the Koran, we should like to know?'

The Porte had been slow to launch a campaign against Ali owing to a fear that the English might intervene on his behalf, but now the Imperial armies advanced. Ismail, at the head of a somewhat medieval rabble of 20,000 men, made for Jannina, while a Bulgarian general, Pehlevan Baba, newly appointed Pasha of Lepanto, drove Odysseus out of Thessaly, took Lepanto, Missolonghi, and Vonitza, and laid siege to Preveza, where Veli was in command. Turkish armies have always been notorious for their ferocious cruelties, and on this occasion they were true to their reputation: besides the usual outrages, they would burn hives after stealing the honey, and after feeding their horses would burn what was left of the hay. Had they only known it, they were fanning the flames of revolution.

Vallona surrendered, Butrinto fell, and Parga was besieged. The siege lasted three days and then the garrison mutinied against young Mehmet, who was left with no alternative but to surrender to the Turkish admiral. He was received very graciously and assured that the Sultan did not extend the bitterness he felt against Ali to the Vizier's sons and grandsons. When Ali heard of the surrender of Parga he was dreadfully upset and tore his clothes in despair. Indeed, Preveza was the only place now left to him on the coast, and in it Veli was besieged by the Turkish fleet on one side and Pehlevan Baba's army on the other. Veli had sent his treasures to Santa Maura, burnt down the palace his father had built, and shut himself up in the fortress. Meanwhile Pehlevan took Arta, which was surrendered by one of Ali's 'faithful' lieu-tenants, who made no attempt at resistance. Ismail, by means of a flanking movement, compelled Mukhtar to retreat from Berat to Argyro Castro, and then set out for Jannina near which he was to combine forces with Pehlevan.

All these disasters and the approach of the Imperial armies created something like panic in Jannina. 'It's time to go,' said the old dervish Yusuf, 'for Nineveh's about to fall,' and accompanied by two attendants and carefully carrying his sacred relic, the alleged hair from the beard of the Prophet, he left the Castro and took the road to Arta, meaning to end his days in Mecca. What was infinitely more momentous was that the Skipetars either lost their nerve or decided to play for safety. The main body of Ali's army, consisting of 15,000 chosen troops, well armed and equipped, led to some extent by European officers, mostly Italians, and commanded by Omer Bey Vrioni, deserted to the enemy. Two other divisions followed their example, and Omer was given the title of Vizier as a reward for his treachery. Before the end of August the position was that Ali found himself without an army; he still held Jannina, which was garrisoned by a few thousand faithful followers, well fortified, provisioned for years, and defended by 200 pieces of artillery under Carretto and by a strong flotilla on the lake; but not far from the southern end of the lake Ismail and Pehlevan were already encamped at the head of 50,000 men, short of artillery and munitions, but eager to take Jannina, sack it, and capture its master. The inhabitants of the town, anticipating pillage and bombardment, began to flee into the country, and the lake was soon covered with boat-loads of refugees. Ali himself thought seriously of escaping to Corfu and applied to the High Commissioner for help, but was told that help could not be given openly to a proclaimed rebel and that not until he had crossed half the channel between the mainland and the island would he be entitled to British protection.

Whether he was unwilling to abandon his treasures or whether his defiant courage had revived, he now set himself to resist till the last. He knew he could not defend the whole town but only the Castro and Litharitza, so he resolved to destroy it in order to prevent its falling into the hands of his enemies, and turned the garrison out to loot it. They made a bee-line for the Greek cathedral where considerable amounts of money and valuables had been sent for safe keeping, and took the opportunity to break open the tombs of the archbishops and to steal the cathedral plate. Then they turned to the houses of the remaining rich. Harems were broken into, and 'displayed the cruel sight of modesty struggling with violence', and groans, cries and threats were heard on all sides.

As soon as the job was done and the garrison recalled Ali ordered that a heavy fire should be opened on the town. He sat on one of the bastions of the Castro, 'like the exterminating angel', and directed the bombardment. Showers of bombs, howitzer shells, grenades, fireballs, and Congreve rockets (made in England) descended on the town, which was soon a raging mass of 'sulphurous and thought-executing fires', in which perished whole streets, Mukhtar's palace, Pouqueville's old consulate, the hospital, the libraries, mosques, churches, the bazaar, the public baths. The remaining inhabitants escaped before the flames, taking with them whatever they could save, but they only ran into the advance guards of the Turkish army, who fell on them, seized whatever bits of property they had saved from Ali, the Skipetars, and the fire, and carried off their sons and daughters. The survivors scattered and fled to the mountains, where they were attacked by brigands or perished from hunger and exposure, and the paths through the passes were littered with the dying and the dead.

On August the 20th, Ismail entered the still smoking ruins, hoisted the three horse-tails which were the emblem of his new rank, and had the decree appointing him Pasha of Jannina and Delvino read aloud, and then that excommunicating the rebel Ali – Black Ali, as he was now called. To this little demonstration Ali made a spirited reply, fired off some salvoes from his cannon and had his flotilla paraded on the lake with all the boats decked out in flags and bunting as if for a fête.

His position was not so desperate as might be imagined. He had several thousand men with him who were apparently ready to stand by him and share his fate, whatever it might be; he had ample supplies of food and munitions, and his treasury was full; he was master of the lake, which besides being useful for purposes of defence served as a channel of communication with the outside world; and he knew that the rainy season was about to set in, which would make things unpleasant for Ismail, whose troops were ill-assorted and short of artillery.

It happened that Odysseus and 1500 of his followers, retreating from Pehlevan Baba, had taken refuge with Ali in the Castro, but they were used to a free and roving life and did not fancy the idea of being shut up in a fortress, and a besieged one at that. They grew impatient and worked out

253

a plan by which they could regain their liberty without losing their heads or harming Ali. Odysseus entered into a correspondence with Ismail, pretending that he and his men were disaffected and wished to desert to the Imperial cause. They duly went over to the Turks and received a hearty welcome, but Odysseus soon slipped off to Ithaca, his native island, and his men took to the mountains and made continual raids on Turkish convoys and outposts.

September was nearly over, and Ismail had accomplished nothing. His troops were on short rations and only remained loyal to him in the hope that they would eventually be able to lay hands on Ali's treasures. Not feeling strong enough to launch an attack on the Vizier, Ismail turned his attention to Veli, who was still being besieged at Preveza. With sixteen ships of his own Veli had been able to prevent the Imperial squadron from entering the Gulf of Arta, but they now deserted to the Turks, and although he had plenty of arms and supplies he was not in an enviable position. His old friend Ismail now wrote to assure him that the Sultan was not going to bear malice against Ali's sons or hold them responsible for their father's behaviour, and had decided, as a proof of goodwill, to give Veli, if he would cease to support his father's rebellion, a pashalik in Syria. An Imperial decree to this effect was sent with the letter. Veli was equally ready to take the Sultan's word and to abandon his father's cause, and his son Selim, who was with him, begged him to surrender at once in order to ensure that nothing unpleasant should happen to his other son Mehmet, in Turkish custody since the fall of Parga. Veli accordingly abandoned Preveza to the Turkish admiral, who received him in state and treated him with great consideration, even obliging him by obtaining doctors from Corfu to treat him for a heart complaint of syphilitic origin from which he had long been suffering.

Veli sent the news of his surrender to his brothers Mukhtar and Sali at Argyro Castro, telling them that the Sultan would pardon them too and give them pashaliks in Anatolia. They decided to follow Veli's example, so Argyro Castro, that great stronghold on which Ali had lavished so much thought and money and labour, was in its turn given up to the Turks. Mukhtar now wrote to his son Mahmud at Tebeleni, telling him to follow suit, and then left for Salonica.

When Ali heard how his three sons had deserted him, he behaved with great dignity, showed no astonishment, and replied coolly, 'I've known for a long time that they're unworthy of my blood. From now on,' he added, addressing his followers, 'I have no other children or heirs but the brave defenders of my cause'. And as if to emphasize his own toughness, he ordered a special bombardment of the besiegers.

That old crocodile Shainitza, shut up in her palace at Liboövo, where the divans were stuffed with the hair of the Gardikiot women, received the bad news with her usual display of temperament, and immediately wrote with a shaking hand to Mahmud at Tebeleni to make him feel ashamed of his father Mukhtar's behaviour. She urged this ten-year-old boy to resist to the last, threatening him with all sorts of curses if he weakened.

'My father, my uncles, and my cousins, whom my grandfather honoured with his confidence, have chosen to betray it,' he said in a speech to the garrison at Tebeleni. 'I know you would not wish me to do the same.' At this they cheered, and replied that they were with him to a man.

A regiment of men from Argyro Castro and Gardiki, knowing that Shainitza was isolated, thought this a suitable moment to pay her out for her crimes, and marched off to Liboövo. When they got there she appeared at her front door, too angry to be frightened, with pistols stuck in her girdle, a musket in her hand, and two large ferocious dogs by her side.

'Stop!' she cried. 'Don't think for a moment that you're going to take my life or lay a finger on my money. Come in, if you dare! But if you do, you'll all be blown sky-high, for the whole place is mined. However, I am prepared to grant you a pardon, which you little deserve. Now clear out, and don't dare to answer me back. Here are a few bags of gold to compensate you for the losses you have lately been made to suffer by my brother's enemies. But don't let me hear or see anything of you again. Life means nothing to me, whether it's mine, or yours, and I have other means of causing death besides gunpowder.'

This dark hint was taken to mean that she knew how to spread the plague. The visitors took the gold, and the châtelaine of Liboövo went back into her house.

In the meantime quarrels had broken out in the Turkish camp near Jannina. Ismail had brought the guns captured at Preveza and was preparing to use them, when Pehlevan, who was jealous of him and eager to get hold of Ali's wealth, urged that a general attack should be made at once. Ismail was against this, and said it would be madness to attack until a breach had been made in the forts, for the troops could not be brought up under cover, as there was none. Pehlevan called Ismail's common sense cowardice, and is said to have entered into a secret understanding with Ali and to have encouraged insubordination in the Turkish army. In order to avoid any further trouble Ismail poisoned him and sent word to Constantinople that he had died of fever. Along with this message he sent Pehlevan's treasures, which he hoped would help to quieten the irritation felt by the Porte at his slowness in conquering Ali.

The Vizier was not without troubles of his own. Some of his men, prompted perhaps by bribes from outside, urged him to let old Ibrahim out of his cell for a little. Now over eighty, Ibrahim had been a prisoner for a good many years. Ali said he could move about within the Castro but would not allow him to shelter in the casemates, an order which naturally left him the chance of stopping a Turkish bullet. However, Ibrahim achieved shortly afterwards the really extraordinary feat of dying a natural death.

The garrison, not in love with their situation and well aware that they were serving an exceedingly rich man, very sensibly asked for a rise in their pay, and although this request was a little in the nature of blackmail, it was granted.

'I never haggle,' said Ali grandiloquently, 'with my family; my adopted children shed their blood for me, and in comparison with the services they render me, gold is nothing.'

What on earth did this mean? That Ali was getting generous in his old age? Not at all, for he at once gave orders to the Jew in charge of his commissariat to raise the prices of the provisions bought by the soldiers. When they heard this they thrashed the quartermasters and made up songs about Ali in which he was called Ali the Huckster. About this time he is supposed to have had some of his treasure enclosed in iron strong-boxes and sunk in the lake by some gipsies, whom he immediately had massacred, so that the secret should remain with him.

Autumn came on and it began to rain, and still Ismail had accomplished nothing of his main purpose: Ali had even made a successful sortie which had obliged him to retreat and pitch his camp further off. His troops were needy and restless and not looking forward to the winter, and there were many desertions. Nor could he rely on his generals. One of them had been accepting presents from Shainitza and had officially recognized the authority of Mahmud at Tebeleni, and this was a source of annoyance. Then there was trouble with some

Suliots who had joined the Turks in the hope that Suli would be restored to them but now began to have doubts. Like some of the Greeks who had also joined Ismail, they had imagined that in fighting against Ali they would be fighting for their own independence, but they began to understand that they could not expect much from a Turkish victory, and many of them deserted.

Towards the end of September Ismail wrote to the Parghiot refugees at Corfu and told them to return to their old home. They would be allowed, he said, to get back their estates in return for the payment of tribute to the Sultan. They replied that 'never having been subjects of His Highness, whom they respected, they owed him neither tribute nor obedience', and were only interested in living in a free country.

In Epirus many people were sick of uncertainties and the depredations of the Turks, and began to sigh for the good old days when Ali was their master!

CHAPTER XXXII

ALI THE DIAMOND

ALI'S meanness was in the long run his worst enemy. Fifteen years before, Leake, inspecting the foundry at Bonila, had asked him where he got copper to make gun-metal, and Ali had replied, 'I collect it from my subjects; one brings an old pot, and another a kettle'. Napier had found him buying bad flour because it was cheap for the men working on the fortifications at Jannina, and as Napier's brother afterwards wrote: 'Possessing millions, and engaged in a struggle for life and death, he would not be at the cost of safety while danger was not close at hand; but when the Turks crossed the Pindus range, when his lieutenants deserted him, and his capital was menaced, he sent to Charles Napier offering unlimited command and money. "Have you fortified the positions pointed out to you when I was at Jannina? No! Then you have neglected to do that in time which would have saved you, and must now abide your fate. You want to give my head to save your own, but you shall not".'

On his visit to Jannina Napier had formed very good opinions as to Ali's geographical position and political prestige before proposing any schemes. 'As to the natural strength of the ground, that occupied by the celebrated lines round Lisbon is not to be compared with the passes over Mount Pindus. One hundred soldiers might have arrested the mob that was dignified with the appellation of the Turkish army.' He had concluded that Ali was *de facto* an independent sovereign and a Greek, and was looked up to by the Greeks as the greatest man of their country. He had told Ali that he would put him on the Sultan's throne in a few months, if he would 'advance a million of money, admit of a new military organization and declare the Christians free'. 'Had he undertaken the enterprise, and proclaimed himself a Christian (he was certainly no Mohammedan) and King of Greece, he would have succeeded, for every Greek chieftain looked upon Ali, virtually, as his sovereign. Fifty thousand pounds would have done it all . . .' Whether Napier's schemes would have succeeded, either with fifty thousand or a million pounds, we shall never know, but Ali thought them sound. When they *might* have succeeded, 'with a miser's madness he refused the money; he afterwards offered two millions but was answered, "Too late! The Turks are in the Aetolian mountains. You are lost!" ' The days were gone when he could defy the Porte and play off foreign powers one against the other, when he had an army at his back and his sons were like kings, when his word was law and his confidence unshaken. If not lost, he was at least cornered.

The best description of the siege of Jannina we owe to Michel, the Parisian carpenter who had lived for many years in Jannina, found himself shut up with Ali in the Castro, and now, at the beginning of December 1820, managed to escape to Preveza. The siege, he said, was conducted in such a casual way that Ali's detachments could pass without hindrance between the Castro and Litharitza. There were surprisingly free communications between the besiegers and the besieged: men in the Turkish camp who had relations in the forts came to see them, bringing them tobacco or brandy, drinking, singing, or effecting an exchange of prostitutes with them, and telling them all the news, so that it was known every day in the Castro what was going on both in Ismail's camp and the countryside generally, and it sometimes happened that Ali heard the latest news before Ismail. A breach had been opened in the walls of Litharitza twelve days before Michel's escape, but it had been followed up by no attack. The Turkish soldiers were mostly looking for something to steal or collecting firewood in order to keep themselves warm and cook their pilaffs: to obtain wood they had destroyed such of the houses in Jannina as had · survived the fire and the bombardment. Altogether they came and went in the most casual way, without orders.

Ismail was afraid to act with any severity, for he trusted nobody and felt quite insecure. Endless councils were held, at which everybody gave his own opinion, which differed from everybody else's, so nothing was ever settled. At night a half-hearted bombardment was sometimes begun, but so ill-directed that most of the shells fell into the lake or otherwise did little harm. About 3500 shells had been fired so far, and had only killed 14 people. In the Castro and Litharitza there were about 5000 people, of whom about 2500 were armed men.

Ali had destroyed the gilded saloons and most of the living apartments in both palaces, partly because the wood was needed and partly to avoid the danger of fire. The only indication that he was profoundly troubled, disappointed and alarmed was that he had got very thin; otherwise his clothes, manners and conversation were all very much as in the days when he was at the height of his power. Rumours had been put about that he now shared his women with his soldiers, and that he had gone back to the rough clothes and habits of his early days, but they were quite untrue. He had preserved a few luxuriously furnished rooms and would rest there on brocade-covered cushions, sleeping little and always armed. He still granted audiences and issued commands (now not always obeyed) and managed to keep as gay and lively as if he were waiting for a festival. He said he was expecting help from the Czar Alexander and from the people of Upper Albania. 'The Turks have taken to calling me Black Ali,' he said, 'but they'd do better to call me Ali the Diamond . . . that would be more suitable'; and he went off into great bursts of laughter. Presently he heard a report which Ismail had spread, to the effect that his sons had been put to death. 'They betrayed their father,' said Ali apparently (but only apparently) without emotion. 'Don't let's think any more about it.'

In his last adversities the monstrous aspects of Ali's character are half forgotten, and his grandeur emerges. Close on eighty, betrayed by his sons, abandoned by his generals, deserted by his army, his power gone, his prospects anything but hopeful, and driven to defend himself in his last strongholds against forces ten times as large as his own and backed by the Imperial authority and the Imperial anger, he remained fearless and dignified in his behaviour and cheerful in his conversation.

Michel complained that he had lost 6000 piastres in the fire.

'Well, and what about me?' said Ali, laughing. 'I've lost something too, you know. But everything will arrange itself. My money's doing its work in the camp over there, and I no longer feel any anxiety.'

Ali's fat fingers, so often loaded with diamond rings, were now like those of a skeleton, and his eyes that used to twinkle in his fresh face were now sunk in his head and glittered with a sultry light. He had taken to resting in a casemate at the entrance to the powder magazine, which he could blow up at a moment's notice; he sat on velvet cushions, resting his head on the knees of the ever-faithful Athanasi Vaya, while a renegade Jew named Abraham Saratch, formerly his post-master-general, kept watch at the door. This individual used to say, 'If I knew anyone more devoted than I am to my master's wishes, I should kill him at once.'

'Greater in misfortune than he had ever been in his glory,' said Pouqueville, 'Ali seemed suddenly to be enjoying a second youth.' A soothsayer announced the approach of a crisis favourable to his cause, and he began to sleep better. 'Only courage and perseverance,' he told his men, 'can save us.' When they grumbled of their losses he reminded them of his own, and promised them all sorts of rewards when his cause was won.

'So the Turks call me Black Ali, do they? Why, you couldn't find my equal, at my age, in the whole of the Turkish Empire. The cowards! They'll be sorry, when they find what troubles I shall leave them, that they didn't learn to value the old Lion and his palikars. They make war on me to get my treasures, but they shall only get them soaked in blood. I'll work up hatred and vengeance against them. In a few months I'll shake the Empire, and those who are attacking me now won't be safe in Constantinople itself. Wretched town! Before he dies Ali will see your palaces burnt to the ground, and his wrongs washed away in the blood of his covetous enemies!'

He treated Ismail with the utmost contempt, speaking of him always as 'the servant', and sneering at his plans of attack. He sent him a present of a small quantity of coffee and sugar with the message 'With the compliments of a master who attends to the wants of a servant', and offered to relieve any shortage from which Ismail might be suffering, by selling him provisions from his own stores! Actually, although he had plenty of flour and rice and such things, he was getting short of fresh meat and green stuff, and the garrison was bothered with fevers and other complaints.

The Suliots in Ismail's camp who had joined him on the understanding that Suli should be restored to them now began to press their claims, but could get no satisfaction. Ali took advantage of their discontent to intrigue with them, and they sent a monk, who crossed the lake at night, to confer with him. Ali offered to restore Suli to them and said he would give them a year's pay in advance. At the same time he said he would order his lieutenant Tahir Abbas to deliver up the fortress which he had built there and which was still held in his name. The Suliots agreed, and hostages were exchanged, the Suliots taking with them Ali's grandson Hussein, son of Mukhtar, who had been in the Castro all this time. While making over to his new allies a large sum of money deposited in banks at Malta and Corfu, Ali sent secretly to Tahir Abbas to tell him *not* to surrender the fortress. However the Suliots went back to Suli and proceeded to wage a guerrilla warfare against the Turks, whose line of communications between Arta and Jannina they succeeded in cutting. Ismail's army continued to be weakened by hunger and desertions, and when some of his troops attempted to regain control over the road to Arta they were sharply defeated by the Suliots, secretly forewarned by Ali.

After long delays Ismail made up his mind to attack the Castro, but Ali promptly decided to lead a counter-attack in person. He mounted his Arab horse Dervish, and his chief armourer brought him his arms, which were famous throughout Epirus and often named in the songs of the Skipetars, like those of heroes in ancient times. A large musket, damasked in blue and powdered with gold stars, which had been made at Versailles and presented by Napoleon to Djezzar Pasha of Acre, was given to Athanasi Vaya to hold; one of Ali's pages carried the gun which he himself had been given by Napoleon in 1806; at his saddlebow he carried the sword of Charles XII that he had had from Gustav Adolf; and he wore at his side a sabre given him by Orkhan Gerai, the exiled heir to the Tartar

Khans of the Crimea, who had been his guest at Jannina from
1811 to 1816. The Skipetars gave vent to their shrieks and
war-whoops, prolonged answering howls came from the
attackers, and while the mountains were echoing with these
strange noises Ali challenged Ismail to single combat. The
challenge was not met. 'He'll neither conquer nor die like
a soldier!' cried Ali, and catching sight of the colonel in command of the Turkish artillery he took up Djezzar Pasha's
gun and shot him dead, crying, 'Ha! You see I can shoot
straighter than the commander of the Sultan's artillery!'
Then with Napoleon's gun he picked off a bey, and was fired
at in return without result. When the smoke cleared he
caught sight of a hostile pasha of his acquaintance and calling
on the sinister spirit of Khamco for aid ('Mother, help me!')
he shot him through the heart. Ismail's attack collapsed in
confusion, and the Turks retired leaving 150 dead, including
22 officers, against 42 of Ali's men, and one officer.

Afraid of further desertions from Omer Bey Vrioni's
army of Greeks and Albanians, Ismail asked them for hostages,
a demand which was very unfavourably received. Ali sent
word to say that he was willing to pardon their treachery if
they would come back to him. One of their leaders, named
Alexis Noutza, at once agreed. About forty, arrogant, depraved in his habits and luxurious in his way of living, Noutza
had been the friend and boyhood companion of Mukhtar and
had long enjoyed the favour of Ali. He had regretted his
desertion, for the Turks had treated him with an even greater
haughtiness than his own, and he now came secretly at night
to the Castro and had a private meeting with Ali. For the
first time Ali showed his feelings about the behaviour of
his sons. No one knew how deeply it had hurt him, for he
had kept up an air of indifference in the matter. But it was
obvious that most of his life had been taken up with the

endeavour to consolidate a vast dominion to hand on to his progeny, and that his whole ambition in the matter had come to nothing. Alone with Alexis Noutza, he wept. But his tears soon gave way to curses, and he urged him to do all that he could to make trouble for the Turks, and this Noutza did, so that there were soon wholesale desertions of Greeks and Mohammedan Albanians from the Turkish camp, and not long after a number of districts in the countryside declared themselves openly in favour of Ali.

In January 1821 Ali's troops made a successful sortie, and the Porte completely lost patience with Ismail's delays and general incompetence. It soon became known that a successor had been appointed, namely Khurschid Pasha, formerly Grand Vizier, lately successful in suppressing a Serbian revolt, and now Pasha of the Morea. Ismail was to be allowed to retain the pashaliks of Jannina and Delvino, but was to hand over the command of the army.

Ali at once wrote to Khurschid at Tripolitza to congratulate him on his appointment, and to say that it was only the intrigues of Ismail that had provoked the Imperial anger against him. He flattered Khurschid and asked him to put in a word with the Sultan on his behalf. Khurschid replied in friendly terms, and set out for Jannina, where he arrived at the end of February. Ali received him with a salute of twenty-one guns and sent him another letter and some presents. Khurschid replied politely, and then proceeded to investigate the state of the Turkish army, sending a bad report on it to Constantinople, and taking steps to obtain reinforcements and munitions.

CHAPTER XXXIII

THE END OF ALI

In the early part of 1821 the first serious outbreak of the Greek revolution took place at Patras. Khurschid knew that Ali had had something to do with the revolutionaries, and in order to put him off any further intrigues in that direction he now sent him a copy of a letter which Alexander Ypsilanti, the head of the Friendly Society, had written to the Greeks suggesting that they should only help Ali so long as it suited them and only with their own aims clearly in view, and that they should use any help which Ali might give them in the way of money and munitions solely to further the revolution. The general who brought the letter urged upon Ali the desirability of arriving at a settlement with Khurschid, but Ali mistook this for weakness and grew haughty. The beginnings of the revolution, and the success which his agents in Epirus and Albania had lately had in winning people over to his side, had given him confidence, and he said that he would only be willing to accept a settlement on his own terms. He asked that he himself should be allowed to retain the government of Epirus for life and that a general amnesty should be granted to all his supporters. Provided that Ismail was handed over to him alive, he engaged to pay at once the tribute with which he was in arrears and the expenses of the war as well. He did condescend to express regret that he had incurred the Sultan's displeasure and said he was willing to sue for pardon, but if his conditions were not accepted as they stood he was ready, he said, to defend himself to the bitter end.

Khurschid sent his proposals to Constantinople, and while

awaiting an answer both sides agreed to an armistice. The answer soon came: the Porte demanded an unconditional surrender. Ali at once took up arms again, explained to the garrison his reasons for not giving up hope of success, set them an example of firmness and cheerfulness, and ordered a bombardment as an expression of his opinion of the besiegers.

The breach in the walls of Litharitza was now six months old and had neither been mended by one side nor taken advantage of by the other. At the end of May Khurschid ordered an attack on the place, but Ali's men rushed out of the Castro to catch them in the rear. Ali himself was suffering from gout and could neither walk nor ride, but he had himself carried out in a litter to direct operations, which he did with such success that the Turks were heavily repulsed and beat a hasty retreat, leaving behind them three hundred dead. After this Ali sent a message to Khurschid to say 'The Bear of Pindus is still alive'; but his pleasure was somewhat spoilt by the news that at Liboövo Shainitza had just died in an apoplectic fit.

It was now the beginning of Ramazan, the Mohammedan Lent, so another truce was declared. On the last day of the fast the besiegers went to celebrate the festival of Bairam, which marks its end, in a mosque which stood not far from the Castro and had survived the fire and the bombardment. They took it for granted that Ali would do nothing to interfere with their religious exercises, but he thought the chance too good to miss, and when they were all inside he opened fire on the mosque, which caught fire and was blown to pieces. When the smoke cleared away there was nothing to be seen where the mosque had stood but a fiery crater and all round it the great cypresses blazing like torches. Two hundred Turks and sixty officers had been either killed or wounded. 'Ali Pasha's not dead yet!' shouted Ali in triumph when he saw what he had done.

In July the Suliot captain Marco Botzaris defeated the Turks in an engagement only fifteen miles from Jannina. In any case the guerrilla warfare carried on by the Suliots was a continual annoyance, and Khurschid was anxious to deal severely with them but felt he must first settle with Ali, to whom he now made new overtures, demanding an immediate surrender of Litharitza and the Castro, and offering Ali in return a complete pardon and the right to go and live quietly in Asia Minor: he took care to remind him that the Greeks were fighting under the Cross and that if he were not careful he would become nothing but a tool in their hands. Ali stuck to his guns and his former conditions, demanding the immediate withdrawal of the Turkish army, insisting on having Ismail delivered up to him, and offering to suppress the revolutionary outbreak in the Morea on his own. He had a conviction that sooner or later the Porte, always so weak and muddled, would have to call on him for help in suppressing the insurrection, since he had so long been responsible for keeping a sort of order in the provinces concerned. Also he felt in a slightly better position at the moment as he was expecting to be joined by an army of 6000 Skipetars that had been raised in the neighbourhood of Tebeleni and Argyro Castro. But these Skipetars were put off by hearing that Khurschid's army had been heavily reinforced and now included 15,000 cavalry, so they took to guerrilla activities in the mountains instead. In August Khurschid succeeded in driving the Suliots back to Suli, so now *he* felt a slight advantage.

A month later news reached Epirus that Ali's three sons and one of his grandsons had been put to death by the orders of the Porte. The news was true. Instead of being given pashaliks, Mukhtar, Veli, Sali, and Veli's son Mehmet had been interned in Asia Minor. The Porte feared that so long as they were alive the Skipetars might remain faithful to them as heirs of Ali, and owing largely to the influence of the Sultan's favourite Halet Effendi, the friend of Ismail, the Sultan was persuaded to get rid of them on the alleged grounds that they were still plotting against his authority. He therefore signed a death warrant against all four of them.

Veli and Mehmet, taken unawares, were quickly and neatly murdered. Their heads were sent to Constantinople and there set up in public with an inscription detailing their faults, ingratitude, treason, etc., and declaring them guilty of plotting even after having been pardoned and allowed to live in peace. When the Sultan saw Mehmet's head he was much struck by its beauty, and made what is perhaps the most idiotic remark in history.

'Dear me,' he said, 'I'm sorry now that I condemned him to death. *I was thinking that he was as old as his father.*'

Mukhtar and Sali, who were living at Angora, were cornered in their house by troops sent by the local governor. They and their attendants put up a fight and went down shooting at their enemies until their ammunition was all spent; then they set fire to the house and tried, sabre in hand, to fight their way out, but fell covered with wounds. Their heads were then cut off and also sent to Constantinople for public exhibition.

There is no record of the way Ali took the news. His own position was worse again. The garrison of Litharitza consisted mostly of Skipetars belonging to a single tribe. It happened that many others of their tribe were in the besieging army, and whether they were anxious to join their relations or whether they yielded to bribes from Khurschid, or both, they presently surrendered the fortress. The news was received in the Turkish camp with loud cheers, and the traitors were rewarded with money and clothes, their leaders being treated with great ceremony. At Constantinople the news made as much impression as if it had been that of a hard-won victory, and the couriers who brought it were presented with handsome sable pelisses.

Ali was now left with the Castro and about one thousand eight hundred men, the rest having deserted or succumbed to wounds or illnesses. The Suliots offered him reinforcements, but he said he could still hold out for years on his own if necessary, the truth being that he did not trust them. 'Old serpents are always old serpents,' he remarked. 'I mistrust the Suliots and their friendship.' He asked that instead of coming to Jannina, they should go to Arta, which was being defended by Ismail, and try and take him alive. They took him at his word and attacked Arta and set fire to it in the middle of November. Ismail found himself cooped up in the citadel, from which he had to be rescued by Khurschid in person, assisted by Omer Bey Vrioni. He was judged unfit for any further command, relieved of his still purely nominal pashaliks, sent into exile, and finally deprived of his head. Imagination boggles at the thought of what Ali would have done to him if he had managed to get hold of him.

Failing to subdue Ali by force of arms, Khurschid attacked him with lies. In order to alienate the Mohammedan Skipetars he gave out that Ali had been converted to Christianity by Vasiliki, who was of course a Christian and still with him in the Castro, and in order to reassure Ali's supporters that it would be in the old Lion's best interests to surrender, he repeated that Ali would be allowed, if he submitted, to take his household and his harem and his treasures to Asia Minor and live there in peace.

In the Castro an epidemic of sorts had broken out, and as the result of privations the resistance of the garrison to disease had been weakened. They were suffering naturally from nervous strain, and a strain was continually put on their

271

loyalty by offers of lavish bribes from Khurschid. Caretto, who had been directing the artillery to good purpose all this time and who had been badly burnt about the face and nearly blinded by the explosion of a shell, could at last stand his situation no longer: it is said that Ali's everlasting meanness finally exasperated him. At all events, he decided to desert, and fastened a rope to a cannon and let himself down into the moat at night. The rope was too short and he fell and broke his arm, but he managed to reach the Turkish camp where he received the lukewarm welcome to be expected by a foreigner and a Christian, who had neither health, money, nor authority, and from whom there was nothing more to be feared.

In January 1822 Ali had only about a hundred men left with him in the Castro, no longer enough even to maintain a proper guard. One night some of Khurschid's men succeeded in penetrating the outer defences. They parleyed with some of the defenders, and by means of threats and promises persuaded them to open one of the gates, whereupon Ali retired with about twenty men to the place he called his 'refuge'. This was an inner fortified tower, which contained the powder magazine, his treasures, and what remained of his food and munitions. The entrance to the magazine was guarded by a young man named Selim Tchami, who had a gentle appearance but had devoted himself absolutely and fanatically to Ali and had vowed to give his life for him if it should be needed. He stood there constantly with a lighted match in his hand, ready to blow up the whole place at a moment's notice.

Khurschid now sent a confidential secretary to invite Ali once more to surrender. Ali received him, but his only reply was to lead him into the magazine which contained two thousand barrels of powder and his money and jewels. In his last miserly madness Ali drew a pistol from his girdle and aimed it at one of the barrels. The secretary made a rush for the door and Ali burst out into a hearty laugh. This time Ali sent to tell Khurschid that he would only surrender after the Turks had left the outer enclosure and he had been shown a decree signed by the Sultan promising him a full pardon: then, he said, he would agree to go to Asia Minor, but if these conditions were not accepted and if he were not guaranteed complete immunity he would blow himself up with his last few faithful followers and all that remained of his possessions.

On January 14th Khurschid sent to Ali to say that a decree was being prepared at Constantinople, and that he wished to have an interview with him. He suggested the island in the lake as a rendezvous, and to this Ali agreed.

The next morning, before leaving the Castro, he spoke to Selim Tchami, who was to remain at his post, and taking a string of amber from his pocket he showed it to him and said he must not deliver up the 'refuge' unless the amber was brought to him.

'And if they kill me on the island,' said Ali, 'you are to blow this place up.'

He next turned to Veli's son Ismail, his favourite grandson, now aged sixteen, put him in command of the little party of soldiers that was left, and after folding him in a tender embrace went down to the boats with Vasiliki and about twelve of his followers, including Athanasi Vaya, and crossed over to the little monastery of St. Panteleimon on the island.

Khurschid pretended to be ill and did not put in an appearance, but sent food to Ali and musicians to play to him. Everybody who came to see Ali assured him that the Sultan had pardoned him, but the old man's thoughts went back, as the thoughts of an old man will, to the scenes of his early years, and he began to hanker for Tebeleni and his native mountains and to wonder if he could escape and go there.

After he had been nine days on the island, word came from Khurschid to say that the decree of pardon had arrived. He suggested at the same time that before it could be officially read aloud Ali should make public submission to his Imperial sovereign by ordering Selim Tchami to give up the 'refuge'. Ali was at once suspicious, and calling aside a man named Costa Botzaris asked him to go at once to Selim Tchami and tell him to blow the place up.

'But,' said Botzaris, 'it's impossible to tell Selim anything, because it's impossible now to get into the Castro. Khurschid has it guarded on every side and anybody who even tries to approach will be stopped at once.'

Ali then turned to Khurschid's messenger and said that Selim Tchami would only surrender the 'refuge' on a verbal order from him. The messenger strongly protested Khurschid's good faith, and said it was simply a matter of form, for obviously it would be difficult to pardon Ali before he had surrendered. He took solemn oaths to convince Ali, but whether Ali was convinced, or felt suddenly weary and longed for peace or for death, he slowly drew the string of amber from his pocket (the act must have had an overwhelming significance for those who saw it) and handed it over. The rattle of a few beads marked the end of Ali's power. They were sent to Khurschid, who had them conveyed at once to Selim Tchami, and that gentle fanatic, acting in good faith on behalf of a man who in eighty years had scarcely learnt the meaning of good faith, gave up the Castro to the Turks.

All day Ali waited impatiently for the decree of pardon to be brought and read to him. Gloomy and anxious, and perhaps expecting the worst, he lay on a sofa in a room on the upper story of the monastery. Late in the afternoon a boat-load of thirty armed men under an officer named Mehmet Pasha approached the island from the direction of Khurschid's camp. Informed at once, Ali got up and came to the top of the staircase to receive the visitors. As soon as he saw Mehmet Pasha and the troop in the courtyard he knew they were not bringing him the decree.

'Stay where you are, Pasha!' he cried. 'What's all this?'

'It's this, pasha,' replied Mehmet, producing a scroll of paper, and then making a sudden dash for the stairs, followed by his men.

Ali drew the pistols from his girdle, and fired twice at Mehmet.

'Scum!' he cried. 'I'll show you how to crack my skull!'

One shot struck Mehmet in the hand; the other embedded itself in his thick cloak.

He fired back and hit Ali in the left arm, and dashed up to prevent Ali firing again, followed by another officer who drew his sabre meaning to slash off Ali's head, but missed and struck one of the beams overhead, the blade cutting right into it. Ali's supporters crowded round shooting, and the Turks retreated into the courtyard. Ali was helped back to his sofa, for he was badly wounded in the arm, and then volleys of shots were exchanged between Ali's men at the window and the Turks in the yard below.

Suddenly Ali heard the voice of a man who had lately deserted him, Elmas Bono, calling up from the yard to his brother Selfo Bono, who was still with Ali. Anger, an emotion ready to the last to take precedence over all others in that turbulent heart, now got the better of pain, and Ali cried out, 'Shoot Elmas! Shoot Elmas!'

While the shooting was going on, Mehmet with eight of his men managed to get into the room below the one where Ali was. He ordered them to fire through the ceiling, which in a few moments was riddled with shots. A bullet caught Ali in the groin, making a frightful wound, and he rolled on the sofa in agony. He called to Athanasi Vaya who was standing at the door shooting at the men in the yard. Almost his last words were concerned with Vasiliki, who was hiding in terror in the next room; he asked Athanasi to kill her rather than let her fall into the hands of the Turks.

'Hold out till the end!' he cried, and fell back dead in Athanasi's arms.

Athanasi ordered the others to cease fire and surrender, and Mehmet and his men dashed upstairs, burst into the room, and took everyone prisoner, including Vasiliki. Then they dragged Ali's corpse to the top of the stairs, cut off his head and carried it to Khurschid. When Khurschid saw it he stood up and tears flowed from his eyes. His men wiped the blood from the head, put it on a silver dish, and showed it to the other generals. Khurschid gave orders that it was to be exposed publicly in Jannina for three days in order to prove to the Skipetars that Ali Pasha was indeed dead. Ali's body was put in a boat, taken over to the Castro in great ceremony, and buried on January 25th, 1822, near the tomb of Eminé.

A month later the head arrived in Constantinople and everybody flocked to see it. A spectator tried to buy it with the idea of putting it on show in London, but he was outbid by a dervish named Suleiman, a friend of Ali's in childhood, who buried it near those of Mukhtar, Veli, Sali, and Mehmet in the cemetery near the Silivri gate, outside the walls of the city.

The memorial stones of the five pashas may still be seen. They were put up by Albanians living in Constantinople. Suleiman composed an epitaph for Ali which says, 'God is the Creator, the Eternal. Here lies the head of the famous Ali Pasha of Tebeleni, former governor of Jannina, who, for more than thirty years, made himself independent in Albania'. One recalls the words of Napier: 'Love of money made and unmade him: first it made him hoard until his riches gave him

THE END OF ALI

power, which enabled him to increase those riches: but when the hour of danger came he would not expend his money, and so fell.' True, perhaps; but the truth is not so easily seized, for it is hidden in the first sentence of Suleiman's epitaph for his old friend.

Those directly responsible for Ali's fall were given immense rewards, partly because the Sultan and his advisers believed that now that Ali was dead, the Greek insurrection could be crushed. Khurschid received two and a half million piastres and a jewelled sabre.

The treasures found in the Castro did not come up to expectations: treasures seldom do. Nevertheless it took fifty horses to bring them to Constantinople and their value was estimated at forty million piastres. There was not very much money left in the Castro, for Ali had heavily subsidized the Greek revolt in the Morea. Khurschid questioned Vasiliki as to the probable whereabouts of other hoards, but she could not or would not tell him anything. Nor could anybody else. She was taken to Constantinople, but retired later to an estate near Trikkala that Ali had settled on her. Still young, she had numerous offers of marriage from both Greeks and Turks, but she turned them all down.

'There's no man living,' she said, 'for the widow of Ali Pasha.'

The last years of her life were spent near Missolonghi, where she took to drink and died in 1835.

> Shall I abide
> In this dull world, which in thy absence is
> No better than a sty?

Of Mukhtar's two sons, Hussein died without issue at Salonica, and Mahmud, the little hero of Tebeleni, was sent into exile at Erzerum. Later he was pardoned, says M.

Remérand, and lived at Constantinople till 1863 – 'he dressed like a dervish and lived like a dervish, lying in rags at the doors of mosques, and wearing the vaguely ecstatic expression to be seen on the faces of certain harmless idiots.' Veli's second son Selim was exiled to Anatolia, but later became governor of Belgrade, where he died, leaving three sons. Veli's third son Ismail, who had been in the Castro with his grandfather till the last, was taken by Khurschid to Constantinople, rose in favour, and died in 1875 a member of the Sultan's Privy Council.

BIBLIOGRAPHICAL NOTE

AMONGST the sources of information about Ali Pasha are the writings of travellers and officials who met him, especially the *Travels in Greece and Albania* (London, 1830) of the Rev. T. S. Hughes; F. C. H. L. Pouqueville's *Voyage en Morée* (Paris, 1805), his *Histoire de la Régénération de la Grèce* (Paris, 1820), and his *Voyage dans la Grèce* (Paris, 1826); the *Mémoires* (Paris, 1827) of Ibrahim Mansur Effendi (Samson Cerfbeer de Medelsheim); Sir H. Holland's *Travels in the Ionian Isles* (London, 1819); W. M. Leake's *Travels in Northern Greece* (London, 1835); J. C. Hobhouse's *Travels in Albania* (London, 1855); C. R. Cockerell's *Travels in Southern Europe* (London, 1903); and of course Byron's *Letters and Journals* and *Childe Harold's Pilgrimage*. The best and most recent biography, to which I am especially indebted in matters relating to Ali's relations with the French in general and Pouqueville in particular, is M. Gabriel Remérand's *Ali de Tébélen* (Les Grands Figures de l'Orient, No. 2. Paris: Paul Geuthner, 1928), a lucid work written from a French and largely a political point of view. The last life of Ali in English was R. A. Davenport's (London, 1837). Since then have appeared *Istoria Ali Pasa tou Tepelenli* (Athens, 1895) by Spiro Aravantinos, and a life in Turkish (Constantinople, 1908) by Ahmed Mufid, a descendant of Shainitza. Ali's career can be seen in perspective in Alison's *History of Europe* (London, 1850–1853); Finlay's *History of Greece* (London, 1877); Gordon's *History of the Greek Revolution* (London, 1832); Mr. W. Miller's *The Ottoman Empire* (London, 1923); and Mr. J. N. Mavrocordato's *Modern Greece* (London, 1931). For special periods and incidentals the following are useful:

279

BIBLIOGRAPHICAL NOTE

Colonel de Bosset's *Proceedings in Parga* (London, 1819);
L. Ciampolini's *Le Guerre dei Sulliotti contro Ali Bascià di
Janina* (Florence, 1827); *Istoria tou Soulliou kai Parga*
(Athens, 1857) by Christophoros Perraivos; Sir W. F. P.
Napier's *Life and Opinions of Sir C. J. Napier* (London,
1857); *Parga* (Prague, 1907) by the Archduke Louis Salvator;
and *Some English Philhellenes*, by Z. D. Ferriman (London,
1917, etc.). The diplomatic correspondence of the time,
French and English, published and unpublished, abounds in
relevancies which the French have taken more trouble to
bring to light than we have. The illustrations in this book are
taken from the *Voyage à Athènes* (Paris, 1825) of Louis
Dupré, who is referred to in Chapter XXIX, and the translation
from Valaorites in Chapter XII, from *Greek Folk-Songs from
the Turkish Provinces of Greece* (London, 1885) by Lucy M.
J. Garnett and J. S. S. Glennie.

INDEX

INDEX

INDEX

Mukhtar, vice-governor of Tebeleni, 18
—— Pasha, son of Ali, born, 36; married, 58; in command against Suli, 65; at Roze's wedding, 85; attacks Preveza, 87; at Bonila, 91; affair with Phrosýne, 102-4; attacks Suli, 107; drinks against Gregory, 128; goes against the Russians, 138-9, 162, captures Vlachavas, 143; murders Gardikiots, 173; visited by Holland, 183; visited by Hughes, 200; his shoot, 205, 206; at Berat, 241, 244, 245; intercedes for Vaya, 243; surrenders at Argyro Castro, 255; interned in Asia Minor, 269; murdered, 270; his head buried, 276
Murad Bey, 61, 62
Murtus, 163, 164
Mustai Pasha of Scutari, 176
Mustapha Aga Koka, 39
—— Bey, son of Hussein, 18
—— Pasha of Delvino, 41, 91, 98, 100, 101, 136, 160, 167, 168, 174, 176, 178, 190, 191
—— Zyguri, 94, 95

NAPIER, SIR C. J., 201, 220, 248, 249, 259, 260, 276
Naples, 71, 116
Napoleon, 11, 84, 89, 124-6, 130, 132, 135, 161, 165, 178, 189, 192, 219, 264
Navarino, 89, 125
Nazif, 17
Nazir of Drama, the, 242
Negropont, 34, 124, 188
Nelson, 88
Nicole, Colonel (Hadji Nicolas), 192, 213, 215
Nicopolis, 183
Noutza, Alexis, 265, 266

ODESSA, 247
Odysseus, 197, 247, 250, 253, 254
Olympus, 144
Omer Bey Vrioni, 139, 142, 155, 166, 243, 251, 265, 271
Orkhan Gerai, 264
Osborne, Lord Sydney, 221
Ossa, 144
Oswald, General, 138, 158

PALASKAS, 93, 94
Paparigopoulos, 247

Paramythia, 99, 101, 108, 118, 241
Parasuli, 61, 63
Parga and the Parghiots, 84, 88, 92, 97, 100, 107, 108, 112, 114-6, 131, 132, 151, 178, 192, 213-6, 219-22, 232, 235, 239, 240, 245, 250
Paris, 67, 91, 126, 219
—— Treaty of, 219
Parker, R. T., 194, 199, 206, 208-10, 218
Pasho, wife of Mukhtar, 58, 103-5
Passano, 82
Pasvan, Oglu of Vidin, 86, 139, 246
Patras, 219, 267
Paul, Czar, 84
Paxos, 84
Pehlevan Baba, 250, 251, 253, 256
Philippopolis, 118, 119
Photomara, 98, 99
Photo of Suli, 235, 237
Phrosýne, 102-6
Pindus, 43, 51, 88, 141, 161, 195, 259
Pirosmanishvili, Niko, 147
Plichivitza, 121, 227
Poitevin, Colonel, 89, 96
Porson, Professor, 199
Porte, the Sublime, 33, 37, 45, 47, 86, 92, 107, 116-9, 131, 133, 155, 159, 163, 178, 186, 190, 191, 219, 232, 239, 245, 250, 266, 268
Porto Panormo, 126
Potemkin, 44
Pouqueville, F. C. H. L., at Navarino, 89; arrival in Epirus, 125-9; consul at Jannina, 130-37, 140, 143, 155, 156, 158-166, 169, 175, 177, 178, 189, 190, 202, 214-16; transferred to Patras, 219; quoted, 136, 263; and Byron, 153; and Cockerell, 203; and Hughes, 206
Preveza, 68, 77, 84, 86-8, 92, 108, 131, 133, 137, 138, 145, 158, 159, 182, 183, 194, 195, 213, 220, 247, 250, 251, 254
Prifti, Chaoush 56, 57
Pronio Aga of Paramythia, 65, 95, 97-101
Psalida, Athanasius, 52, 74, 132, 182, 196, 198, 199
Pyrrhus, 75, 210, 217, 236

RAGUSA, 126
Rasselas, 183

INDEX

Remérand, M. G., 227, 278
Riniassa, 115
Rousseau, Douanier, 147
Roze, Adj.-Gen., 84-7
Rumelia, 37, 41, 92, 119, 120
Russia, 44, 84, 130, 131, 138, 188

SAIKAKU, 28
St. George, 26
St. Panteleimon, Monastery of, 273-6
Sakellario, Dr., 80
Salamanca, 180
Sali Bey, son of Ali, 120, 183, 184, 210, 272, 230, 244, 269, 280, 276
Salona, 121
Salonica, 229, 255, 277
Samanioti, 134, 135
Samuel ('Last Judgment'), 108, 111-13, 115
Santa Maura, 84, 86, 131, 132, 138, 152, 155, 158, 166, 189, 251
Saratch, Abraham, 262
Savannah, H.M.S., 214
Scanderbeg (George Castriotes), 21, 60, 155
Schindriada, 169, 170
Scutari, 45
Sébastiani, General, 130, 133
Sefer Bey, 57, 58, 159
Selim Pasha of Delvino, 39-41
—— son of Veli, 254, 278
Seltzo, 115
Septinsular Republic, 91, 114, 132
Serbs in revolt, 191-3
Serio, 229
Shakespeare, 11
Shainitza, sister of Ali, 20, 30, 38, 46, 61, 120, 140, 141, 168, 169, 172, 255-7, 268
Sicily, 138
Silivri Gate, 276
Sistruni, 94
Sofia, 119, 192
Somerset, Lord Charles, 221
Spartans, 24
Spencer, Capt. R., R.N., 201
Stuart, Sir J. (the Hero of Maida), 207
Suleiman, a dervish, 276, 277
—— husband of Shainitza, 38
Suli and the Suliots, 33, 55, 58-67, 85, 87, 92-101, 103, 107-9, 111-18, 142, 178, 234, 258, 263, 264, 269, 271

Susman, 121-3
Syria, 89

TAHIR ABBAS, 264
Talleyrand, 132
Tchami, Selim, 272-4
Tebeleni, 17-20; Khamco and, 30-32, 45; Ali leaves, 34; Ali at, 40, 46, 56, 57, 77, 146-52, 173; Mustapha escapes from, 41; dervishes at, 76; Bailey at, 78; treasures at, 77, 92, 192, 230, 241; palace at, 77; Yusuf Arab at, 183; Holland at, 183; Ali ordered to retire to, 191; fire at, 230; palace rebuilt, 231; Mahmud defends, 245, 255, 257
Thebans, 27
Theocritus, 24
Thesprotia, 58
Thessaly, 34, 42-4, 46, 142, 143, 161, 186, 250
Thomas the Despot, 48, 50, 69
Thrace, 118, 241
Tilsit, 132
Toulon, 124, 219
Tozzoni, 90, 110
Trikkala, 42, 43, 45, 47, 49, 57, 120, 241, 277
Tripolitza, 126
Turkish Empire, state of, 246, 247
Tzaras, Niko, 142
Tzavellas, Captain, 63, 64, 94
—— Moscho, 65, 94, 100, 116, 117, 235
—— Photo (Kalilyros), 64, 65, 94-7, 100, 101, 108, 112, 116, 117, 235

VALAORITES, 112, 143
Vallona, 35, 42, 139, 155, 159-61, 166, 241, 250
Vasiliki, wife of Ali, 121, 227, 271, 273, 276, 277
Vaudoncourt, Colonel Baron Guillaume de, 21, 79, 82, 131
Vaya, Athanasi, 80, 166, 170, 171, 182, 241, 243, 262, 264, 273, 276
—— Lucas, 80, 182
Veli Bey, father of Ali, 18-20, 30, 32
—— Pasha, son of Ali, born, 36; pasha of Trikkala, 57; married; 61; threatens Photo Tzavellas, 64, 65; at Bonila, 91; at blockade of Suli, 103; negotiaties with Suliots, 111;

287

INDEX

Veli Bey—*contd.*
breaks treaty, 114; murders Susman, 121-3; closes ports to the French, 133; Byron given letter to him, 152; trouble in Morea, 162; daughters married, 176, 177; character, 182; loses Morea, 186; friendship with Ismail Pasho Bey, 186-8; deprived of Trikkala, 244; defends Preveza, 245, 250, 251, 254; surrenders Preveza, 254; his example followed, 255; interned in Asia Minor, 269; murdered, 270; head buried, 276

Venetians, 39, 45, 50, 84, 221

Victoria, Queen, 153, 185

Vienna, 67, 80

Vivian, 234

Vlachavas, Evthymio, 142-4, 146

Voiussa, 17, 77

Vonitza, 84, 131, 220, 250

Vurgareli, 115

WARREN, SIR JOHN, 68

Wedgwood, Josiah, 179

Wellington, 180

YPSILANTI, PRINCE ALEXANDER, 267

Yusuf Arab (the Blood-Drinker), 56, 85, 131, 183, 188

—— the dervish, 174, 175, 230, 251

ZAGORI, 222

Zalongo, 114, 115

Zante, 84, 151

Zerva, Dimo, 99

Zobeidé, wife of Veli, 61, 104, 186, 187

Zoitza (Black-Eyed), 85

Zosima family, 51